Introduction

Developing Reading Skills: Advanced, Third Edition, is a completely new book. This thoroughly revised program is based on an interactive process model of reading, and it follows the organizational scheme of *Expanding Reading Skills: Advanced*, Second Edition (1990), *Expanding Reading Skills: Intermediate*, Second Edition (1993), *Developing Reading Skills: Beginning*, Second Edition (1994), and *Developing Reading Skills: Intermediate* (1995).

Developing Reading Skills: Advanced is intended for college students or other adults who want to develop their reading skills for academic, personal, and/or career purposes. The text is also appropriate for high school students. These materials have been used successfully with English as a Second Language and English as a Foreign Language students, as well as with native-speaking adults in developmental reading classes in both academic and nonacademic settings.

Developing Reading Skills: Advanced is the fourth in a five-book reading program designed to meet the needs of students from beginning through advanced levels. The program is designed as follows:

- *Developing Reading Skills*, Beginning
- *Developing Reading Skills*, Intermediate 1
- *Expanding Reading Skills*, Intermediate 2
- *Developing Reading Skills*, Advanced 1
- *Expanding Reading Skills*, Advanced 2

This thoroughly revised edition is composed of five thematic units and a research and writing skills unit:

- *Leaving Home* (an exploration of the painful effects of leaving one's home)
- *You Are What You Eat* (a look at nutrition and food)
- *Why Do People Behave the Way They Do?* (why we behave the way we do)
- *The Human Brain and Its Workings* (how the human brain has evolved and how it functions)
- *Opening up the Mind* (how reading transforms one's inner world)
- *Developing Research and Writing Skills* (a writing resource unit)

Each thematic unit has three readings and a variety of reading, writing, discussion, and structure exercises designed to help learners develop comprehension and integrate new ideas with their knowledge and experiences. The readings are on challenging and relevant topics and have been selected from a wide variety of published sources including newspaper and magazine articles and chapters from both fiction and nonfiction books. Excerpts from college textbooks are included as well. Students and teachers at City University of New York and New York University have helped us select the unit themes, and they generously offered us feedback on the materials in the experimental stages. The materials were tested and revised before publication.

Some of the major features of *Developing Reading Skills: Advanced* are:

- **Extensive prereading activities:** Before they begin reading, learners work together in guided discussion to activate their awareness of each topic. The prereading activities (1) introduce the text in the context of what is already known by the learners, (2) promote a sharing of information by members of the group, (3) encourage speculation on textual content and, finally, (4) set the stage for the learners' successful integration of new ideas and concepts in the text with their knowledge and experience of the world. We recommend that students working together in small groups choose one or two questions to discuss in detail and that a spokesperson from each group later summarize the main points of the group discussion for the whole class. However, students working on their own can still profit from thinking carefully about the questions before they begin the reading.

- **Thematic organization:** Each of the five units has three readings centered around a common theme. The thematic approach allows for a natural recycling and spiraling of concepts, vocabulary, and syntactic structures as well as an appreciation for the effect of genre on theme. The result is that learners develop their reading, thinking, and writing skills more quickly and are highly motivated to expand their efforts as they successfully cope with increasingly challenging material. Finally, we have carefully selected the thematic readings so that learners will be exposed to a variety of content demands, text densities, and genres.

- **Solid reading-writing connection:** Students write about what they read. They explore their own ideas and feelings about each selection in writing, and they read their writing to their classmates. Furthermore, students have the opportunity to develop their writing research skills through a multistep process approach. They learn how to develop and elaborate on their ideas in writing, and they are given guidance in continuing the thematic spiral through their own independent research if they wish. The process writing and research

Developing Reading Skills

advanced

3rd Edition

Linda Markstein
The Borough of Manhattan Community College,
The City University of New York

Louise Hirasawa
University of Washington

Heinle & Heinle Publishers
I(T)P An International Thomson Publishing Company

Pacific Grove • Albany • Bonn • Boston • Cincinnati • Detroit • London
Madrid • Melbourne • Mexico City • New York • Paris
San Francisco • Tokyo • Toronto • Washington

The publication of *Developing Reading Skills, Advanced, Third Edition* was directed by the members of the Newbury House Publishing Team at Heinle & Heinle:

Erik Gundersen, Editorial Director
Jonathan Boggs, Market Development Director
Kristin M. Thalheimer, Senior Production Services Coordinator
Stanley J. Galek, Vice President and Publisher

Also participating in the publication of this program were:
Project Manager/Desktop Pagination: LeGwin Associates
Managing Developmental Editor: Amy Lawler
Manufacturing Coordinator: Mary Beth Hennebury
Associate Editor: Ken Pratt
Associate Market Development Director: Mary Sutton
Assistant Editor: Jill Kinkade
Photo/video Specialist: Jonathan Stark
Media Services Coordinator: Jerry Christopher
Interior Designer: LeGwin Associates
Photo Reasearcher: Martha Leibs Heckly
Cover Designer: Ha Nguyen

Photo Credits
p. x: © by Jean-Claude Lejeune/Stock•Boston
p. 2: © Dan Gair/The Picture Cube, Inc.
p. 16: © 1994 Michael Justice/The Image Works
p. 30: © MCMXCII Ulrike Welsch. All rights reserved.
p. 50: © Bob Daemmrich/The Image Works
p. 62: © 1992 by Newsweek, Inc.
p. 76: © 1996 Frank Pedrick/The Image Works
p. 79: © Archive Photos/Popperfoto
p. 90: © Heinle Image Resource Bank/Jonathan Stark
p. 92: Courtesy of Louise Hirasawa
p. 106: © Joseph Schuyler/Stock•Boston
p. 109: © Rhoda Sidney/Stock•Boston
p. 129: © John Nordell/The Picture Cube, Inc.
p. 142: © Heinle Image Resource Bank/Jonathan Stark
p. 144, 146, 148, 149, 150 from "The Old Brain and the New," in *The Enchanted Loom: Mind in the Universe* © 1981 by Robert Jastrow. The Reader's Library a division of Simon and Schuster. Used by permission.
p. 158 © Heinle Image Resource Bank/Jonathan Stark
p. 175 © AP Photos for *The New York Times*
p. 186 © Heinle Image Resource Bank/Jonathan Stark
p. 188: © Corbis-Bettmann
p. 202: © Corbis-Bettmann
p. 218: © Heinle Image Resource Bank/Jonathan Stark
Charts and graphs
p. 24 immigration statistics, courtesy of U.S. Immigration & Naturalization Services
p. 52 food pyramid, courtesy of U.S. Dept. of Argiculture
p. 59 circle chart, "The Changing Tastes of Canadians," from *Macleans* Magazine, Oct. 22, 1990, p. 47.
p. 66: tomato chart used with permission of Newsweek, Inc.
p. 161 © Harriet Gans/The Image Works

For permission to use copyrighted material, grateful acknowledgment is made to the copyright holders on pages 279–280 which are hereby made part of this copyright page.

Manufactured in the United States of America

ISBN: 08384-5276-0

10 9 8 7 6

Contents

section has been placed at the end of the book so students can refer to it as a resource handbook as needed.

- **Process approach to reading and writing:** Learners are shown how to interact with text in a logical, systematic manner and how to vary their reading approach to suit their reading purpose as well as the content and text density demands of the reading. They are encouraged to use text features—headings, different print sizes and types—as pointers to meaning and to use context clues to figure out meanings of new words and phrases. They are guided in how to relate their prior knowledge and experience to the text. Finally, they learn that systematic rereading is as important to reading as systematic rewriting is to writing.

- **Vocabulary games:** Each unit closes with a series of challenging vocabulary and logic games to reinforce vocabulary in the unit. We encourage learners to work through the quizzes on their own without the aid of a dictionary and then compare their results with those of their groupmates. Dictionaries may be used at this point to resolve differences of opinion.

- Glossary: A glossary, with definitions and example sentences, has been added at the end of the text as a quick, convenient reference. Students will still need to use their own dictionaries for examining the range of meanings of a word and for words not included in the glossary.

How to Use the Text

We recommend that instructions within the units be followed as closely as possible. For example, every unit begins with an extensive headnote to provide contextual orientation. This headnote helps learners get their bearings before they begin reading by providing useful social and historical information about the topic. This is especially helpful for readers approaching unfamiliar topics. Prereading discussion activities follow. We emphasize the importance of giving careful attention to these activities (as outlined above) because they help learners relate the text to their previous knowledge and experience. Furthermore, the prereading activities promote cooperative learning and encourage a sharing of social and cultural information. It is not necessary to discuss all the prereading questions in detail (small groups can choose one or two to examine), but the prereading activities definitely set the stage for successful interaction with the text later on.

In the first unit we recommend that the teacher work directly with the students in helping them recognize the significance of textual features (e.g., headings, subheadings, and different print sizes and fonts) and how these features point to meaning and are essential to effective skimming and scanning. We further recommend that the teacher draw attention to the relationship of illustrations, graphs, and photographs to the printed text. We encourage attention to footnotes as well.

We continue to believe that reading speed is important. However, we have not recommended specific reading times because, in the testing stage, we found that different individuals had significantly different reading abilities and could read and comprehend at varying rates. We encourage teachers to evaluate the reading abilities of their students and to help students set reading times that are challenging, yet not frustrating. We note that ESL and EFL students must be consistently encouraged to break the word-by-word reading habit, which in fact interferes with comprehension. Particularly in the beginning, it is important to emphasize to students that they can understand the main ideas of a text without understanding every word.

The second reading is designed to give the students time to go back over difficult passages of text and look up words in their glossaries or dictionaries if they wish. We do not encourage students to look up every unfamiliar word and, in the experimental testing, we noted that very few students attempted to do so. Generally, students chose to confer with each other on the meanings of certain words and to look up other words, or words they were still unsure of, on their own.

The third reading is designed to help students integrate old and new concepts and vocabulary found in the text. It is important to encourage students to recognize the purposes and benefits of rereading because many students are not familiar with a process approach to reading and, in fact, may consider rereading a sign of poor reading skills without careful instruction in this area. In certain cases of densely packed text, we have recommended more than three readings.

We recognize that the level of the readings in this book is challenging. Reading is developmental: We learn to read by reading; we learn to read difficult material only by reading difficult material. Finally, we believe that learners at the advanced level must undertake new reading challenges if they are to reach their personal, professional, and vocational goals in the future.

Linda Markstein   Louise Hirasawa
New York, New York   *Seattle, Washington*

In Memory of Steve Markstein

Acknowledgments

Many people have helped us along the way in the writing, testing, and production of this book. We would like to thank Bill DeYoung, Anthony Greenwald, Dorien Grunbaum, William Harshbarger, Anne Habiby, Danielle Kaplan, Ken Levinson, Suzanna Markstein, Paulette Plonchak, Cynthia Richards, and Elizabeth Upton for assistance they provided with content selection and development. We would further like to thank our pre-publication reviewers for their valuable suggestions. We have had the continuing good fortune to have the encouragement and support of a knowledgeable and enthusiastic team at Heinle & Heinle guided by Erik Gundersen. We express our deep gratitude for the generous comments and suggestions made by the many teachers and students at Borough of Manhattan Community College who tested out various units for us. And finally, we must thank, as always, Allan Kent Dart, Barbara Gonzales, Janis Jones, Katsushige Hirasawa, Otto Markstein, Nina Percy, Steve Rooney, and Billie Schildkraut for their unflagging support and encouragement, particularly in this season of great personal sadness and difficulty. Without these people, this book would not have been possible.

Leaving Home

Leaving home is one of the biggest changes in any person's life. Some-times people move from the country to a city for better educational or economic opportunities. Sometimes people immigrate to a new country, also for better opportunities. Whatever form the leaving takes, the change brings both the excitement of new possibilities and a disruption of traditional values and old patterns. In this unit you will read about the clash between new and old ways in the first two chapters; the third chapter examines both positive and negative effects of immigration on U.S. society.

Discussion

Before you begin reading, think about the following questions and discuss your answers. *Note:* You may wish to choose one or two questions to explore in detail either on your own or with a small group of students from your class.

1. Have you had the experience of leaving home? If so, why did you leave and where did you go? What were some of the advantages you gained by moving? What were some of the difficulties? Make a chart like the one below to help you organize your ideas.

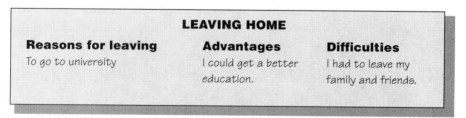

LEAVING HOME		
Reasons for leaving	**Advantages**	**Difficulties**
To go to university	I could get a better education.	I had to leave my family and friends.

2. Have you ever had a disagreement with older members of your family about values? What was the disagreement? Explain the situation in detail. Did the disagreement involve a conflict in values?

3. What effects do you think immigration has on society? Are the effects generally good or bad? What do immigrants contribute to their new society? Do immigrants cause problems for other groups? Use information from your own experience, the experiences of others, or the news media to answer these questions.

Marriage Is a Private Affair

When people move from one country to another, they frequently encounter different lifestyles and cultural values and, after they have lived in the new country for a while, they may adopt some of the values and customs of their new home. At times they may feel a conflict between their new and old values. Likewise, when people move from a rural to an urban area within their own country, they experience some of these same differences in values and customs. As rural people adapt to the ways of the city, for example, they often come into conflict with the values of their family still living in the countryside. Chinua Achebe, a world-famous writer from Nigeria, tells a story of this kind of urban-rural conflict in "Marriage Is a Private Affair." Nene and Nnaemeka, the young couple who want to marry, are now living in Lagos, the modern, cosmopolitan capital of Nigeria. However, Nnaemeka is a member of the Ibo tribe, and he comes from a very traditional rural background where arranged marriages are customary. Nnaemeka's father cannot understand or accept his son's marriage because it conflicts with his strongly held traditional values. This story is reprinted by permission.

1.1
First Reading

Read this story quickly for the main ideas. The main characters are a young woman named Nene, a young man named Nnaemeka, and Nnaemeka's father, Okeke. As you read, think about what kind of person each one is and what kind of background each comes from. Think about how each confronts the problem presented in this story. What is the problem? Do you think it will be resolved? Do *not* stop to look up words in your dictionary.

1 "Have you written to your dad yet?" asked Nene one afternoon as she sat with Nnaemeka in her room at 16 Kasanga Street, Lagos.

2 "No. I've been thinking about it. I think it's better to tell him when I get home on leave!"

3 "But why? Your leave is such a long way off yet—six whole weeks. He should be let into our happiness now."

4 Nnaemeka was silent for a while, and then began very slowly as if he groped for his words: "I wish I were sure it would be happiness to him."

5 "Of course it must," replied Nene, a little surprised. "Why shouldn't it?"

6 "You have lived in Lagos all your life, and you know very little about people in remote parts of the country."

7   "That's what you always say. But I don't believe anybody will be so unlike other people that they will be unhappy when their sons are engaged to marry."

8   "Yes. They are most unhappy if the engagement is not arranged by them. In our case it's worse—you are not even an Ibo."

9   This was said so seriously and so bluntly that Nene could not find speech immediately. In the cosmopolitan atmosphere of the city it had always seemed to her something of a joke that a person's tribe could determine whom he married.

10 At last she said, "You don't really mean that he will object to your marrying me simply on that account? I had always thought you Ibos were kindly-disposed to other people."

11 "So we are. But when it comes to marriage, well, it's not quite so simple. And this," he added, "is not peculiar to the Ibos. If your father were alive and lived in the heart of Ibibio-land he would be exactly like my father."

12 "I don't know. But anyway, as your father is so fond of you, I'm sure he will forgive you soon enough. Come on then, be a good boy and send him a nice lovely letter . . ."

13 "It would not be wise to break the news to him by writing. A letter will bring it upon him with a shock. I'm quite sure about that."

14 "All right, honey, suit yourself. You know your father."

15 As Nnaemeka walked home that evening he turned over in his mind different ways of overcoming his father's opposition, especially now that he had gone and found a girl for him. He had thought of showing his letter to Nene but decided on second thoughts not to, at least for the moment. He read it again when he got home and couldn't help smiling to himself. He remembered Ugoye quite well, an Amazon of a girl who used to beat up all the boys, himself included, on the way to the stream, a complete dunce at school.

16 *I have found a girl who will suit you admirably—Ugoye Nweke, the eldest daughter of our neighbor, Jacob Nweke. She has a proper Christian upbringing. When she stopped schooling some years ago her father (a man of sound judgment) sent her to live in the house of a pastor where she has received all the training a wife could need. Her Sunday School teacher has told me that she reads her Bible very fluently. I hope we shall begin negotiations when you come home in December.*

17 On the second evening of his return from Lagos Nnaemeka sat with his father under a cassia tree. This was the old man's retreat where he went to read his Bible when the parching December sun had set and a fresh, reviving wind blew on the leaves.

18 "Father," began Nnaemeka suddenly, "I have come to ask for forgiveness."

19 "Forgiveness? For what, my son?" he asked in amazement.

20 "It's about this marriage question."

21 "Which marriage question?"

22 "I can't—we must—I mean it is impossible for me to marry Nweke's daughter."

23 "Impossible? Why?" asked his father.

24 "I don't love her."

25 "Nobody said you did. Why should you?" he asked.

26 "Marriage today is different . . ."

27 "Look here, my son," interrupted his father, "nothing is different. What one looks for in a wife are a good character and a Christian background."

28 Nnaemeka saw there was no hope along the present line of argument.

29 "Moreover," he said, "I am engaged to marry another girl who has all of Ugoye's good qualities, and who . . ."

30 His father did not believe his ears. "What did you say?" he asked slowly and disconcertingly.

31 "She is a good Christian," his son went on, "and a teacher in a Girls' School in Lagos."

32 "Teacher, did you say? If you consider that a qualification for a good wife I should like to point out to you, Emeka, that no Christian woman should teach. St. Paul in his letter to the Corinthians says that women should keep silence." He rose slowly from his seat and paced forwards and backwards. This was his pet subject, and he condemned vehemently those church leaders who encouraged women to teach in their schools. After he had spent his emotion on a long homily he at last came back to his son's engagement, in a seemingly milder tone.

33 "Whose daughter is she, anyway?"

34 "She is Nene Atang."

35 "What!" All the mildness was gone again. "Did you say Neneataga, what does that mean?"

36 "Nene Atang from Calabar. She is the only girl I can marry." This was a very rash reply and Nnaemeka expected the storm to burst. But it did not. His father merely walked away into his room. This was most unexpected and perplexed Nnaemeka. His father's silence was infinitely more menacing than a flood of threatening speech. That night the old man did not eat.

37 When he sent for Nnaemeka a day later he applied all possible ways of dissuasion. But the young man's heart was hardened, and his father eventually gave him up as lost.

38 "I owe it to you, my son, as a duty to show you what is right and what is wrong. Whoever put this idea into your head might as well have cut your throat. It is Satan's work." He waved his son away.

39 "You will change your mind, Father, when you know Nene."

40 "I shall never see her," was the reply. From that night the father scarcely spoke to his son. He did not, however, cease hoping that he would realize how serious was the danger he was heading for. Day and night he put him in his prayers.

Review

1. What is the problem in this story? Why is Okeke, the father, so upset? Why is Nnaemeka, the son, so upset?

Prediction

2. What do you think is going to happen in the future?
3. Will Okeke forgive his son? Why or why not?
4. How do you think this story will end?

41 Nnaemeka, for his own part, was very deeply affected by his father's grief. But he kept hoping that it would pass away. If it had occurred to him that never in the history of his people had a man married a woman who spoke a different tongue, he might have been less optimistic. "It has never been heard," was the verdict of an old man speaking a few weeks later. In that short sentence he spoke for all of his people. This man had come with others to commiserate with Okeke when news went round about his son's behavior. By that time the son had gone back to Lagos.

42 "It has never been heard," said the old man again with a sad shake of his head.

43 "What did Our Lord say?" asked another gentleman. "Sons shall rise against their Fathers; it is there in the Holy Book."

44 "It is the beginning of the end," said another.

45 The discussion thus tending to become theological, Madubogwu, a highly practical man, brought it down once more to the ordinary level.

46 "Have you thought of consulting a native doctor about your son?" he asked Nnaemeka's father.

47 "He isn't sick," was the reply.

48 "What is he then? The boy's mind is diseased and only a good herbalist can bring him back to his right senses. The medicine he requires is *Amalile*, the same that women apply with success to recapture their husbands' straying affection."

49 "Madubogwu is right," said another gentleman. "This thing calls for medicine."

50 "I shall not call in a native doctor." Nnaemeka's father was known to be obstinately ahead of his more superstitious neighbors in these matters. "I will not be another Mrs. Ochuba. If my son wants to kill himself let him do it with his own hands. It is not for me to help him."

51 "But it was her fault," said Madubogwu. "She ought to have gone to an honest herbalist. She was a clever woman, nevertheless."

52 "She was a wicked murderess," said Jonathan, who rarely argued with his neighbors because, he often said, they were incapable of reasoning. "The medicine was prepared for her husband, it was his name they called in its preparation and I am sure it would have been perfectly beneficial to him. It was wicked to put it into the herbalist's food, and say you were only trying it out."

53 Six months later, Nnaemeka was showing his young wife a short letter from his father:

54 *It amazes me that you could be so unfeeling as to send me your wedding picture. I would have sent it back. But on further thought I decided just to cut off your wife and send it back to you because I have nothing to do with her. How I wish that I had nothing to do with you either.*

55 When Nene read through this letter and looked at the mutilated picture her eyes filled with tears, and she began to sob.

56 "Don't cry, my darling," said her husband. "He is essentially good-natured and will one day look more kindly on our marriage." But years passed and that one day did not come.

57 For eight years, Okeke would have nothing to do with his son, Nnaemeka. Only three times (when Nnaemeka asked to come home and spend his leave) did he write to him.

58 "I can't have you in my house," he replied on one occasion. "It can be of no interest to me where or how you spend your leave—or your life, for that matter."

59 The prejudice against Nnaemeka's marriage was not confined to his little village. In Lagos, especially among his people who worked there, it showed itself in a different way. Their women, when they met at their village meeting, were not hostile to Nene. Rather, they paid her such excessive deference as to make her feel she was not one of them. But as time went on, Nene gradually broke through some of the prejudice and even began to make friends among them. Slowly and grudgingly they began to admit that she kept her home much better than most of them.

60 The story eventually got to the little village in the heart of the Ibo country that Nnaemeka and his young wife were a most happy couple. But his father was one of the few people in the village who knew nothing about this. He always displayed so much temper whenever his son's name was mentioned that everyone avoided it in his presence. By a tremendous effort of will he had succeeded in pushing his son to the back of his mind. The strain had nearly killed him but he had persevered, and won.

61 Then one day he received a letter from Nene, and in spite of himself he began to glance through it perfunctorily until all of a sudden the expression on his face changed and he began to read more carefully.

62 *. . . Our two sons, from the day they learnt that they had a grandfather, have insisted on being taken to him. I find it impossible to tell them that you will not see them. I implore you to allow Nnaemeka to bring them home for a short time during his leave next month. I shall remain here in Lagos . . .*

63 The old man at once felt the resolution he had built up over so many years falling in. He was telling himself that he must not give in. He tried to steel his heart against all emotional appeals. It was a reenactment of that other struggle. He leaned against a window and looked out. The sky was overcast with heavy black clouds and a high wind began to blow filling the air with dust and dry leaves. It was one of those rare occasions when even Nature

takes a hand in a human fight. Very soon it began to rain, the first rain in the year. It came down in large sharp drops and was accompanied by the lightning and thunder which mark a change of season. Okeke was trying hard not to think of his two grandsons. But he knew he was now fighting a losing battle. He tried to hum a favorite hymn but the pattering of large rain drops on the roof broke up the tune. His mind immediately returned to the children. How could he shut his door against them? By a curious mental process he imagined them standing, sad and forsaken, under the harsh angry weather—shut out from his house.

64 That night he hardly slept, from remorse—and a vague fear that he might die without making it up to them.

Number of words: 2,250

Reading Times   **Reading Speed**

1st reading _____ minutes   10 minutes = 225 words per minute
3rd reading _____ minutes   9 minutes = 250 wpm
                                       8 minutes = 281 wpm
                                       7 minutes = 321 wpm
                                       6 minutes = 375 wpm

1.2
Second Reading

Go back and read the story again. Take as much time as you need. Look up some of the unfamiliar words in the glossary at the end of the book or in your dictionary if you wish.

1.3
Third Reading

Read the story quickly a third time. Concentrate on understanding the main ideas of the story and the meanings of new vocabulary words in the contexts in which they appear.

1.4
Reader Response

You, the reader, are part of the reading process. Your ideas and your reactions to what you read are important and valuable because the meaning of the reading depends in part on you and the knowledge and experience that you bring to the reading. In order to explore your response to this reading, write for 15 minutes about anything that interested you in this story. You may wish to write about your reactions to some of the themes and ideas presented here—or you may wish to disagree with something in the story. Try to explore *your own thoughts and feelings* as much as possible. Do *not* merely summarize or restate the ideas in the story. For sample reader responses, turn to pages 44–45.

1.5
Response Sharing

Read your response to two or three other people in your class. Listen carefully to what the others have written. After you have discussed each other's responses, talk about other points of interest in the story.

1.6
Outlining the Plot

Working with the same small group, make an outline of the plot of this story. In other words, tell what happened in the order that it happened.

> **Example:**
>
> *A young couple in Lagos, Nigeria, fall in love and decide to get married.*
>
> [Continue explaining what happened in this story.]

1.7
Analyzing the Text

Work with your group members on this exercise. Discuss the answers carefully, particularly if there are disagreements among members of your group. In some cases, there may be more than one possible interpretation.

1. One of the main themes of this story is:

    a. arranged marriages in Nigeria.

    b. conflict between rural and urban values.

    c. reasons why young people move from the countryside to cities.

2. How does the title relate to the story? Do you think all of the characters in this story would agree that marriage is a private affair? Who would not agree? Why?

3. Read each statement carefully, decide if it is true or false according to this story, and then write *T* (true) or *F* (false) on the line in front of the statement.

    a. ___F___ Nene comes from Lagos, a large, cosmopolitan city; this is why she is more conservative than Nnaemeka.

    b. _____ Arranged marriages are customary in traditional tribal cultures in Nigeria.

    c. _____ Nnaemeka does not want to defy his father.

    d. _____ The women from the village who are now living in Lagos gradually overcome their prejudice and begin to accept Nene.

e. _____   At the end of the story Okeke, the father, remains as determined as ever not to see or recognize Nnaemeka or his children.

4. Write the words *village* and *city* on a piece of paper and then make a list of
words that you associate with each. After you finish, compare your list with
the lists of others in your group. What are the similarities and differences
in your lists? What words would you like to add to your list now?

Village	*City*
friendly	crowds
old fahioned	cosmopolitan

5. What is the main problem or issue in this story? How does each of the three
main characters try to resolve the problem? Do you believe there will be a
resolution? Why or why not? Be as specific as possible in your answer.

1.8
Vocabulary Study

It is important to learn how to figure out word meanings from the context in
which they appear. Study the italicized words and phrases in their contexts and
guess at their meanings. Write your guess in the first blank. Then look up the
word or phrase in your dictionary and write the definition in the second blank.

1. (paragraph 4) Nnaemeka was silent for a while, and then began very slowly
as if he *groped* for his words: "I wish I were sure it would be happiness to
him."

a. (guess)   searched for, looked for _____

b. (dictionary)   to feel about blindly in search _____

2. (paragraph 6) "You have lived in Lagos all your life, and you know very little
about people in *remote* parts of the country."

a. (guess)   _____

b. (dictionary)   _____

3 and 4. (paragraph 9) This was said so seriously and so *bluntly* that Nene
could not find speech immediately. In the *cosmopolitan* atmosphere of the
city it had always seemed to her something of a joke that a person's tribe
could determine whom he married.
bluntly

a. (guess)   _____

b. (dictionary)   _____

cosmopolitan

a. (guess) _____

b. (dictionary) _____

5 and **6.** (paragraph 17) On the second evening of his return from Lagos Nnaemeka sat with his father under a cassia tree. This was the old man's retreat where he went to read his Bible when the *parching* December sun had set and a fresh, *reviving* wind blew on the leaves.

parching

a. (guess) _____

b. (dictionary) _____

reviving

a. (guess) _____

b. (dictionary) _____

7, 8, 9, and **10.** (paragraph 32) "Teacher, did you say? If you consider that a qualification for a good wife I should like to point out to you, Emeka, that no Christian woman should teach. St. Paul in his letter to the Corinthians says that women should keep silence." He rose slowly from his seat and paced forwards and backwards. This was his *pet* subject, and he *condemned vehemently* those church leaders who encouraged women to teach in their schools. After he had spent his emotion on a long *homily* he at last came back to his son's engagement, in a seemingly milder tone.

pet

a. (guess) _____

b. (dictionary) _____

condemned

a. (guess) _____

b. (dictionary) _____

vehemently

a. (guess) _____

b. (dictionary) _____

homily

a. (guess) _____

b. (dictionary) _____

11, 12, 13, and **14.** (paragraph 36)". . . . She is the only girl I can marry." This was a very *rash* reply and Nnaemeka expected the storm to burst. But it did not. His father merely walked away into his room. This was most unexpected and *perplexed* Nnaemeka. His father's silence was *infinitely* more *menacing* than a flood of threatening speech. That night the old man did not eat.

rash

a. (guess) _____

b. (dictionary) _____

perplexed

a. (guess) _____

b. (dictionary) _____

infinitely

a. (guess) _____

b. (dictionary) _____

menacing

a. (guess) _____

b. (dictionary) _____

15 and **16.** (paragraph 41) "It has never been heard," was the *verdict* of an old man speaking a few weeks later. In that short sentence he spoke for all of his people. This man had come with others to *commiserate* with Okeke when news went round about his son's behavior. By that time the son had gone back to Lagos.

verdict

a. (guess) _____

b. (dictionary) _____

commiserate

a. (guess) _____

b. (dictionary) _____

17. (paragraph 55) When Nene read through this letter and looked at the *mutilated* picture her eyes filled with tears and she began to sob.

a. (guess) _____

b. (dictionary) _____

18, 19, and **20.** (paragraph 59) The *prejudice* against Nnaemeka's marriage was not confined to his little village. In Lagos, especially among his people who worked there, it showed itself in a different way. Their women, when they met at their village meeting, were not hostile to Nene. Rather, they paid her such excessive *deference* as to make her feel she was not one of them. But as time went on, Nene gradually broke through some of the prejudice and even began to make friends among them. Slowly and *grudgingly* they began to admit that she kept her home much better than most of them.

prejudice

a. (guess) _____

b. (dictionary) _____

deference

a. (guess) _____

b. (dictionary) _____

grudgingly

a. (guess) _____

b. (dictionary) _____

1.9
Drawing Inferences

It is important to be able to draw inferences, i.e., to read between the lines, to understand the deeper meaning of a passage. To draw an inference, you must first read the passage carefully, think carefully about the context and the facts that are given, and then go on to make a decision about the underlying meaning that is implied but not stated. To practice this reading skill, study the following passages and explain deeper meanings that you can infer from the underlined sentences.

Example:

Nnaemeka was silent for a while, and then began very slowly as if he groped for his words: "I wish I were sure [the news of our engagement] would be happiness to him."

"Of course it must," replied Nene, a little surprised. "Why shouldn't it?"

"You have lived in Lagos all your life, and you know very little about people in remote parts of the country."

(paragraphs 4–6)

The inference here is that Nene does not understand tribal traditions and customs because she has lived in a large, cosmopolitan city all of her life; therefore, she has lost touch with her tribal background, and this is why she cannot understand why Nnaemeka's father could possibly be unhappy about their engagement.

1. I have found a girl who will suit you admirably. . . . She has a proper Christian upbringing. When she stopped schooling some years ago her father . . . sent her to live in the house of a pastor where she has received all the training a wife could need. Her Sunday School teacher has told me that she reads her Bible very fluently. (from Okeke's letter to Nnaemeka; paragraph 16)

Reread the underlined sentences carefully. What is Okeke suggesting about the proper education for a good wife?

2. "I can't—we must—I mean it is impossible for me to marry Nweke's daughter."

    "Impossible? Why?" asked his father.

    "I don't love her."

    "Nobody said you did. Why should you?" he asked.

    "Marriage today is different. . ."

    "Look here, my son," interrupted his father, "nothing is different. What one looks for in a wife are a good character and a Christian background." (paragraphs 22–27)

Reread the underlined sentence. What is Nnaemeka trying to explain to his father before his father interrupts him?

3. "I owe it to you, my son, as a duty to show you what is right and what is wrong. Whoever put this idea into your head might as well have cut your throat. It is Satan's work." He waved his son away.

    "You will change your mind, Father, when you know Nene."

    "I shall never see her," was the reply. From that night the father scarcely spoke to his son. He did not, however, cease hoping that he would realize how serious was the danger he was heading for. Day and night he put him in his prayers. (paragraphs 38–40)

Reread the underlined sentences. What is written between the lines here?

4. "I shall not call in a native doctor." Nnaemeka's father was known to be obstinately ahead of his more superstitious neighbors in these matters. "I will not be another Mrs. Ochuba. If my son wants to kill himself let him do it with his own hands. It is not for me to help him." (paragraph 50)

    Reread the underlined sentences. What can you infer about Mrs. Ochuba?

5. The story eventually got to the little village in the heart of the Ibo country that Nnaemeka and his young wife were a most happy couple. But his father was one of the few people in the village who knew nothing about this. He always displayed so much temper whenever his son's name was mentioned that everyone avoided it in his presence. By a tremendous effort of will he had succeeded in pushing his son to the back of his mind. The strain had nearly killed him but he had persevered, and won. (paragraph 60)

    Reread the underlined sentences. What can you infer about the father?

1.10
Application, Critical Evaluation, and Synthesis

Choose one or more topics to discuss with your small group or to write about.

1. Okeke objects to his son's marriage on principle; he believes in arranged marriages within the tribe. Nnaemeka, however, insists on choosing his own wife. What do you think Okeke would state as the advantages and merits of arranged marriages? By the same token, what do you think Nnaemeka and Nene would state as the advantages and merits of love marriages? Make a chart like the one below to help you organize your ideas.

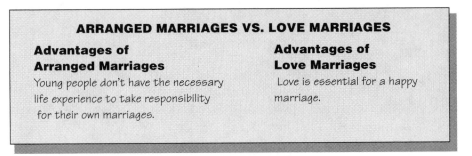

ARRANGED MARRIAGES VS. LOVE MARRIAGES

Advantages of Arranged Marriages	Advantages of Love Marriages
Young people don't have the necessary life experience to take responsibility for their own marriages.	Love is essential for a happy marriage.

2. Okeke is a moral and principled man and a highly respected member of his tribe and yet he refuses to see Nnaemeka and to meet Nene and their children. Why does he do this? How would you explain his position and his actions from his point of view? Can you understand Okeke's point of view?

3. At the end of the story, Okeke experiences a dilemma. It is stated that "he knew he was fighting a losing battle." Reread the end of the story and explain what inner conflict he is experiencing, what the battle is, and why he knows he is fighting a losing battle. What do you think Okeke is going to do and why is he going to do it?

4. All of us have had experiences that have brought us into conflict with others in our family because of differences in our perspectives and values. Describe your experience and explain the conflict. Was the problem ever resolved? If so, how? Explain in detail and be as specific as possible. What did you learn from the experience, if anything? Were you changed by the experience? If so, how? What about your family members? Were they changed by the experience? If so, how?

5. Societies with arranged marriages have much lower divorce rates than societies in which people choose their own mates. How do you explain this? Give clear reasons and examples to support your point of view. Does this mean that arranged marriages are preferable to nonarranged marriages?

An Indian Family in New York

Immigrants usually come to their new country with high hopes and the desire to start a new life of opportunity. However, especially at the beginning, many of them experience great difficulties and a painful period of adjustment as they face life in a strange and confusing new culture. Bharati Mukherjee, the author, came to the United States from India more than 30 years ago; she has written extensively about Indian-American life. The following selection comes from the novel *Jasmine* (Grove Press, Inc., 1989) , and it has been reprinted by permission.

2.1
First Reading

Read this story quickly for the main ideas. Jasmine, the narrator, is a young widow from India who has come to the United States to live with the family of her dead husband's teacher. She has entered the country illegally, and she is quite restricted in where she can go and what she can do in the United States. As you read, think about how people in this story live their lives in their new country. Do *not* stop to look up words in your dictionary.

1 Professorji[1] and his family put me up for five months—and it could have been five years, given the elasticity of the Indian family—just because I was the helpless widow of his favorite student. I was also efficient and uncomplaining, but they would have tolerated a clumsy whiner just as easily.

2 I want to be fair. Professorji is a generous man. Somehow, the trouble is in me. I had jumped a track. His kind of generosity wasn't good enough for me. It wasn't Prakash's, it wasn't Lillian Gordon's.[2]

3 The family consisted of his aged parents and his recent bride, Nirmala, a girl of nineteen fresh from a village in the Patiala district. The marriage had been arranged about a year before. She was pretty enough to send a signal to any Indian in Flushing[3]: *He may not look like much over here, but back in India this guy is considered quite a catch.*

4 In what I already considered "real life," meaning America, he was at least forty, thickening and having to color his hair. He had a new name in New York. Here he was "Dave," not Devinder, and not even Professor, though I

---

1. **Professorji**—This is a title of respect for a professor. It is a combination of English and Hindi, one of the main languages in India.
2. **Prakash**—The narrator's dead husband, who had been a student of Professorji. **Lillian Gordon** is a friend.
3. **Flushing**—A district in the Queens borough of New York City where many Indians as well as other ethnic groups live.

never called him anything but Professorji. When he answered the phone, "Dave Vadhera here," even the Vadhera sounded English. It sounded like "David O'Hara."

5 They had no children. He had avoided marriage until he had saved enough to afford two children, and to educate them in New York. Male or female did not matter, he was a progressive man. They'd been trying, according to Nirmala, who blushingly confided the occasional marital intimacy. I took enough interest in their problem to look and listen for signs of dedicated activity. Perhaps they were more imaginative than I gave them credit for. Nirmala was nineteen: According to my forged passport, I was nineteen too, but I was a widow. She was in the game, I was permanently on the sidelines. Professorji blamed his long hours and back pains. She blamed impurities in the food.

6 Pleading lab work, Professorji was out of the house by seven o'clock, five days a week. They both came back at six o'clock, harassed and foul-tempered, looking first for snacks and tea, later for a major dinner.

7 Should anyone ask, I was her "cousin-sister."

8 Nirmala worked all day in a sari store on our block. Selling upscale fabrics in Flushing indulged her taste for glamour and sophistication. The shop also sold 220-volt appliances, jewelry, and luggage. An adjacent shop under the same Gujarati ownership sold sweets and spices, and rented Hindi movies on cassettes. She was living in a little corner of heaven.

9 Every night, Nirmala brought home a new Hindi film for the VCR. Showings began promptly at nine o'clock, just after an enormous dinner, and lasted till midnight. They were Bombay's "B" efforts at best, commercial failures and quite a few famous flops, burnished again by the dim light of nostalgia. I could not unroll my sleeping mat until the film was over.

10 I felt my English was deserting me. During the parents' afternoon naps, I sometimes watched a soap opera. The American channels were otherwise never watched (Professorji's mother said, "There's so much English out there, why do we have to have it in here?"), but for the Saturday morning Indian shows on cable. Nirmala brought plain saris and salwar-kameez outfits[4] for me from the shop so I wouldn't have to embarrass myself or offend the old people in cast-off American T-shirts. The sari patterns were for much older women, widows.

11 I could not admit that I had accustomed myself to American clothes. American clothes disguised my widowhood. In a T-shirt and cords, I was taken for a student. In this apartment of artificially maintained Indianness, I wanted to distance myself from everything Indian. . . . To them, I was a widow who should show a proper modesty of appearance and attitude. If not, it appeared I was competing with Nirmala.

12 Flushing, with all its immigrant services at hand, frightened me. I, who had every reason to fear America, was intrigued by the city and the land beyond

---

4. **Saris and salwar-kameez outfits**—Traditional Indian clothing for women. *Saris* are long pieces of fabric that are wrapped around and draped to make a long dress. *Salwar-kameez* outfits are pants worn with knee-length shirts.

the rivers. The Vadheras, who would soon have saved enough to buy a small apartment building in Astoria,[5] had retired behind ghetto walls.

13 To date in her year in America, Nirmala had exhausted the available stock of Hindi films on tape and was now renting Urdu[6] films from a Pakistani store. She faced a grim future of unintelligible Bengali and Karnataka films. Everyone in Flushing seemed to know her craving. Visitors from India left tapes of popular Indian television series, and friends from Flushing were known to drive as far as New Jersey to check out the film holdings in the vast India emporia. They had a bookcase without books, stacked with television shows.

14 Professorji and Nirmala did not go out at night. "Why waste the money when we have everything here?" And truly they did. They had Indian-food stores in the block, Punjabi[7] newspapers and Hindi film magazines at the corner newsstand, and a movie every night without having to dress up for it. They had a grateful servant who took her pay in food and saris. The parents were long asleep, no need to indulge ritual pleasantries. In the morning, the same film had to be shown again to the parents. Then I walked the rewound cassette back to the rental store.

15 Professorji's parents, both in their eighties and rather adventurous for their age, demanded constant care. There were thirty-two Indian families in our building of fifty apartments, so specialized as to language, religion, caste, and profession that we did not need to fraternize with anyone but other educated Punjabi-speaking Hindu Jats. There were six families more or less like Professorji's (plus Punjabi-speaking Sikh families who seemed friendly in the elevator and politically tame, though we didn't mingle), and three of the families also had aged parents living in. Every morning, then, it was a matter of escorting the senior Vadheras to other apartments, or else serving tea and fried snacks to elderly visitors.

16 Sundays the Vadheras allowed themselves free time. We squeezed onto the sofa in the living room and watched videos of Sanjeev Kumar movies or of Amitabh. Or we went to visit with other Punjabi families in sparsely furnished, crowded apartments in the same building and watched their videos. Sundays were our days to eat too much and give in to nostalgia, to take the carom board out of the coat closet, to sit cross-legged on dhurries and matchmake marriages for adolescent cousins or younger siblings. Of course, as a widow, I did not participate. Remarriage was out of the question within the normal community. There were always much older widowers with children to look after who might consider me, and this, I know, was secretly discussed, but my married life and chance at motherhood were safely over.

17 Professorji's father always lost a little money at poker. Professorji always got a little drunk. When he got drunk he complained that America was killing

---

5. **Astoria**—Another area in Queens, close to Flushing where many immigrant groups live.
6. **Urdu**—A language spoken primarily in parts of northern India and Pakistan.
7. **Punjabi**—A regional language spoken in the province of Punjab in northern India and Pakistan.

him. "You want stress," he asked anyone who would listen, "or you want big bank balance?"

18 The old folks' complaints were familiar ones. In India the groom's mother was absolute tyrant of the household. The young bride would quiver under her commands. But in New York, with a working wife, the mother-in-law was denied her venomous authority. The bent old lady who required my arm to make her way from the television to the bathroom had been harboring hatred and resentment of *her* mother-in-law for sixty-five years. Now that she *finally* had the occasion to vent it, Nirmala wasn't around to receive it. This was the tenor of all the old people's complaints—we have followed our children to America, and look what happens to us! Our sons are selfish. Our daughters want to work and stay thin. All the time, this rush-rush. What to do? There are no grandchildren for us to play with. This country has drained my son of his dum. This country has turned my daughter-in-law into a barren field. If we are doomed to die here, at least let us enjoy the good things of America: friends from our village, plentiful food, VCRs, air conditioning.

19 I felt myself deteriorating. I had gained so much weight I couldn't get into the cords even when I tried. I couldn't understand the soap operas. I didn't know the answers to game shows. And so I cooked, shopped, and cleaned, tended the old folks, and made conversation with Professorji when he got home.

20 Professorji was a good man, by his lights, but he didn't seem the same caring teacher who, in sleek blue American aerograms only months before, had tempted Prakash, his best engineering student, to leave the petty, luckless world of Jullundhar.[8] Flushing was a neighborhood in Jullundhar. I was spiraling into depression behind the fortress of Punjabiness. Some afternoons when Professorji was out working, and Nirmala was in her shop, and the old Vadheras were snoring through their siestas, I would find myself in the bathroom with the light off, head down on the cold, cracked rim of the sink, sobbing from unnamed, unfulfilled wants. In Flushing I felt immured. An imaginary brick wall topped with barbed wire cut me off from the past and kept me from breaking into the future. I was a prisoner doing unreal time. Without a green card, even a forged one (I knew at least four men in our building who had bought themselves resident alien cards for between two and three thousand dollars), I didn't feel safe going outdoors. If I had a green card, a job, a goal, *happiness* would appear out of the blue.

Review

1. What is the problem in this story? Why is the narrator so depressed?

Prediction

2. What do you think is going to happen in the future?
3. Will the narrator's predicament change?
4. How do you think this story will end?

---

8. **Jullundhar**—A small town in northern India in the Punjab province.

21 One Monday—after a particularly boisterous Sunday—Professorji came home around two in the afternoon and caught me crying as he barged into the dark bathroom. He seemed helpless before my grief. I tried to stop my sobbing and swallowing, but the more I tried, the harder the tears came.

22 Professorji turned on the light, and with it the noisy, hateful fan. "You're like a daughter to me," he said, in his stiff, shy way. "Has anybody been treating you like a servant?"

23 Disappointments tumbled out of me. I told him I wanted a green card more than anything else in the world, that a green card was freedom.

24 Professorji put the toilet lid down and sat on it cautiously. He lit a cigarette and held it pinched between thumb and index finger, as my brothers used to. "A green card," he said, "is an expensive but not an impossible proposition. For the rich, such a matter is arranged daily."

25 "Then arrange it!" I begged. "Please! I'm dying in this limbo." I'd sign any IOU he wanted, at any interest rate he fixed, if he would advance the two or three thousand.

26 "You?" Professorji smiled. "You think you have enough skills to pay me back so much money within my lifetime?" He suggested I send word to my brothers to see if they could pay him in rupees. "For Prakash's sake," he said, "I'll make this concession. I'll take rupees." He quoted black-market exchange rates that weren't outrageously unfair.

27 I calculated in my head. Three thousand dollars would come to fifty thousand rupees. My brothers were generous, loyal, ingenious men, but they couldn't get together fifty thousand fixing motor scooters in Hasnapur. I wouldn't demand it of them. Still, Professorji didn't have to know that.

28 I glared down at the embarrassed and unhappy man sitting on the toilet lid. "The card is for me, and I shall make the payments." I had to believe that given a chance I could make the payments.

29 "And how do you think you'll do that?" he said. He stood up and flushed his cigarette. Then he said, "All right. I shall make all the necessary arrangements. But this is not something we want to discuss with my wife and parents."

30 I was so thrown by his quick turnaround that I dropped to my knees and touched his feet to thank him, as I would have done in Hasnapur. He walked slowly out into the hall, as though my desperation hadn't gone head to head with his generosity in the tiny bathroom.

31 Professorji came through, but he was emotionally tight, with Nirmala, with his parents, with me. I was grateful, and I admired him, but I didn't understand him. He was secretive, he was parsimonious with his affections. I remembered Prakash's rage . . ., his depressions, his glee. He told me everything, took pleasure in my adventures, small as they were. Nirmala had no idea where her husband worked—he never told her. "What if there's an accident?" I asked, and she smiled, like a child. "*He* will know," she said, using the pronoun. She had no idea what he did. He was following an ancient prescription for marital accord: silence, order, authority. So was she: submission, beauty, innocence.

32 One day his father cut his head open on the bathtub faucet. I couldn't decide, because I didn't know enough about the old man's immigration status and medical insurance, if I should rush him by taxi to a hospital or call the emergency squad. Old Mrs. Vadhera was screaming for a doctor, a priest, and her son. I called Queens College and asked for Professor Vadhera. They asked which department, and I didn't know. They checked every variant spelling, every department, and couldn't find him. Try Queensborough College, the woman suggested. Or LaGuardia Community. I did. Nothing.

33 Leaving the old woman in charge, I hurried down to Nirmala's sari shop. She was sitting in the back with a Coke, watching an Urdu film. Scurrying through old papers, she found an address for *him*. The Almighty Him. It was a street number, not a college.

34 Flushing was not the downtown of dreams I'd conjured from the aerogram back in Jullundhar. And Professorji was not a professor. He was an importer and sorter of human hair. The hair came in great bundles from middlemen in villages as small as Hasnapur all over India. The middlemen shipped the hair in switches. Every weekday Professorji sat from eight so'clock till six on a kitchen ladder-stool in a room he rented in the basement of the Khyber Bar BQ measuring and labeling the length and thickness of each separate hair.

35 Junk hair he sold to wigmakers. Fine hair to instrument makers. Eventually, scientific instruments and the U.S. Defense Department. It was no exaggeration to say that the security of the free world, in some small way, depended on the hair of Indian village women. His integrity as a man of science, and as a businessman, rested on the absolute guarantee that hair from Dave Vadhera met the highest standards and had been personally selected.

36 As for his father, he said he'd call a doctor friend, an uncertified but still hopeful Delhi doctor working as a technician for a blood bank, who lived three floors down, to come around and bandage the wound. He acted more upset that I'd found him; *found him out.* He suspected that I'd deliberately shamed him, using the excuse of an injured father to pry information out of Nirmala. Now she'd get suspicious if *I* didn't talk about the university and his labs and all his assistants.

37 I told him not to worry. I would.

38 Actually, he said, he still was a scientist. America hadn't robbed him of his self-respect. "No synthetic material has the human hair's tensile strength. How to gauge humidity without strands?" He picked out a long black hair from the 24-inch tray. "Like this beautiful one. How to read the weather?"

39 A hair from some peasant's head in Hasnapur could travel across oceans and save an American meteorologist's reputation. Nothing was rooted anymore. Everything was in motion.

40 "You could sell your hair, if you wanted to. It is eighteen inches at least, I think. We are purchasing Indian ladies' hair only. Indian women are purists, they're cleansing their hair with berries or yogurt only, they're not ruining their hair with shampoos, gels, dyes, and permanents. American

women have horrible hair—this I have learned since settling here. Their hair lacks virginity and innocence."

41 I got the point. He needed to work here, but he didn't have to like it. He had sealed his heart when he'd left home. His real life was in an unlivable land across oceans. He was a ghost, hanging on.

42 That's when he offered to introduce me to the master forger, another renter in the Khyber basement. He made up a fake bill of sale, my future hair when it was twenty-four inches, for three thousand dollars. He was buying my silence for his shame, and I felt the shame as well.

Number of words: 3,025

Reading Times	Reading Speed
1st reading _____ minutes	15 minutes = 202 words per minute
3rd reading _____ minutes	13 minutes = 233 wpm
	10 minutes = 303 wpm
	9 minutes = 336 wpm
	8 minutes = 378 wpm

2.2
Second Reading

Go back and read the passage again. Take as much time as you need. Look up some of the unfamiliar words in the glossary at the end of the book or in your dictionary if you wish.

2.3
Third Reading

Read the passage quickly a third time. Concentrate on understanding the main ideas of the passage and the meanings of new vocabulary words in the contexts in which they appear.

2.4
Reader Response

In order to explore your response to this reading, write for 15 minutes about anything that interested you in this passage. You may wish to write about your reactions to some of the themes and ideas presented here—or you may wish to disagree with something in the passage. Try to explore *your own thoughts and feelings* as much as possible. Do *not* merely summarize or restate the ideas in the passage.

2.5
Response Sharing

Read your response to two or three other people in your class. Listen carefully to what the others have written. After you have discussed each other's responses, talk about other points of interest in the passage.

2.6
Character Development

Working with the same small group, choose a couple of the characters in this passage and then talk about how the writer makes us understand these characters. Look at the actions and words of each of these characters and talk about how these actions and words give us a picture of the person. What conclusions can we reach about the person and his or her character from these details?

Example:

Nirmala: She is a 19-year-old village girl with an arranged marriage. She works in an Indian store selling material for saris, traditional Indian dresses. She is generous; she gives the narrator traditional Indian clothing from the shop. She brings home Indian movies to watch every night with her family. She has a craving for Indian movies, and people give her tapes of Indian television shows and bring her movies they think she may not have seen. Nirmala and her husband do not go out at night because they feel they have everything they could ever want at home: Indian food, Indian magazines, Indian newspapers, Indian movies. Nirmala does not know where her husband works and shows no curiosity about his job; she has to look through a stack of old papers to find his work address. Conclusion: Nirmala is a traditional Indian woman even though she lives in New York City. She surrounds herself with everything Indian in her daily life. She shows no interest in American life outside her ethnic community. She is not adaptable or curious about new things. She does not value change. For her, immigration means only living an Indian life in a different country.

2.7
Analyzing the Text

Work with your group members on this exercise. Discuss the answers carefully, particularly if there are disagreements among members of your group. In some cases there may be more than one possible interpretation.

1. How does the title relate to the text? How does this family relate to the setting, New York City? To what extent does the family live in New York?

   Explain and give examples from the text.

2. Give three examples of how the family tries to maintain its Indian cultural identity in the middle of New York.

3. Read each statement carefully, decide if it is true or false according to this passage, and then write *T* (true) or *F* (false) on the line in front of the statement.

a. _____ Jasmine, the narrator, feels trapped in her ethnic community in Flushing.

b. _____ Nirmala is interested in American life and customs.

c. _____ Nirmala's mother-in-law likes the fact that Nirmala has a job.

d. _____ Jasmine is unhappy because she is mistreated by Professorji and his family.

e. _____ Professorji is sympathetic to Jasmine's position.

4. Write the words *ghetto* and *neighborhood* on a piece of paper and then make a list of ideas that you associate with each word. After you finish, compare your list with those of others in your group. What are the similarities and differences? What words would you like to add to your list now?

5. What is the main problem or issue in this passage? Do you think there will be a resolution? Why or why not? Be as specific as possible in your answer.

2.8
Vocabulary Study

Study the italicized words and phrases in their contexts and guess at their meanings. Write your guess in the first blank. Then look up the word or phrase in your dictionary and write the definition in the second blank.

1, 2, 3, and **4.**   (paragraph 1) Professorji and his family put me up for five months—and it could have been five years, given the *elasticity* of the Indian family—just because I was the helpless widow of his favorite student. I was also efficient and uncomplaining, but they would have *tolerated* a *clumsy whiner* just as easily.

elasticity

a. (guess) _____

b. (dictionary) _____

tolerated

a. (guess) _____

b. (dictionary) _____

clumsy

a. (guess) _____

b. (dictionary) _____

whiner

a. (guess) _____

b. (dictionary) _____

5 and **6.** (paragraph 6) They both came back at six o'clock, *harassed* and *foul-tempered,* looking first for snacks and tea, later for a major dinner.

harassed

a. (guess) _____

b. (dictionary) _____

foul-tempered

a. (guess) _____

b. (dictionary) _____

7. (paragraph 8) Nirmala worked all day in a sari store on our block. . . . An *adjacent* shop under the same Gujarati ownership sold sweets and spices, and rented Hindi movies on cassettes.

a. (guess) _____

b. (dictionary) _____

8. (paragraph 11) I could not admit that I had accustomed myself to American clothes. American clothes *disguised* my widowhood.

a. (guess) _____

b. (dictionary) _____

9. (paragraph 12) Flushing, with all its immigrant services at hand, frightened me. I, who had every reason to fear America, was *intrigued* by the city and the land beyond the rivers.

a. (guess) _____

b. (dictionary) _____

10. (paragraph 16) Sundays were our days to eat too much and give in to *nostalgia*, to take the carom board out of the coat closet, to sit cross-legged on dhurries and matchmake marriages for adolescent cousins or younger siblings.

a. (guess) _____

b. (dictionary) _____

11. (paragraph 20) Some afternoons when Professorji was out working, and Nirmala was in her shop, and the old Vadheras were snoring through their siestas, I would find myself in the bathroom with the light off, head down on the cold, cracked rim of the sink, sobbing from unnamed, unfulfilled wants. In Flushing I felt *immured*. An imaginary brick wall topped with barbed wire cut me off from the past and kept me from breaking into the future. I was a prisoner doing unreal time.

a. (guess) _____

b. (dictionary) _____

12 and **13.** (paragraphs 24 and 25) "A green card," he said, "is an expensive but not an impossible *proposition*. For the rich, such a matter is arranged daily."

"Then arrange it!" I begged. "Please! I'm dying in this *limbo*." I'd sign any IOU he wanted, at any interest rate he fixed, if he would advance the two or three thousand.

proposition

a. (guess) _____

b. (dictionary) _____

limbo

a. (guess) _____

b. (dictionary) _____

14. (paragraph 27) I calculated in my head. Three thousand dollars would come to fifty thousand rupees. My brothers were generous, loyal, *ingenious* men, but they couldn't get together fifty thousand fixing motor scooters in Hasnapur.

a. (guess) _____

b. (dictionary) _____

2.9
Drawing Inferences

It is important to be able to draw inferences, i.e., to read between the lines, to understand the deeper meaning of a passage. To draw an inference, you must first read the passage carefully, think carefully about the context and the facts that are given, and then go on to make a decision about the underlying meaning that is implied but not stated. To practice this reading skill, study the following passages and explain deeper meanings you can infer from the underlined sentences.

1. Professorji and his family put me up for five months—and it could have been five years, given the elasticity of the Indian family—just because I was the helpless widow of his favorite student. I was also efficient and uncomplaining, but they would have tolerated a clumsy whiner just as easily. (paragraph 1)

What is the underlying meaning of the this sentence?

2. Every night, Nirmala brought home a new Hindi film for the VCR. Showings began promptly at nine o'clock, just after an enormous dinner, and lasted till midnight. They were Bombay's "B" efforts at best, commercial failures and quite a few famous flops, burnished again by the dim light of nostalgia. I could not unroll my sleeping mat until the film was over. (paragraph 9)

What inference can you draw from the underlined sentence?

3. <u>I could not admit that I had accustomed myself to American clothes.</u> <u>American clothes disguised my widowhood.</u> In a T-shirt and cords, I was taken for a student. In this apartment of artificially maintained Indianness, I wanted to distance myself from everything Indian. . . . To them, I was a widow who should show a proper modesty of appearance and attitude. If not, it appeared I was competing with Nirmala. (paragraph 11)

   What do you understand from the underlined sentences?

4. Professorji and Nirmala did not go out at night. <u>"Why waste the money when we have everything here?" And truly they did. They had Indian-food stores in the block, Punjabi-newspapers and Hindi film magazines at the corner newsstand, and a movie every night without having to dress up for it.</u> (paragraph 14)

   What can you infer about Professorji's and Nirmala's interests from the underlined sentences?

2.10
Application, Critical Evaluation, and Synthesis

Choose one or more topics to discuss with your small group or to write about.

1. The narrator of this passage is unhappy and depressed. Why? How do the conditions of her present life contribute to her feelings? What are the constraints and limitations of her life? Describe her life and explain why she feels trapped. Find some sentences that show how she feels. Have you ever had a period in your life when you felt trapped? If so, explain your situation in detail and compare and contrast it with the narrator's situation. What was happening in your life at that time? Why were you frustrated? What did you do, if anything, to resolve or change the situation? Did you get help from others, as the narrator did? Explain in detail. Were you successful in making the change you wished? What advice would you give others who feel trapped in a particular situation? Be specific.

2. Jasmine, the narrator, and Nirmala are the same age, and they both come from traditional village backgrounds. Yet they are very different in personality and outlook on life. They have different goals. They are neither pleased nor frustrated by the same things. Compare and contrast Jasmine and Nirmala. Give specific examples to make your points about the differences between them. What predictions would you make about their lives ten years after the story? Why? Explain in detail. Why do you think they are so different from each other?

3. Describe the relationship between Professorji and his wife in detail. What does their relationship tell the reader about traditional roles for husband and wife in Indian society? Compare these roles with traditional roles in your society.

4. The image of the video movie is important in this passage. What is the main theme of this passage and how does the video image relate to it? How do the different characters relate to the videos?

5. "The Vadheras . . . had retired behind ghetto walls." What point is the writer trying to make in this sentence? Do you think this is a valid point about immigrant life in general? Explain and give examples from your own experience, the experiences of others, or from your reading.

© Ulrike Welsch

Immigrants:
How They're Helping
to Revitalize the U.S. Economy

How do immigrants affect the U.S. economy? Do they contribute to economic growth and development? Or do they use up more than their share of welfare and other societal resources? *Business Week* (July 13, 1992) takes an in-depth look at the impact of immigrants on the U.S. economy in this article, written by Michael J. Mandel and Christopher Farrell with assistance from Dori Jones Yang in Seattle, Gloria Lau in Los Angeles, Christina Del Valle in Washington, S. Lynne Walker in San Diego, and *Business Week* bureau reports. Reprinted by permission.

3.1
First Reading

Read the article quickly for the main ideas. Pay attention to the title and the text headings as you read. Do *not* stop to look up words in your dictionary.

Give me your tired, your poor,
Your huddled masses yearning to breathe free. . . .

1 Those words carved into the base of the Statue of Liberty speak to America's vision of itself. We were, and still are, a nation of immigrants. In the 1980s alone, a stunning 8.7 million people poured into the U.S., matching the great immigration decade of 1900–10. But with the country facing difficult economic and social problems, is it time to put aside our romantic past and kick away the immigrant welcome mat?

2 A lot of Americans feel the answer is "yes." In a *Business Week*/Harris poll, 68% of respondents said today's immigration is bad for the country, even though most thought it was good in the past. . . . And in areas like recession-weary Southern California, immigrants are being blamed for everything from rising unemployment to a rocketing state budget deficit. "I understand, in the past, 'give me your tired, your poor.' Today, the U.S. has to look at our own huddled masses first," says former Colorado Governor Richard D. Lamm.

3 This rising resentment against immigrants is no surprise. The million or so immigrants—including 200,000 illegals—that will arrive in the U.S. this year are coming at a time when unemployment is high and social services strained. Unlike past waves of immigration, the new immigrants are mainly

from Asia and Latin America. And just like the American work force, these immigrants are split between the highly skilled and well-educated and those with minimal skills and little education. Hungry for work, the newcomers compete for jobs with Americans, particularly with the less skilled. The large number of untrained immigrants, especially those from Mexico, are finding it harder to move up the employment ladder than did past generations of newcomers. And in the cities, the new immigrants seem to inflame racial and ethnic conflicts.

4 But on balance, the economic benefits of being an open-door society far outweigh the costs. For one thing, the U.S. is reaping a bonanza of highly educated foreigners. In the 1980s alone, an unprecedented 1.5 million college-educated immigrants joined the U.S. work force. More and more, America's high-tech industries, from semiconductors to biotechnology, are depending on immigrant scientists, engineers, and entrepreneurs to remain competitive. And the immigrants' links to their old countries are boosting U.S. exports to such fast-growing regions as Asia and Latin America.

5 Even immigrants with less education are contributing to the economy as workers, consumers, business owners, and taxpayers. Some 11 million immigrants are working, and they earn at least $240 billion a year, paying more than $90 billion in taxes. That's a lot more than the estimated $5 billion immigrants receive in welfare. Immigrant entrepreneurs, from the corner grocer to the local builder, are creating jobs—and not only for other immigrants. Vibrant immigrant communities are revitalizing cities and older suburbs that would otherwise be suffering from a shrinking tax base. Says John D. Kasarda, a sociologist at the University of North Carolina at Chapel Hill: "There is substantial evidence that immigrants are a powerful benefit to the economy, and very little evidence that they are negative."

Review

1. Why do many people in the U.S. resent new immigrants at this time?
2. What are some of the ways new immigrants can benefit the economy and society in general?

Prediction

3. Patterns of immigration have changed. Where do you think most new immigrants in the U.S. come from now?
4. How do you think immigrants now are different from earlier immigrants?

---

6 In 1965, when Congress overhauled the immigration laws, nobody expected this great tide of new immigrants. But that law made it easier to bring close relatives into the country and, influenced by the civil-rights movement, eliminated racially-based barriers to immigration. Prior to that, it was difficult for anyone who was not European or Canadian to settle here. The result: a surge of immigrants from Asia and Latin America, especially

from countries like South Korea and the Philippines that had close economic and military ties to the U.S. And once a group got a foothold in the U.S., it would continue to expand by bringing over more family members.

7 **New Wave.** The aftermath of the Vietnam War provided the second powerful source of immigrants. Over the last 10 years, the U.S. granted permanent resident status to about 1 million refugees, mostly from Vietnam, Cambodia, and Laos. And now the end of the cold war is tapping another immigrant stream: Between 1989—1992, the fastest growing group of new settlers was refugees from Eastern Europe and the former Soviet Union.

8 Throughout the 1970s and 1980s, a total of some 5 million illegal immigrants from Mexico and other countries settled in the U.S., drawn by opportunity here and fleeing economic troubles at home. Many settled in Southern California and Texas. In 1986, Congress passed the Immigration Reform & Control Act (IRCA), which imposed penalties on employers who hired illegal immigrants but also gave amnesty to many illegal immigrants. About 2.5 million people have become permanent residents under the amnesty program. And the pending North American Free Trade Agreement, by strengthening economic ties between Mexico and the U.S., might very well increase illegal immigration in the short run rather than diminish it.[1]

9 Opening the gates to Asians and Latin Americans dramatically altered the face of immigration. In the 1950s, 68% of legal immigrants came from Europe or Canada. In the 1980s, the percentage fell to only 13%. Conversely, the proportion of legal immigrants coming from Latin America and Asia rose from 31% to 84%, including illegal aliens granted amnesty under the 1986 law.

10 As the ethnic mix of the new immigrants changed, so did their levels of skill. At the low end, the plethora of low-wage service-sector jobs drew in a large number of unskilled, illiterate newcomers. About one-third of immigrant workers are high school dropouts, and one-third of those entered the U.S. illegally.

11 But the number of skilled immigrants has been increasing as well. "The level of education of recent immigrants has definitely increased over the last 10 years," says Elaine Sorensen, an immigration expert at the Urban Institute. About one-quarter of immigrant workers are college graduates, slightly higher than for native-born Americans. Some groups, such as Indians, are on average much better educated than today's Americans. Observes Steven Newman, an executive at the New York Association for New Americans, which will resettle about 20,000 from the former Soviet Union this year, including many engineers, computer programmers, and other skilled workers: "The only thing they lack is English skills."

12 **Talent Base.** Even immigrants who were doing well in their home countries are being drawn to the U.S. Take Subramonian Shankar, the 43-year-old president of American Megatrends Inc., a maker of personal-computer

---

1. The North American Free Trade Agreement was passed in November 1993; its effect on immigration is not yet clear as of this writing.

State of Residence	Legal Permanent Residents		Eligible to Apply for Naturalization	
	Number	Percent	Number	Percent
All States	10,525,000	100.0%	5,776,000	100.0%
California	3,717,000	35.3%	2,265,000	39.2%
New York	1,498,000	14.2%	669,000	11.6%
Texas	825,000	7.8%	483,000	8.4%
Florida	790,000	7.5%	405,000	7.0%
New Jersey	462,000	4.4%	231,000	4.0%
Illinois	457,000	4.3%	194,000	3.4%
Massachusetts	310,000	2.9%	177,000	3.1%
Virginia	183,000	1.7%	97,000	1.7%
Maryland	178,000	1.7%	97,000	1.7%
Washington	174,000	1.7%	84,000	1.5%
Other States	1,931,000	18.3%	1,074,000	18.6%

Population estimates by state of residence: Legal permanent residents and aliens eligible to apply for naturalization as of April 1996. (Courtesy of U.S. INS)

motherboards and software based in Norcross, Georgia. He was director of personal-computer R & D [research and development] at one of India's largest conglomerates. Then in 1980, he came to the U.S. In 1985, he and a partner founded AMI, which last year had sales of $70 million and employed 130 workers, both immigrants and native-born Americans. ""I couldn't have done this in India," says Shankar. "That's one good thing about America. If you're determined to succeed, there are ways to get it done."

13   And U.S. industry has been eager to take advantage of the influx. About 40% of the 200 researchers in the Communications Sciences Research wing at AT&T Bell Laboratories were born outside the U.S. In Silicon Valley, the jewel of America's high-tech centers, much of the technical work force is foreign-born. At Du Pont Merck Pharmaceutical Co., an $800 million-a-year joint venture based in Wilmington, Del., losartan, an antihypertensive drug now in clinical trials, was invented by a team that included two immigrants from Hong Kong and a scientist whose parents migrated from Lithuania. People from different backgrounds bring a richness of outlook, says Joseph A. Mollica, chief executive of Du Pont Merck, "which lets you look at both problems and opportunities from a slightly different point of view."

14   The next generation of scientists and engineers at U.S. high-tech companies will be dominated by immigrants. While about the same number of Americans are getting science PhDs, the number of foreign-born students receiving science doctorates more than doubled between 1981 and 1991, to 37% of the

total. In biology, the hot field of the 1990s, the number of non-U.S. citizens getting doctorates tripled over the last 10 years. And about 51% of computer-science doctorates in 1991 went to foreign-born students. "We are getting really good students—very, very smart people," says Victor L. Thacker, director of the office of international education at Carnegie Mellon University, which has doubled its foreign enrollment since 1985.

15 **Up The Ladder.** Attracted by the research opportunities and the chance to use what they know, about half of them stay in the U.S. after graduation, estimates Angel G. Jordan, a professor and former provost at Carnegie Mellon, who himself emigrated from Spain in 1956. And the 1990 changes to the immigration law, by increasing the number of visas for skilled immigrants, will increase the number of foreign graduates who remain in the U.S.

16 Besides boosting the nation's science and engineering know-how, the latest wave of immigrants is loaded with entrepreneurs. Korean greengrocers and other immigrant merchants are familiar sights in many cities, but the entrepreneurial spirit goes far beyond any one ethnic group or single line of business. Almost by definition, anyone who moves to a new country has a lot of initiative and desire to do well. Says Dan Danilov, an immigration lawyer based in Seattle, "They're willing to put in more hours and more hard work."

17 And do they work. Paul Yuan, for example, left Taiwan with his wife in 1975, seven days after their marriage, eventually settling in Seattle with several thousand dollars in life savings and no work visas. For two years Yuan, a college graduate, worked in Chinese restaurants. Then, in 1978, he became a legal resident and opened his own travel agency while working nights as a hotel dishwasher. Today, at age 43, Yuan owns a thriving Seattle travel business, and he and his family live in a $4 million house. In 1965, 21-year-old Humberto Galvez left Mexico City for Los Angeles. He started pumping gas and busing tables, working his way up the ladder, with a lot of bumps along the way. After starting, then selling, the chain of 19 "El Poco Loco" charbroiled chicken restaurants in the Los Angeles area, he now owns six Pescado Mojado (wet fish) seafood diners, employing 100 workers.

18 Immigrant entrepreneurs have also made big contributions to the U.S. export boom. Businesses run by immigrants from Asia, for example, have ready-made connections overseas. Immigrants bring a global perspective and international contacts to insular American businesses. And it is not just Asians. From Poles to Mexicans, "the utility of the immigrant groups is that they bring their fearless spirit of competing globally," observes Michael Goldberg, dean of the University of British Columbia's business school.

19 That's certainly true for Benjamin and Victor Acevedo, two brothers whose family moved from Tijuana, Mexico, to California in 1960, when they were 3 and 8. In 1984, the Acevedos started up a wood-products company in the south San Diego community of San Ysidro, just across the U.S.-Mexico border. Cal-State Lumber Sales Inc. now commands 10% of the architectural molding market in the U.S. and had 110 employees and $147 million in sales last year. And as long-term trade barriers with Mexico crumbled over the past few years, the Acevedos have been able to take advantage of their

bicultural heritage. "My brother and I started shipping all over Mexico, and our export business boomed," says Ben Acevedo.

20 **Urban Boosters.** Perhaps the least-appreciated economic benefit from the new immigrants is the contribution they are making to American cities. Immigrants have been drawn to the major metropolitan areas. They are invigorating the cities and older suburbs by setting up businesses, buying homes, paying taxes, and shopping at the corner grocery. In the past decade, population in the nation's 10 largest cities grew by 4.7%, but without new immigrants it would have shrunk by 6.8%, according to calculations done by *Business Week* based on the 1990 census. Almost a million immigrants came to New York City in the 1980s, more than offsetting the 750,000 decline in the rest of the city's population. Indeed, about a third of adults in New York, 44% of adults in Los Angeles, and 70% of adults in Miami are now foreign-born, according to the 1990 census.

21 Immigrants have turned around many a decaying neighborhood. Ten years ago, Jefferson Boulevard in south Dallas was a dying inner-city business district filled with vacant storefronts. Today, there are almost 800 businesses there and on neighboring streets, and about three-quarters of them are owned by Hispanics, many of them first- and second-generation immigrants. "They were hungry enough to start their own businesses," says Leonel Ramos, president of the Jefferson Area Assn. And sociologist Kasarda adds: "There is a whole multiplier effect throughout the community."

22 Moreover, immigrants provide a hardworking labor force to fill the low-paid jobs that make a modern service economy run. In many cities industries such as hotels, restaurants, and child care would be hardpressed without immigrant labor. At the Seattle Sheraton, 28% of the hotel's staff of 650 is foreign-born, and most work in housekeeping, dishwashing, and other low-paying jobs. "We don't have American-born people apply for those positions," says Carla Murray, hotel manager for the Seattle Sheraton.

Review

1. Were your predictions about changing immigration patterns correct? According to this article, where are most recent U.S. immigrants from? How is this a change from the past?

2. Give some specific examples of ways new immigrants have benefited the economy and society.

Prediction

3. You are now going to read about some problems associated with immigration. What do you think some of these problems could be?

4. Which groups of people do you think are hurt most by immigrants?

5. Do you think immigrants use more than their share of social services (e.g., welfare, healthcare)?

6. On the whole, do you think immigration offers more advantages or disadvantages to U.S. society? What do you think the conclusion of this article will be?

23 **Margin Dwellers.** But all the economic vitality immigrants add comes at a price. While economists and employers may celebrate industrious immigrants, many barely survive on the economy's margins. "They don't go to the doctor, don't buy insurance, don't buy glasses, don't buy anything you or I are used to," says Hannah Hsiao, head of the Employment Program at the Chinese Information & Service Center in Seattle. A firing, unpaid wages, a deportation, or some other calamity is always threatening. And racial discrimination makes their lot even harder, especially those who don't speak English. Some, like economist George J. Borjas of the University of California at San Diego, worry that these poor and unskilled immigrants are condemned to years of poverty.

24 In many cities, newcomers and long-time residents struggle over jobs and access to scarce government resources. Immigrants are straining health and education services in some cities and suburbs. And many African-Americans believe the apparent success of immigrants is coming at their expense. In New York City, blacks picketed a number of Korean greengrocers. According to the *Business Week*/Harris poll, 73% of blacks said businesses would rather hire immigrants than black Americans.

25 The people hurt worst by immigrants are native-born high school dropouts, who already face a tough time. They compete for jobs against a large number of unskilled immigrants, including illegals from Mexico and the Caribbean who are poorly educated, unable to start their own businesses, and willing to work harder for lower wages than most longtime residents.

26 For Americans who have at least a high school education, however, the influx of immigrants hasn't had much negative impact. High school graduates, for example, saw their real wages decline by 10% in the 1980s. But almost all of that drop came from import competition and rising skill requirements of many jobs, and only a fraction from immigrant competition, according to a study by Borjas of UC, San Diego, and Richard Freeman and Lawrence Katz of Harvard University. "It is extremely convenient to point a finger at immigrants," says Muzaffar Chishti, director of the Immigration Project for the International Ladies' Garment Workers' Union in New York. "But the problems of black employment are outside the immigrant domain."

27 Moreover, for all their struggles, most immigrants are hardly wards of the state. Illegals are not eligible for welfare, and even many legal immigrants shun it, fearing that it will make it harder to become a citizen in the future. A study by Borjas shows that in 1980—the latest national data available— only 8.8% of immigrant households received welfare, compared to 7.9% of all native-born Americans. And with the education and skill levels of immigrants rising in the 1980s, the expectations are that the spread between the two hasn't worsened, and may have even narrowed. In Los Angeles County, for example, immigrants amount to 16% of the 722,000 people on Aid to Families with Dependent Children, the government's main welfare program. Yet immigrants are more than 30% of the county's population. "Immigrants benefit natives through the public coffers by using less than their share of services and paying more than their share of taxes," says Julian L. Simon, a University of Maryland economist.

28 **School Daze.** One real concern is whether urban school systems can handle the surge of immigrant children. "The public school is the vehicle through which the child of immigrants becomes Americanized," says Jeffrey S. Passel, a demographer for the Washington-based Urban Institute. But in many cities, the task of educating immigrant students has become an enormous burden. In Los Angeles, 39% of the city's students don't speak English well, and in Seattle, 21% come from homes where English is not the family's first language. In the nation's capital, the school system is nearly overwhelmed by a huge number of Vietnamese, Haitians, and Salvadorean children. "If the school system is inadequate, then it's much more difficult to help immigrants move up the economic ladder," says Robert D. Hormats, vice-chairman of Goldman, Sachs International and head of the Trilateral Commission's working group on immigration.

29 City schools, despite the constraint of tight resources, are finding innovative ways to reach immigrant children. In Seattle, about half the immigrant students speak such limited English that they qualify for a program where they are taught subjects in simplified English. The Los Angeles schools offer dual language classes in Spanish, Korean, Armenian, Cantonese, Filipino, Farsi, and Japanese. Other organizations, such as unions, are also teaching immigrants English. In New York, the Garment Workers Union, often called the immigrant union, offers English classes to its members and their families.

30 In the coming decade, it won't be easy to assimilate the new immigrants, whether they come from Laos or Russia. But the positives far outweigh any short-term negatives. In today's white-hot international competition, the U.S. profits from the ideas and innovations of immigrants. And by any economic calculus, their hard work adds far more to the nation's wealth than the resources they drain. It is still those "huddled masses yearning to breathe free" who will keep the American dream burning bright for most of us.

Number of Words: 3,157		
Reading Times		**Reading Speed**
1st reading _____ minutes		20 minutes = 158 words per minute
3rd reading _____ minutes		18 minutes = 175 wpm
		16 minutes = 197 wpm
		14 minutes = 225 wpm
		12 minutes = 263 wpm

3.2
Second Reading

Go back and read the article again. Take as much time as you need. Look up some of the unfamiliar words in the glossary at the end of the book or in your dictionary if you wish.

3.3
Third Reading

Read the article quickly a third time. Concentrate on understanding the main ideas of the article and the meanings of new vocabulary words in the contexts in which they appear.

3.4
Reader Response

In order to explore your response to this reading, write for 15 minutes about anything that interested you in this article. You may wish to write about your reactions to some of the ideas presented here—or you may wish to disagree with something in the article. Try to explore *your own thoughts and feelings* as much as possible. Do *not* merely summarize or restate the ideas in the article.

3.5
Response Sharing

Read your response to two or three other people in your class. Listen carefully to what the others have written. After you have discussed each other's responses, talk about other points of interest in the article.

3.6
Identifying Main Ideas

Working with the same small group, make a list of the main ideas in this article. Be sure to state the main ideas in your own words. Don't just copy sentences directly from the text. Think carefully about what the writers are trying to tell you.

3.7
Analyzing the Text

Work with your group members on this exercise. Discuss the answers carefully, particularly if there are disagreements among members of your group. In some cases there may be more than one possible interpretation.

1. The subject of this article is:

    a. the effects immigrants have on the U.S. economy.

    b. the reasons immigrants come to the U.S.

    c. the objections people have to the U.S. immigration policy.

2. How does the title relate to the article? Does the title fit the article? Explain and give examples.

3. Read each statement carefully, decide if it is true or false according to this article, and then write *T* (true) or *F* (false) on the line in front of the statement.

   a. _____ A majority of people responding to the poll cited in this article said they thought immigration was good for the U.S. today.

   b. _____ Former Colorado governor Richard D. Lamm stated that the U.S. should take care of the people already in the U.S. first instead of encouraging new immigration.

   c. _____ Immigrants contribute far more to the economy than they receive in welfare and other societal benefits.

   d. _____ On average, recent immigrants are not as well educated as former immigrants were.

   e. _____ Since 1965, immigration from Asia and Latin America has greatly increased.

4. The thesis of this article is that

   a. immigration has neutral value; it is neither positive nor negative for the U.S. economy.

   b. immigration has a strongly negative impact on the U.S. economy.

   c. immigration has a strongly positive impact on the U.S. economy.

   Give examples to support your answer.

5. What is the relationship between resentment against immigrants and high unemployment and strained social services (see paragraph 3)?

3.8
Vocabulary Study

Study the italicized words and phrases in their contexts and guess at their meanings. Write your guess in the first blank. Then look up the word or phrase in your dictionary and write the definition in the second blank.

1. (paragraph 1) In the 1980s alone, a *stunning* 8.7 million people poured into the U.S., matching the great immigration decade of 1900–10.

   a. (guess) _____

   b. (dictionary) _____

2. (paragraph 2) And in areas like recession-weary Southern California, immigrants are being blamed for everything from rising unemployment to a *rocketing* state budget deficit.

   a. (guess) _____

   b. (dictionary) _____

3. (paragraph 3) This *rising* resentment against immigrants is no surprise.

a. (guess) _____

b. (dictionary) _____

4. (paragraph 3) And in the cities, the new immigrants seem to *inflame* racial and ethnic conflicts.

a. (guess) _____

b. (dictionary) _____

5 and **6.** (paragraph 4) For one thing, the U.S. is *reaping* a *bonanza* of highly educated foreigners.
reaping

a. (guess) _____

b. (dictionary) _____

bonanza

a. (guess) _____

b. (dictionary) _____

7, 8, and **9.** (paragraph 5) *Vibrant* immigrant communities are *revitalizing* cities and older suburbs that would otherwise be suffering from a *shrinking* tax base.
vibrant

a. (guess) _____

b. (dictionary) _____

revitalizing

a. (guess) _____

b. (dictionary) _____

shrinking

a. (guess) _____

b. (dictionary) _____

10. (paragraph 10) At the low end, the *plethora* of low-wage service-sector jobs drew in a large number of unskilled, illiterate newcomers.

a. (guess) _____

b. (dictionary) _____

3.9
Distinguishing Fact from Opinion

It is important to be able to distinguish fact from opinion in all forms of communication. Study these statements, decide whether they are facts or opinions, and then write *F* (fact) or *O* (opinion) on the line. Remember that a fact is something that can be verified or checked. An opinion is a personal belief, it is subjective, and it may or may not be true.

Example:

_____*O*_____ Immigration is good for the U.S. economy. (This may or may not be true. Supporting data would be needed to verify it.)

_____*F*_____ In a *Business Week*/Harris poll, 68% of respondents said today's immigration is bad for the country. (This is a fact because it can be verified by looking at the poll results.)

1. _____ In the 1980s alone, a stunning 8.7 million people poured into the U.S., matching the great immigration decade of 1900–10.

2. _____ Unlike past waves of immigration, the new immigrants are mainly from Asia and Latin America.

3. _____ On balance, the economic benefits of being an open-door society far outweigh the costs.

4. _____ In 1965, Congress changed the immigration laws.

5. _____ Immigrants have turned around many decaying neighborhoods.

6. _____ Today, three-quarters of the almost 800 businesses on Jefferson Boulevard in south Dallas are owned by Hispanics, many of them first- and second-generation immigrants.

7. _____ Throughout the 1970s and 1980s, a total of some 5 million illegal immigrants from Mexico and other countries settled in the U.S.

8. _____ Immigrants are hardworking and eager to make progress in their new country.

9. _____ "The utility of the immigrant groups is that they bring their fearless spirit of competing globally," observes Michael Goldberg, dean of the University of British Columbia's business school.

10. _____ In 1984, the Acevedos started up a wood-products company in the south San Diego community of San Ysidro, just across the U.S.-Mexico border. Cal-State Lumber Sales Inc. now commands 10% of the architectural molding market in the U.S. and had 110 employees and $147 million in sales last year.

3.10
Application, Critical Evaluation, And Synthesis

Choose one or more topics to discuss with your small group or to write about.

1. What are some of the benefits of immigration to the U.S. economy and to society in general? Make a chart like the one below to help you organize your ideas. After you list a benefit, explain it and, if possible, give an example from the article or from some other source, including your own experience.

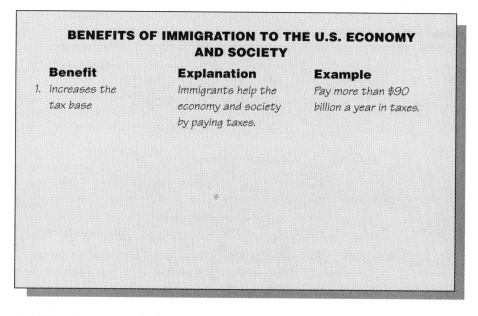

BENEFITS OF IMMIGRATION TO THE U.S. ECONOMY AND SOCIETY

Benefit	Explanation	Example
1. Increases the tax base	Immigrants help the economy and society by paying taxes.	Pay more than $90 billion a year in taxes.

2. Why do you think that a majority of Americans surveyed in the *Business Week*/Harris poll said they thought today's immigration is bad for the country, even though most thought it was good in the past? What are some of the reasons they may have had for their negative opinion of immigration? How do you explain the differences in opinions between respondents to this poll and the writers of the article you have just read?

3. What is the effect of immigration (or emigration) on the area in which you live? Give specific examples of the effects. In general, has immigration (or emigration) had a positive or a negative effect on your area? Have you had any personal experience with immigration? If so, explain in detail.

4. What were the most interesting points in this article in your opinion? Were you surprised by any parts? If so, which ones and why? In general, how would you evaluate this article? How carefully do you think it was researched? Do you think that the writers' opinions were adequately supported by facts? Give examples. Would you recommend this article to someone interested in this topic? Why or why not?

5. Go to a library and look up recent articles on immigration. (For help in doing library research, turn to page 243) Are these articles positive or negative toward immigration? Explain and give examples. What are the main points made in each article?

AT THE END OF EVERY UNIT YOU ARE INVITED TO TURN TO THE EXPANSION SECTION BEGINNING ON PAGE 233. THIS SECTION CONCENTRATES ON THE FUNDAMENTALS OF LIBRARY RESEARCH AND REPORT WRITING.

Sample Reader Response #1 (see Ex. 1.4, page 8)

> I remember very well the day I left my home in Jamaica to come to the United States to go to university. I had planned for this day and dreamed about it for so many month and years. My brother and sister were livin in England. I could have gone there but I wanted to be completly on my own in a new ~~contry~~ country. I was so excite — but at the last moment, I was terrified. "What is waiting for me?" I wondered. And I was afraid I would never see my dear grandmother alive again. I cried and I cried. My grandmother cried too but she said, "You must go, my dear little one. It's time you go and try your wings." My lovely childhood was over.
>
> — Victoria A.

Sample Reader Response #2

I had never been on an airplane before when I left Cairo to go to England. I was so fascinated about the experience. How could we be so far up in the skye seeing a movie and having a lovely dinner??? I felt I was literally in the heaven as I looked down on the clouds. I felt then my life was perfect. It was a lovely time. I wish it would last forever.

– Samir S.

Vocabulary Games

Here is a chance to review some of the vocabulary you have encountered in this unit. After you finish the game quizzes on your own, discuss your answers with your group members. You may use your dictionary to look up items to resolve disagreements. Scoring: 5 points for each correct answer.

Synonyms

Read each passage carefully and then draw a circle around the word or phrase that means the same thing (or almost the same thing) as the italicized word or phrase. If a word or phrase has more than one meaning, choose the meaning that fits the context in the passage.

Example: Mexico City is a large, *cosmopolitan* city.

a. crowded   b. sophisticated   c. polluted

Passage One

Juan Pablo Alvarez traveled from Lima, the capital, to a *remote* province in Peru to study local farming conditions. The local farmers spoke to Mr. Alvarez very *bluntly* and *vehemently* about the lack of *support* they had received from local government officials. They said the hot sun had *parched* the earth and destroyed their corn crop.

1. *remote*

   a. distant   b. poor   c. backward

2. *bluntly*

   a. angrily   b. approvingly   c. directly

3. *vehemently*

   a. angrily   b. cautiously   c. passionately

4. *support*

   a. control   b. assistance   c. money

5. *parched*

   a. scorched   b. revived   c. nourished

Passage Two

When the jury announced its *verdict*, many people who had followed the trial carefully were shocked and *perplexed*. "This seems like a *rash* decision," the judge said to the jury. One juror explained, "Your Honor, we realize the defendant *threatened* his wife on several occasions, but we don't think he killed her. Furthermore, we don't think he is a *menace* to society."

6. *verdict*

a. judge's sentence   b. jury's decision   c. lawyer's closing argument

7. *perplexed*

a. surprised   b. angered   c. confused

8. *rash*

a. thoughtful   b. thoughtlesss   c. thought-provoking

9. *threatened*

a. said he would hurt [her]   b. said he would not hurt [her]   c. said he hated [her]

10. *menace*

a. danger   b. victim   c. murderer

Antonyms

Antonyms are words that have opposite meanings, e.g., cold-hot; tall-short; dark-light. Read each passage carefully and then draw a circle around the word or phrase that means the opposite (or almost the opposite) of the italicized word or phrase. If a word or phrase has more than one meaning, choose the meaning that fits the context in the passage.

Example: At Central Savings Bank it is *customary* to give new customers a small gift for opening a checking account.

a. usual   b. unusual   c. necessary

[*Unusual* is the antonym of *customary*.]

Passage Three

Mr. Versace did not want to *defy* his supervisor's instructions and the *traditional* policy of the bank, but he *was determined* to help Mrs. Mastroianni with her account problems. He spoke to his supervisor very quietly and *deferentially*. Finally, his supervisor *grudgingly* admitted Mr. Versace had brought up an important point.

11. *defy*

a. support   b. question   c. go against

12. *traditional*

a. customary   b. new   c. former

13. *was determined* (to help)

   a. fully intended   b. refused   c. tried

14. *deferentially*

   a. carefully   b. rudely   c. politely

15. *grudgingly*

   a. quickly   b. unwillingly   c. willingly

Logical Relationships

Look at the first pair of words, determine the relationship between them (are they synonyms or antonyms?). Then circle the word or phrase that fills in the blank to logically make a similar type of relationship.

   Example: tall : high = short : *low*
          a. high   ⟨b. low⟩   c. fat

         [*Tall* is related to *high* in the same way as *short* is related to *low*.]

16. hate : strongly dislike = prejudice : _____

   a. discrimination   b. acceptance   c. tolerance

   [*Hate* is related to *strongly dislike* in the same way as *prejudice* is related to _____.]

17. visitor : guest = immigrant : _____

   a. emigrant   b. illegal alien   c. person born elsewhere

18. open : closed = restricted : _____

   a. forbidden   b. free   c. controlled

   [*Hint: Open* and *closed* are antonyms]

19. destroy : ruin = revitalize : _____

   a. invigorate   b. weaken   c. support

20. tolerate : refuse = permit : _____

   a. allow   b. consent   c. forbid

SCORE: Number of correct answers _____ × 5 = _____

You Are What You Eat

A round the world, people eat many different kinds of food to get the nourishment they need. In an effort to increase the world's food supply, modern technology is making some dramatic changes in how food is grown, stored, and sold, but not everyone agrees that these changes are wise or healthy for people. Food also has some social functions. For example, some families think it is important to eat meals together as a way of maintaining a sense of "family". Also, when people get together—to visit, to celebrate a special occasion, to do business—they often eat or drink.

Discussion

Before you begin reading, think about the following questions and discuss your answers. You may wish to choose two or three questions to explore in detail with a small group of students in your class.

1. Do you think you eat a healthy diet? Are the foods you eat nutritious? Give some examples.

2. Some people think special foods or drinks will make them stronger, healthier, or smarter. Do you know about any such foods? Do they really work?

3. Have you ever been surprised at the foods in other countries? What were these foods? Why were you surprised?

4. New technologies are changing food production. Genetic engineering can put chicken genes into a potato to protect it from disease, or insert bacteria genes into corn to kill insects. Strawberries that are irradiated with strong gamma rays can stay on the supermarket shelf for a few weeks without refrigeration. What do you think of such technologies? Are they useful or harmful? Are the benefits more important than the problems they may cause?

5. What are some of the major issues that you see in feeding the world's population? Make a list of these issues and think of some ways they might be solved.

Major issue	How solved

6. Do you like to celebrate special occasions with food (for example, enjoying a big dinner with family or friends, or bringing a friend a bottle of wine)? Is the food important at this time or does it just add to the celebration? Why?

The Food Guide Pyramid

A Guide to Daily Food Choices

KEY
- Fat (naturally occurring and added)
- Sugars (added)

These symbols show fat and added sugars in foods.

Fats, Oils, & Sweets
USE SPARINGLY

Milk, Yogurt, & Cheese Group
2-3 SERVINGS

Meat, Poultry, Fish, Dry Beans, Eggs, & Nuts Group
2-3 SERVINGS

Vegetable Group
3-5 SERVINGS

Fruit Group
2-4 SERVINGS

Bread, Cereal, Rice, & Pasta Group
6-11 SERVINGS

Courtesy of the US Department of Agriculture

What Do You Know about Nutrition?

How much do you know about good nutrition? Take this "nutrition quiz," which is based on current ideas about food and health. Then read the selection to find out the answers. The information in this reading comes from articles in *Newsweek*, *Family Circle*, *Time*, and *Delicious* magazines; the *New York Times*; and *Jane Brody's Good Food Book*.

1. Rice is a good source of protein. (True False)

2. Potatoes are a nutritious, low-calorie food. (True False)

3. Fresh vegetables are always better for you than frozen or canned vegetables. (True False)

4. All vitamin and mineral pills are equal in quality. (True False)

5. Vitamin pills can be dangerous to your health. (True False)

6. It is better not to eat any salt. (True False)

7. You can get enough protein without eating meat or fish. (True False)

8. You should eat equal amounts of protein (meat, fish, milk products, beans), starches (bread, rice, noodles), and fruits/vegetables. (True False)

9. There will be a time in the future when people can get all the nutrition they need by taking "food pills." (True False)

1.1

First Reading

Read the article quickly for the main ideas. Pay attention to the title and the general concepts as you read. Do *not* stop to look up words in your dictionary.

A. All of us eat every day, but most of us don't understand nutrition. How much do you know about nutrition? And what can you do to improve your eating habits? Decide whether these statements are true or false to see how much you know about current ideas on food and health. The answers may surprise you.

    1. Rice is a good source of protein.

        This is true. Rice is a major source of protein for over half the people in the world today. Brown rice (i.e., rice in its natural, whole grain form) is especially nutritious, but most people eat white rice, which contains less protein than brown rice. Rice is also a good source of the B vitamins and minerals.

2. Potatoes are a nutritious, low calorie food.

   True. Potatoes contain a vegetable protein that is almost as nutritious as milk protein, and they have almost no fat. The potato skin contains a wide variety of essential vitamins and minerals. With only 90 calories per 100 grams, potatoes are a low calorie food and become fattening only when you fry them or put butter, cheese, or other high calorie sauces on them.

3. Fresh vegetables are always better for you than frozen or canned vegetables.

   False. While this may seem surprising, the nutritional value of vegetables depends on how the vegetables are handled or cooked. Vegetables that are frozen immediately after they are picked will retain more nutrients than fresh vegetables that have been in storage or on a grocery store shelf for a long time. Overcooking, or cooking in too much water, also destroys vitamins.

4. All vitamin and mineral pills are equal in quality.

   False. Vitamin pills can give you a false sense of security. While most vitamin products are high-quality and can be a good, safe source of nutrients, not all vitamin products meet the same standards. The accuracy of dosages can vary, so you may not be getting the same dosage in each pill. Poorly-made pills might not dissolve completely in your stomach, so you would be getting less of the vitamin than you had expected. So look for high-quality products—ones that you can digest easily and that have reliable dosages.

5. Vitamin pills can be dangerous to your health.

   Yes, if you take too many. With certain vitamins, the body uses as much as it needs and passes the rest out. Other vitamins, especially Vitamins A and D, accumulate in the body and can cause damage if taken in extremely high amounts over a period of time. Extremely high amounts of Vitamin A, for example, can eventually lead to liver damage and blurred vision. On the other hand, it is safe to take a multiple-vitamin pill regularly, and some vitamins are even prescribed for medical purposes (e.g., niacin is used in very large dosages, under strict medical supervision, to lower cholesterol levels).

6. It is better not to eat any salt.

   False. We all need some salt, but most people eat more salt than they realize. Some salt occurs naturally in everything we eat. The problem occurs when we add salt to food, or eat food that already has a lot of salt added to it. Canned foods, frozen foods, snack foods and soy sauce contain a surprising amount of salt. Even ice cream and other sweet foods contain added salt.

7. You can get enough protein without eating meat or fish.

    Yes, you can. Many vegetarians do not eat any animal products. They get their protein by combining grains (such as rice, wheat, or corn) with beans, peas or lentils. Soybeans, which are eaten mostly in Asia, are a very good source of protein. Also, some vegetarians eat eggs or dairy products (such as yoghurt, milk, or cheese), which contain high quality proteins since they come from animals.

8. You should eat equal amounts of protein (meat, fish, milk products, beans), starches (bread, rice, noodles), and fruits/vegetables.

    Not true. In 1992, the U.S. Department of Agriculture developed a "food pyramid" that shows the proportions of different foods that make up a healthy diet. Rice and other starches make up the largest part at the base of the pyramid. In the middle are fruits and vegetables; you should eat plenty of these. Near the top are foods you should eat in smaller amounts—meat, fish, milk products, beans. At the very top are sugar and fats, which you should eat in very small amounts.

9. There will be a time in the future when people can get all the nutrition they need by taking "food pills."

    Probably not. The science of nutrition is very complex, and scientists still do not know everything about all the nutrients in food. It would be very difficult for pills to contain all the protein, carbohydrates, other nutrients, and fiber that we need to maintain the body and give it energy. Besides, most people like the taste and texture of food, so they probably would not want to take pills instead.

B. How did you do on this quiz? The best advice from nutritionists is to eat a well-balanced variety of foods every day based on the food pyramid. Then you will probably be getting enough vitamins, minerals, and other nutrients that your body needs. Combine this with some basic exercise a few times a week and you should stay healthy. Now, here's a bonus question to see what you know about exercise.

C. Bonus question: Walking isn't really exercise.　　　　　True or False

    False. Walking is an excellent exercise. Regular walks of 30 to 60 minutes, three or four times a week, will help you to stay healthy and fit. Of course, if you like to swim, run, play tennis or soccer (football), those are good exercise choices too, so by all means, do them. Have fun, eat well, and stay healthy!

Number of words: 963	
Reading Time	**Reading Speed**
1st reading _____ minutes	7 minutes = 138 wpm
3rd reading _____ mintues	6 minutes = 161 wpm
	5 minutes = 193 wpm
	4 minutes = 241 wpm
	3 minutes = 321 wpm

1.2
Second Reading

Go back and read the selection again. Take as much time as you need this time. Look up some of the unfamiliar words in the glossary at the end of this book or in your dictionary if you wish.

1.3
Third Reading

Read the selection quickly a third time. Concentrate on understanding the main ideas and the meanings of new vocabulary words in the contexts in which they appear.

1.4
Reader Response

In order to explore your response to this reading, write for 15 minutes about anything that interests you in this selection. You may wish to write about a personal experience this reading reminded you of—or you may wish to agree or disagree with something in the reading. Try to explore *your own thoughts and feelings* as much as possible. Do *not* merely summarize or restate the ideas in the selection.

1.5
Response Sharing

Read your response to two or three other people in your class. Listen carefully to what the others have written. After you have discussed each other's responses, talk about other points of interest in the selection.

1.6
Identifying Main Ideas

Working with the same small group, make a list of the main ideas in this selection. Be sure to state the main ideas in your own words. Don't just copy sentences directly from the text. Think carefully about what the writer is trying to tell you.

1.7
Analyzing the Text

Work with your group members on this exercise. Discuss the answers carefully, particularly if there are disagreements among members of your group. In some cases there may be more than one possible interpretation.

1. According to paragraph 1, which is more nutritious, brown or white rice? Why?

2. Paragraph 5 says "With certain vitamins, the body uses as much as it needs and passes the rest out."

It refers to	*The rest* refers to
a. vitamins not used.	a. vitamins not used.
b. the body.	b. the body.
c. only Vitamins A and D.	c. only Vitamins A and D.

3. a. What are some characteristics of high-quality vitamins?
   b. Why do you need to be careful when choosing vitamin pills?

4. "Canned foods, frozen foods, snack foods, and soy sauce contain a surprising amount of salt" (paragraph 6) means that these foods contain:

   a. an unknown amount of salt.

   b. not much salt.

   c. a lot of salt.

   Why does the author say this is "surprising"?

5. According to paragraph 8, which statement is *not* true about the food pyramid?

   a. You should eat more from the rice/bread group than from the meat/fish group.

   b. Sugar and fat are at the top because they taste the best.

   c. The food pyramid represents a healthy diet.

   Explain your answer.

1.8
Vocabulary Study

Study the italicized words and phrases in their contexts and guess their meanings. Write your guess on the first line. Then look up the word or phrase in your dictionary and write the definition on the second line.

1. (paragraph 2) Potatoes contain a vegetable protein that is almost as *nutritious* as milk protein, and they have almost no fat.

   a. (guess) _____

   b. (dictionary) _____

2 and 3. (paragraph 3) While this may seem surprising, the nutritional value of vegetables depends on how the vegetables are *handled* or cooked. Vegetables that are frozen immediately after they are picked will *retain* more nutrients than fresh vegetables that have been in storage or on a grocery store shelf for a long time.
   handled

   a. (guess) _____

   b. (dictionary) _____

retain

a. (guess) _____

b. (dictionary) _____

4 and **5.** (paragraph 4) The *accuracy* of dosages can vary, so you may not be getting the same *dosage* in each pill.
accuracy

a. (guess) _____

b. (dictionary) _____

dosage

a. (guess) _____

b. (dictionary) _____

6. (paragraph 8) In 1992, the U.S. Department of Agriculture developed a "food pyramid" that shows the *proportions* of different foods that make up a healthy diet. Rice and other starches make up the largest part . . . . In the middle are fruits and vegetables.

a. (guess) _____

b. (dictionary) _____

7. (paragraph 9) Besides, most people like the taste and *texture* of food, so they probably would not want to take pills instead.

a. (guess) _____

b. (dictionary) _____

1.9
Reading Charts

Look at the circle chart and the food pyramid. Then, working with your small group, answer the following questions. (Note: *Per capita* means each person. *Consumption* means the amount eaten.)

1. Look at the circle chart from a Canadian magazine. It shows

a. the foods that Canadians like to eat most.

b. why Canadians have gotten healthier between 1970 and 1988–89.

c. how many pounds of each food an average Canadian eats each year.

How do you know?

2. What do the dates 1970 and 1988–89 mean?

a. These are the only years that Canada gathered this information.

b. These are the years when people ate these foods the most.

c. These are the years used for comparison.

Why do you think so?

THE CHANGING TASTES OF CANADIANS
Per capita consumption of selected foods, in pounds per year

BEEF
1970 **84.2**
1989 **82.6**

BROCCOLI
1970 **0.66**
1988 **5.4**

POULTRY
1970 **45.1**
1989 **60.9**

PEAS
1970 **7**
1988 **3.9**

FISH
1970 **10.8**
1988 **15**

MUSHROOMS
1970 **1.7**
1988 **5.8**

FRUIT
1970 **236.7**
1988 **258.3**

BEANS
1970 **5.3**
1988 **4.3**

CANNED VEGETABLES
1970 **17.9**
1988 **11.6**

FRESH VEGETABLES
1970 **83.8**
1988 **125.1**

3. What two foods show the biggest increase in consumption? What are they? Do you think they indicate some pattern in the eating habits of Canadians?

4. How many foods show a decrease in consumption between 1970 and 1988–89? Do you think they indicate some pattern in the eating habits of Canadians?

5. Compare the consumption of fruit and fish.

   a. Both went up.

   b. Both went down.

   c. Fish went up and fruit went down.

6. Now look at the food pyramid, which was published by the U.S. Department of Agriculture in 1992. It is organized to show that

   a. the foods you should eat most are at the bottom.

   b. the foods you should eat most are at the top.

   c. you should eat any amount of any foods shown on the pyramid.

   What words in the pyramid helped you choose your answer?

7. The nutritionists who developed the pyramid hope that you will

a. eat more fats and oils than breads, rice, and pasta (noodles).

b. eat more vegetables and fruits than meat or milk products.

c. eat 4 to 5 servings of bread, rice, and pasta every day.

8. The little dots (• • •) indicate:

a. how much fat is in each food group.

b. how much sugar is in each food group.

c. how much of each food group you should eat.

How do you know?

9. Why are there lots of dots and triangles (• ▼ • ▼ •) in the top section of the pyramid?

a. This is the only section that has any fats or added sugars.

b. This is the smallest section.

c. The foods in this section contain the most fats and added sugars.

What part of the chart explains this?

1.10

Application, Critical Evaluation, and Synthesis

Choose one or more topics to discuss with your small group or to write about.

1. This article says people should use the food pyramid to choose a healthy diet. In different regions of the world people use different foods for their own food pyramid. For example, people in Asia generally eat rice, while Europeans generally eat bread and potatoes. What foods make up the typical diet in the region where you grew up? Show how these foods fit into the food pyramid below. Then describe some typical meals using these foods.

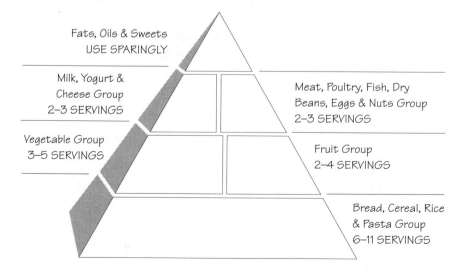

2. Many people believe that certain foods are especially good or bad for their health. There are also some foods, drinks, powders, and other supplements that are eaten by certain people or for special reasons (e.g., by sick people, children, older people; to become strong, to stay youthful, etc.) Describe some of the foods that people eat for special reasons in the region where you grew up and explain why these foods are considered important (e.g., a food contains large amounts of certain vitamins; it improves memory, etc.). Be sure to give examples.

3. Do you think it is good to take extra vitamins? Why or why not? What are some of the benefits or disadvantages of taking vitamins? Explain and give several examples. You may wish to make a chart like the following to help you organize your answer.

VITAMINS

Benefits   **Disadvantages**

4. If you could meet all your nutritional requirements by simply taking a "food pill" every day (and not eating), would you do this? Why or why not? Describe several benefits or disadvantages of taking a food pill. Then explain why you agree or disagree with the statements in paragraph 9 of this reading.

5. If you had to choose only three food items to live on for the rest of your life (for example, apples, fish, cake), which three would you choose? Why? Give several reasons for your answers.

6. Go to a library and look up two or three magazine or newspaper articles on nutrition using the card catalog (see Expansion 4.7.1), the *Reader's Guide to Periodical Literature* (Expansion 4.7.3) or some other magazine or newspaper index. Write a short summary of each article (Expansion 4.8). If you can, bring a copy of the articles to class and present a brief report about them to your small group.

A Calgene researcher working on a long-lasting tomato.

CHAPTER TWO

What's for Lunch?

Tomatoes that contain flounder genes can resist freezing. Corn with firefly genes can resist insects. Pigs that contain human growth hormone genes grow faster. What kind of foods are these? They are foods that have been changed by a new scientific technology, called genetic engineering. In genetically altered food, a gene can be taken from any animal or plant and inserted into any other animal or plant. For example, if a gene that allows a fish to live in cold water is inserted into a tomato, this produces a tomato that resists damage from freezing. The seeds of this altered tomato will contain this new trait and will pass "freeze resistance" on to future generations. As you read the two selections, think about the benefits and hazards of genetically altered food.

2.1
First Reading

Read these two selections quickly for the main ideas. Think about the titles and how the readings relate to each other. Do *not* stop to look up words in your dictionary.

I. Genetically-altered Foods in Our Future

This selection considers the future of genetically-altered foods. Excerpted from *Megatrends 2000* by John Naisbitt (Avon Books, 1990). Reprinted by permission.

1 Jesse Jaynes, a Louisiana State University biochemist, is working in collaboration with John Dodds of the International Potato Center in Lima, Peru. He hopes he can engineer the lowly potato so that it will have the protein value of meat. . . ." It may take another four or five years," says Jaynes. "But we will have plants including potatoes, cassava, and rice—those are the three that we're focusing on—that are going to be more nutritious and, hopefully, prevent the protein malnutrition that one sees [in many parts of the world]."

2 At the same time Jaynes and his colleagues have already found a possible way to help these food plants resist the attacks of bacteria and fungi that account for the annual loss of 40 percent of the world's crops.

3 Jaynes is very optimistic. "I really think that biotechnology and genetic engineering can do some great things to help people in the developing world. I know a lot of people talk about all the great things that are going to happen in the United States. And certainly we will be beneficiaries of that. But I think, overall, the prospects for improving the lot of those people are much brighter in the developing world through this technology."

Superplants

4 A biotech breakthrough from Monsanto has developed a tomato with a built-in resistance to parasites, viruses, and herbicides. The supertomatoes are the grandchildren of tomatoes genetically engineered for endurance. At Cornell University, scientists are breeding new types of apples that will not brown when the inside is exposed to the air. The Japanese have developed a seedless watermelon.

5 At the University of California at Davis, biologists are trying to insert other species' genes into seeds of walnuts, apples, oranges, and other fruits to create hardy, disease-resistant trees. In coming years, these biologists hope to add genes that will protect walnut trees from major pests like the codling moth, navel orange worm, and a virus infection called black line disease, which together cost the industry $10 to $20 million annually. During the next decade or so, scientists will start on apples, oranges, peaches, and cherries.

6 Farmers will be shifting their spending priorities from fertilizers and pesticides to genetically altered seeds that do the same job. Eventually plants could be given desirable traits from animals. [For example,] a gene from bacteria that kill insects can be put into a plant. Insects will then avoid it. Biotechnology reseachers realized early that if the genetic instructions for the manufacture of a desirable protein are inserted in a living cell's DNA,[1] that cell not only manufactures the protein but also passes it on to future generations. To create an insect-repellant plant, the appropriate gene need be injected only into the parent plant, which subsequently hands down the characteristic to its offspring.

Superanimals

7 Chinese researchers have demonstrated how genes from other animals could alter the inherent characteristics of fish. They introduced the gene that produces human growth hormones into goldfish, which is similar to carp and an important food in Asia. The fish promptly grew up to four times faster than normal. . . . In Australia, Robert Seamark and colleagues at the University of Adelaide are nurturing the seventh generation of pigs descended from animals with an extra growth hormone gene. These pigs convert feed into meat 30 percent more efficiently and reach market weight seven weeks earlier than normal pigs. The Australian researchers expect the pigs will be available to farmers within five years.

8 Despite the fears about them, genetic engineers are still limited in what they can do. They can't add more than a few genes to an animal, for example. A cow has tens of thousands of genes; science can't turn a cow into a kangaroo. Scientific capability will expand, however. In a few decades it may be possible to insert genes that change an animal's fertility, size, and behavior (altering salmon migration patterns for example). It's just a matter of time. . . .

---

1. **DNA:** The molecules in the cell that contain genetic information.

Ethical Questions

9 We are moving to "the day when geneticists can custom-design chickens to resist disease, lay bigger eggs, or have other traits valued by producers," says Dr. Lyman B. Crittenden at the U.S. Department of Agriculture's East Lansing, Michigan, research station.

10 Suppose it hurts or injures the chicken to lay bigger eggs. What if milk production *is* up 30 percent, but the cow's udder becomes so huge it can barely walk? Dr. Sheldon Krimsky of Tufts University says he knows of no religious or philosophical principle that forbids transplanting genes from one animal to another. But he sees potential problems of several kinds, economic, environmental, and humane. Jeremy Rifkin [an anti-genetic engineering activist] says his biggest objections to genetic engineering are ethical. He believes the building blocks of life are too precious to be tampered with in laboratories.

II. A Mystery in Your Lunchbox

The next selection looks at the controversy over genetically altered (bioengineered) foods. Try to understand the general ideas. Do not worry about understanding every word or detail. Excerpted from *Newsweek*, June 8, 1992. Reprinted by permission.

1 Hungry? Sit right down, we're having catfish, corn on the cob, baked potatoes and fresh tomatoes. This might turn out to be the most nutritious meal of your life. It might even be the best-tasting dinner you ever had. On the other hand, it might expose your body to a toxic combination no human has ever experienced before. Or it might induce an allergic reaction—even though you're not allergic to any of these foods. Still hungry? *Bon appetit!*

2 Last week's announcement that the federal government would impose no special regulations on bioengineered foods, in effect permitting them to be marketed exactly like nature's own, heralds a potentially vast change in our food supply. Virtually any characteristic of a living organism may now be transferred to another organism; with a few exceptions, the resulting product may be placed on supermarket shelves without federally mandated testing or special labeling. "We will not compromise safety one bit " Vice President Dan Quayle told the press. "[And] the consumer will enjoy better, healthier food products at lower prices."

3 Many specialists in biotechnology agree—in fact, they see consumers around the world benefiting from a new, genetically engineered green revolution—but critics are urging the government to move ahead more cautiously. A potato that resists disease with the help of a chicken gene? A catfish that grows like lightning, thanks to a gene from a virus? Some believe new products like these, which may be on the market by the end of the decade, call for a new regulatory system. "We should have learned from the history of regulating pesticides that we never knew the long-term consequences until it was too late," says Ellen Haas, executive director of Public Voice for Food

and Health Policy, a Washington, D.C.-based advocacy group. The Food and Drug Administration (FDA) maintains that most bioengineered foods present no special safety issues. "We're saying this is just another plant-breeding technique," says Eric Flamm, deputy director of the FDA's Office of Biotechnology.

4 Here's how bioengineering works: all cells contain DNA, the long molecule shaped like a double helix. A gene is a swatch[2] of DNA that controls a certain characteristic of the organism. In the 1970s scientists discovered they could clip off a gene-length swatch from a DNA molecule, and later they learned to affix it to a different DNA molecule—a cut-and-paste job that became known as gene splicing and results in what's called recombinant DNA. Immediately, visions of carrots with the flavor of peanut butter began dancing in the imaginations of scientists and food writers alike. But most current experiments are less exotic. In many ways the new technology differs little from traditional crossbreeding. "One of the powers of the technology is that you make simple and direct changes and alter the food as little as possible," says William Belknap, a plant physiologist at the Department of Agriculture's Agricultural Research Service in Albany, Calif.

5 The first example of recombinant DNA in a form suitable for lunch makes its debut next summer: the Flavr Savr tomato (See chart below). Scientists at Calgene, Inc., a biotech company based in Davis, Calif., isolated the gene in the tomato that triggers the enzyme responsible for rotting and rendered it inactive. Rather than having to be picked hard and green for easy shipping, the tomatoes stay on the vine about five days longer than usual. They can be shipped without refrigeration, which also helps retain flavor, and they'll resist rotting for more than three weeks, twice as long as their conventionally grown cousins. They aren't perfect: like other supermarket tomatoes they're grown with pesticides, they may be waxed, and they still

How to Build a Better Tomato, Step by Step

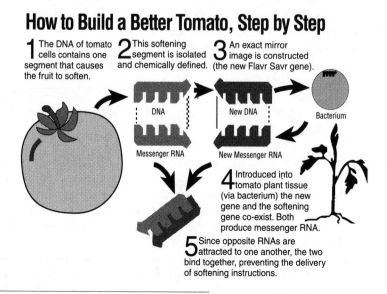

1 The DNA of tomato cells contains one segment that causes the fruit to soften.

2 This softening segment is isolated and chemically defined.

3 An exact mirror image is constructed (the new Flavr Savr gene).

DNA

New DNA

Bacterium

Messenger RNA

New Messenger RNA

4 Introduced into tomato plant tissue (via bacterium) the new gene and the softening gene co-exist. Both produce messenger RNA.

5 Since opposite RNAs are attracted to one another, the two bind together, preventing the delivery of softening instructions.

2. **swatch:** A small piece.

lack the last three to five days of vine-ripening that homegrown tomatoes enjoy. Sampled at Calgene's headquarters, the Flavr Savr tasted fine; whether consumers will find it worth a dollar more per pound remains to be seen. . . .

6 Environmentalists and other consumer advocates don't claim the new foods are unsafe by definition, but they do call for tougher scrutiny than the FDA believes is necessary. "The regulations do a lot more to protect the industry than they do to protect the American consumer," says Rebecca Goldburg, a senior scientist at the Environmental Defense Fund, an advocacy group. "The public has a right to know what's in its food."

7 Goldburg and other critics are especially concerned about potential allergens that may be hiding in new products—an orange touched up with a gene from a cherry, for instance. The FDA requires no special testing or labeling unless the new food is substantially different from its traditional version. If the new orange had no vitamin C, for example, it would have to be labeled. A new food containing a "common allergen" would also have to be labeled, but as examples of common allergens the FDA suggests only eggs, milk, fish, shellfish, tree nuts, wheat and legumes. The truth is, almost any food is an allergen to someone; just because the FDA doesn't cite zucchini as a frequent danger to the public doesn't mean a consumer biting into an apple might not get a very unwelcome surprise . . . .

8 Other critics are uneasy about making such dramatic changes with such speed. "We ought to be testing these changes in large populations over large periods of time," says Greg Drescher, a director of Oldways Preservation & Exchange Trust, a Boston-based think tank[3] for food issues. He also questions how useful the new foods really are. "We don't *need* to play sorcerer's apprentice[4] with agriculture," he says. "We know how to produce good-tasting food in this country. There are much better ways to eat healthfully than a food supply based on techno-foods." . . . At the very least, these critics may persuade the FDA to require more labeling of the new foods.

Number of words: 1,745	
Reading Times	**Reading Speed**
1st reading _____ minutes	12 minutes = 145 wpm
3rd reading _____ minutes	10 mintues = 175 wpm
	8 minutes = 218 wpm
	6 minutes = 291 wpm
	5 minutes = 349 wpm

---

3. A **think tank** is an organization in which specialists consider important issues and try to develop solutions to problems.
4. The **"sorcerer's apprentice"** is a story about a young man who was learning how to be a magician. He created a big problem when he tried to perform some magic before he had enough skill or experience to do it correctly.

2.2
Second Reading

Go back and read the selection again. Take as much time as you need. Look up some of the unfamiliar words in the glossary at the end of this book or in your dictionary, if you wish.

2.3
Third Reading

Read the selection quickly a third time. Concentrate on understanding the main ideas and the meanings of new vocabulary words in the contexts in which they appear.

2.4
Reader Response

In order to explore your response to this reading, write for 15 minutes about anything that interests you in this selection. You may wish to write about a personal experience this reading reminded you of—or you may wish to agree or disagree with something in the reading. Try to explore *your own thoughts and feelings* as much as possible. Do *not* merely summarize or restate the ideas in the selection.

2.5
Response Sharing

Read your response to two or three other people in your class. Listen carefully to what the others have written. After you have discussed each other's responses, talk about other points of interest in the selection.

2.6
Identifying Main Ideas

Working with the same small group, make a list of the main ideas in this selection. Be sure to state the main ideas in your own words. Don't just copy sentences directly from the text. Think carefully about what the writer is trying to tell you.

2.7

Analyzing the Text

Work with your group members on this exercise. Discuss the answers carefully, particularly if there are disagreements among members of your group. In some cases, there may be more than one possible interpretation.

1. Some of the people interviewed in this reading think genetically altered foods are a good idea; others think they are not. Look through the reading for three people who are for this technology and three who are against. Find quotes and other information in the reading to support your answers. Working with your group, make a chart to show the supporting evidence.

Person's name	*For/Against*	*Supporting evidence*
Ex: Jesse Jaynes	for	• hopes he can engineer the potato so it will have the protein value of meat • thinks biotechnology can do some great things • hopes to prevent malnutrition in many parts of the world

2. According to paragraph 6 in "Genetically altered Foods," why are farmers shifting their spending priorities to genetically altered seeds?

3. What is the meaning of the title "A Mystery in Your Lunchbox"?

4. Look at "Mystery" paragraph 5 and the "How to Build a Better Tomato" chart. Which sentence in paragraph 5 describes in words what the chart shows?

5. In your opinion, which sentence summarizes these readings the best?

   a. I really think that biotechnology and genetic engineering can do some great things to help people in the developing world.

   b. We will not compromise safety one bit . . . and the consumer will enjoy better, healthier food products at lower prices.

   c. The public has a right to know what's in its food.

   d. We don't need to play sorcerer's apprentice with agriculture.

   e. None of the above.

   Please give some reasons why you chose your answer. If you chose *e,* write your own sentence to summarize the readings.

2.8
Vocabulary Study

Study the italicized words and phrases in their contexts and guess their meanings. Write your guess on the first line. Then, look up the word or phrase in your dictionary and write the definition on the second line.

1 and 2. (chapter introduction) In genetically *altered* food, a gene can be taken from any animal or plant and *inserted* into any other animal or plant.
altered

a. (guess) _____

b. (dictionary) _____

inserted

a. (guess) _____

b. (dictionary) _____

"Genetically-altered Foods"

3 and 4. (paragraph 7) These pigs *convert* feed into meat 30 percent more efficiently and reach *market weight* seven weeks earlier than normal pigs.
convert

a. (guess) _____

b. (dictionary) _____

market weight

a. (guess) _____

b. (dictionary) _____

5, 6, and 7. (paragraph 10) He believes the *building blocks* of life are too *precious* to be *tampered* with in laboratories.
building blocks

a. (guess) _____

b. (dictionary) _____

precious

a. (guess) _____

b. (dictionary) _____

tampered

a. (guess) _____

b. (dictionary) _____

"Mystery"

8 and 9. (paragraph 5) They can be shipped without refrigeration, which also
helps *retain* flavor, and they'll resist rotting for more than three weeks, twice
as long as their *conventionally* grown cousins.
retain

    a. (guess) _____

    b. (dictionary) _____

conventionally

    a. (guess) _____

    b. (dictionary) _____

10. (paragraph 8) At the very least, these critics may *persuade* the FDA to require
more labeling of the new foods.

    a. (guess) _____

    b. (dictionary) _____

2.9
Interpreting the Meaning

Working with your small group, choose the answer that explains the meaning
of each sentence. Then discuss why you chose that answer.

1. In coming years, these biologists hope to add genes that will protect walnut
   trees from major pests . . . which together cost the industry $10 to $20
   million annually.

   a. The walnut tree industry makes a profit of $10 to $20 million each year
      from genetically altered trees.

   b. The walnut tree industry loses $10 to $20 million each year from dam-
      age caused by pests.

   c. Adding genes to protect the walnut trees will cost $10 to $20 million
      each year.

2. Farmers will be shifting their spending priorities from fertilizers and
   pesticides to genetically altered seeds that do the same job.
   a. Genetically altered seeds will have fertilizers and pesticides within them.

   b. Farmers think that genetically altered seeds will be cheaper than fertil-
      izer and pesticides.

   c. Fertilizer and pesticides will still be needed to protect genetically altered
      seeds.

3. To create an insect-repellant plant, the appropriate gene need be injected only into the parent plant, which subsequently hands down the characteristic to its offspring.

   a. It is not yet possible to create an insect repellant plant.

   b. The ability to repel insects will also appear in the next generation.

   c. Only the parent plant injected with the appropriate gene will be insect repellant.

4. Last week's announcement that the federal government would impose no special regulations on bioengineered foods, in effect permitting them to be marketed exactly like nature's own, heralds a potentially vast change in our food supply.

   a. Because bioengineered foods can be sold without any special labeling, there could be great changes in our food suply.

   b. Bioengineered foods won't cause any great change in our food supply because they look just like foods created by nature.

   c. Neither a nor b.

   If you chose *c*, please write a sentence that means the same thing as the example.

   Like nature's own means:

   d. As if they were natural (not genetically-engineered).

   e. As if they were bioengineered foods.

5. A catfish that grows like lightning thanks to a gene from a virus?

   a. A virus causes the fish to grow slowly.

   b. The virus gene comes from a cat.

   c. The fish grows very quickly.

6. Scientists at Calgene, Inc., a biotech company based in Davis, Calif., isolated the gene in the tomato that triggers the enzyme responsible for rotting and rendered it inactive.

   a. The scientists removed the gene that causes the tomato to rot and put in another enzyme instead.

   b. The scientists used a special enzyme to make the tomato rot more quickly.

   c. The scientists found the gene that causes the tomato to rot and turned off this gene's activity.

7. Goldburg and other critics are especially concerned about potential allergens that may be hiding in new products—an orange touched up with a gene from a cherry, for instance.

   Why are they concerned?

   a. Someone may be allergic to cherries and would not know the cherry gene was in the orange.

b. Someone may be allergic to oranges and would not know the orange gene was in the cherry.

c. Both a and b.

d. Neither a nor b.

If you chose *d*, write a sentence that explains why the critics are concerned.

8. The truth is, almost any food is an allergen to someone; just because the FDA doesn't cite zucchini as a frequent danger to the public doesn't mean a consumer biting into an apple might not get a very unwelcome surprise.

What is the "unwelcome surprise" a consumer might get?

a. An apple that tastes like zucchini.

b. The truth about some popular foods.

c. An allergic reaction.

2.10
Application, Critical Evaluation, and Synthesis

Choose one or more topics to discuss with your small group or to write about.

1. Read the examples given in paragraphs 4 to 7 of "Genetically-altered Foods in our Future." Do you think it is good to change plants and animals in this way? Why or why not? If you agree, describe some of the benefits to society. If you disagree, discuss problems or concerns. Give several examples to explain your answer.

2. Imagine that you and your small group are biochemists working in the food industry. What kinds of changes would you make in some foods? Why? Brainstorm some ideas (see section 4.2.1 on page 235) and give reasons why you chose those foods.

3. Imagine that you have just read about genetically altered foods in the newspaper. You feel very strongly about this issue, so you decide to write a letter to the editor. Write a letter either supporting or opposing some aspect of this issue. For example, you might support the labeling of genetically altered food, or you might think that labeling isn't necessary, or you might feel this is an excellent solution to food shortages in the developing world. Outline your ideas before writing your letter (see Expansion section 5.1, page 252).

4. The situation described in this reading is complex. It is important to produce enough food for all the people in the world. Yet not everyone agrees that genetic engineering, while technically possible, is a good way to increase food production. Using the technique of freewriting, explore your thoughts on technology (see Expansion section 4.2.2, page 238). Some ideas you may want to explore: Is technology always good for people? If a type of technology is possible, should it always be used? What are some of the chances society takes when a new technology is first used?

5. Write your thoughts about one or more of the following statements, which appeared in recent books and newspapers. Give examples to explain your opinion.

   a. All biotechnology would do is speed up the natural process which farmers have done since time began. (*Diversity: Journal for International Genetics*)

   b. Animals will be able to produce valuable biological products for humans, almost like factories—which some people think very wrong, but they will thereby save many human lives. (*Megatrends*)

   c. If you are a vegetarian, or if you have some religious traditions, or if you are allergic to certain foods, you will be unable to be certain about the content of your food. (*PCC Sound Consumer*)

   d. The idea that genetic-engineering is simply a variation of old-fashioned plant and animal breeding is repeated quite often. The plants and animals bred by farmers for generations have always, until now, been within the same species. Now, species can be crossed—an act never done before in human history. (*PCC Sound Consumer*)

CHAPTER THREE

Cody Loves Ruth

This reading comes from a novel by Anne Tyler, *Dinner at the Home-sick Restaurant.* Cody and Ezra are brothers. Cody is a successful business-man and Ezra owns a restaurant. Ruth is a cook at the restaurant. Cody is secretly in love with Ruth, and in this scene he finally tells her that he loves her. As you read this selection, think about what food means to people. Reprinted by permission, Berkeley Books, 1982.

3.1

First Reading

Read the selection and try to understand the story. Do *not* worry about under-standing every word or detail.

1 "I guess I'm not saying it right," he told her.

2 "Saying what? What are you talking about?"

3 "Ruth. I really, truly love you," he said. "I'm sick over you. I can't even eat. Look at me. I've lost eleven pounds."

4 He held out his arms, demonstrating. His jacket hung loose at the sides. Lately he'd moved his belt in a notch; his suits no longer fit so smoothly but seemed rumpled, gathered, bunchy.

5 "It's true you're kind of skinny," Ruth said slowly.

6 "Even my shoes feel too big."

7 "What's the matter with you?" she asked.

8 "You haven't heard a word I said!"

9 "Over me, you said. You must be making fun."

10 "Ruth, I swear—" he said.

11 "You're used to New York City girls, models, actresses; you could have any-one."

12 "It's you I'll have."

13 She studied him a moment. It began to seem he'd finally broken through; they were having a conversation. Then she said, "We got to get that weight back on you."

14 He groaned.

15 "See there?" she asked. "You never eat a thing I offer you."

16 "I can't," he told her.

17 "I don't believe you ever once tasted my cooking."

18 She set the skillet aside and went over to the tall black kettle that was simmering on the stove. "Country vegetable," she said, lifting the lid.

19 "Really, Ruth . . ."

20 She filled a small crockery bowl and set it on the table. "Sit down," she said. "Eat. When you've tried it, I'll tell you the secret ingredient."

21 Steam rose from the bowl, with a smell so deep and spicy that already he felt overfed. He accepted the spoon that she held out. He dipped it in the soup reluctantly and took a sip.

22 "Well?" she asked.

23 "It's very good," he said. In fact, it was delicious, if you cared about such things. He'd never tasted soup so good. There were chunks of fresh vegetables, and the broth was rich and heavy. He took another mouthful. Ruth stood over him, her thumbs hooked into her blue jeans pockets.

24 "Chicken feet," she said.

25 "Pardon?"

26 "Chicken feet is the secret ingredient."

27 He lowered the spoon and looked down into the bowl.

28 "Eat up," she told him. "Put some meat on your bones."

29 He dipped the spoon in again.

30 After that, she brought him a salad made with the herbs she'd grown on the roof and a basketful of rolls she'd baked that afternoon—a recipe from home, she said. Cody ate everything. As long as he ate, she watched him. When she brought him more butter for his rolls, she leaned close over him and he felt the warmth she gave off.

31 Now two more cooks had arrived and a Chinese boy was sauteing black mushrooms, and Ezra was running a mixer near the sink. Ruth sat down next to Cody, hooking her combat boots on the rung of his chair and hugging her ribs. Cody cut into a huge wedge of pie and gave some thought to food—to its inexplicable, loaded meaning in other people's lives. Couldn't you classify a person, he wondered, purely by examining his attitude toward food? Look at Cody's mother—a nonfeeder, if ever there was one. Even back in his childhood, when they'd depended on her for nourishment . . . why, mention you were hungry and she'd suddenly act rushed and harassed, fretful, out of breath, distracted. He remembered her coming home from work in the evening and tearing irritably around the kitchen. Tins toppled out of the cupboards and fell all over her—pork 'n' beans, Spam, oily tuna fish, peas canned olive-drab. She cooked in her hat, most of the time. She whimpered when she burned things. She burned things you would not imagine it possible to burn and served others half raw, adding jarring extras of her own design such as crushed pineapple in the mashed potatoes. (Anything, as long as it was a leftover, might as well be dumped in the pan with anything else.) Her only seasonings were salt and pepper. Her only gravy was Campbell's cream of mushroom soup, undiluted. And till Cody was grown, he had assumed that roast beef had to be stringy—not

something you sliced, but a leathery dry object which you separated with a fork, one strand from the other, and dropped with a clunk upon your plate.

32 Though during illness, he remembered, you could count on her to bring liquids. Hot tea: she was good at that. And canned consomme. Thin things, watery things. Then she'd stand in the door with her arms folded while you drank it. He remembered that her expression, when others ate or drank, conveyed a mild distaste. She ate little herself, often toyed with her food; and she implied some criticism of those who acted hungry or over-interested in what they were served. Neediness: she disapproved of neediness in people. Whenever there was a family argument, she most often chose to start it over dinner.

33 Biting into Ruth's flaky, shattering crust, Cody considered his mother's three children—Jenny, for instance, with her lemon-water and lettuce-leaf diets, never allowing herself a sweet, skipping meals altogether, as if continually bearing in mind that disapproving expression of her mother's. And Cody himself was not much different, when you came right down to it. It seemed that food didn't count with him; food was something required by others, so that for their sakes—on dates, at business luncheons—he would obligingly order a meal for himself just to keep them company. But all you'd find in his refrigerator was cream for his coffee and limes for his gin and tonics. He never ate breakfast; he often forgot lunch. Sometimes a gnawing feeling hit his stomach in the afternoon and he sent his secretary out for food. "What kind of food?" she would ask. He would say, "Anything, I don't care." She'd bring a Danish or an eggroll[1] or a liverwurst on rye; it

---

1. A **Danish** is a sweet roll. An **eggroll** is a Chinese fried roll.

was all the same to him. Half the time, he wouldn't even notice what it was—would take a bite, go on dictating, leave the rest to be disposed of by the cleaning lady. A woman he'd once had dinner with had claimed that this was a sign of some flaw. Watching him dissect his fish but then fail to eat it, noticing how he refused dessert and then benignly, tolerantly waited for her to finish a giant chocolate mousse, she had accused him of . . . what had she called it? Lack of enjoyment. Lack of ability to enjoy himself. He hadn't understood, back then, how she could draw so many implications from a single meal. And still he didn't agree with her.

34 Yes, only Ezra, he would say, had managed to escape all this. Ezra was so impervious—so thickheaded, really; nothing ever touched him. He ate heartily, whether it was his mother's cooking or his own. He liked anything that was offered him, especially bread—would have to watch his weight as he got older. But above all else, he was a feeder. He would set a dish before you and then stand there with his face expectant, his hands clasped tightly under his chin, his eyes following your fork. There was something tender, almost loving, about his attitude toward people who were eating what he'd cooked them.

35 Like Ruth, Cody thought.

36 He asked her for another slice of pie.

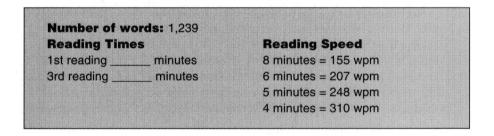

Number of words: 1,239
Reading Times   **Reading Speed**
1st reading _____ minutes   8 minutes = 155 wpm
3rd reading _____ minutes   6 minutes = 207 wpm
                                               5 minutes = 248 wpm
                                               4 minutes = 310 wpm

3.2
Second Reading

Go back and read the selection again. Take as much time as you need. Look up some of the unfamiliar words in the glossary at the end of this book or in your dictionary if you wish.

3.3
Third Reading

Read the selection quickly a third time. Concentrate on understanding the main ideas and the meanings of new vocabulary words in the contexts in which they appear.

3.4
Reader Response

In order to explore your response to this reading, write for 15 minutes about anything that interests you in this selection. You may wish to write about a personal experience this reading reminded you of—or you may wish to agree or disagree with something in this reading. Try to explore *your own thoughts and feelings* as much as possible. Do *not* merely summarize or restate the ideas in the selection.

3.5
Response Sharing

Read your response to two or three other people in your class. Listen carefully to what the others have written. After you have discussed each other's responses, talk about other points of interest in the selection.

3.6
Identifying Main Ideas

Working with the same small group, make a list of the main ideas in this selection. Be sure to state the main ideas in your own words. Don't just copy sentences directly from the text. Think carefully about what the writer is trying to tell you.

3.7
Analyzing the Text

Work with your group members on this exercise. Discuss the answers carefully, particularly if there are disagreements among members of your group. In some cases there may be more than one possible interpretation.

1. Read paragraphs 1 to 12. It is clear that:

   a. Cody has some kind of illness and Ruth is worried about his health.

   b. Ruth really loves Cody but is too shy to tell him.

   c. Ruth doesn't believe what she is hearing (i.e., that Cody loves her).

   Find a few examples in their conversation to support your answer.

2. Read paragraphs 24 to 27. How does Cody feel about chicken feet? Why do you think so?

3. What does the information in paragraphs 31 and 32 tell you about Cody's mother's attitude toward food? Give several examples to explain your answer.

4. In paragraph 33, what is the flaw that the woman claims Cody has? Why does she think it is a flaw?

5. Read paragraphs 34 to 36. Which statement is true?

   a. Cody and Ezra have similar ideas about food.

   b. Ruth and Cody have similar ideas about food.

   c. Ruth and Ezra have similar ideas about food.

   What are these ideas?

6. What is the main point the author wants to make in this selection?

   a. People who don't like food tend to be poor cooks and poor eaters.

   b. You should give some thought to food—to its inexplicable, loaded meaning in people's lives.

   c. You can classify a person purely by examining his or her attitude toward food.

   d. Disliking food is a sign of a lack of ability to enjoy oneself.

   Why do you think so? Support your choice with examples from this selection.

3.8
Vocabulary Study

Study the italicized words and phrases in their contexts and guess their meanings. Write your guess on the first line, then look up the word or phrase in your dictionary and write the definition on the second line.

1, 2, and **3.** (paragraphs 3–4) "Look at me. I've lost eleven pounds." He held out his arms, *demonstrating*. His jacket hung loose at the sides. Lately he'd moved his belt in a *notch*; his suits no longer fit so smoothly but seemed *rumpled*, gathered, bunchy.

demonstrating

a. (guess) _____

b. (dictionary) _____

notch

a. (guess) _____

b. (dictionary) _____

rumpled

a. (guess) _____

b. (dictionary) _____

4. (paragraph 20) She filled a small crockery bowl and *set* it on the table.

   a. (guess) _____

   b. (dictionary) _____

5. (paragraphs 24–26) "Chicken feet," she said. "Pardon?" "Chicken feet is the secret *ingredient*."

    a. (guess) _____

    b. (dictionary) _____

6. (paragraph 31) She burned things you would not *imagine* it possible to burn.

    a. (guess) _____

    b. (dictionary) _____

7, 8, 9, and **10.** (paragraph 33) It seemed that food *didn't count* with him; food was something required by others, so that *for their sakes* —on dates, at business luncheons—he would *obligingly* order a meal for himself just to *keep them company*.

didn't count

    a. (guess) _____

    b. (dictionary) _____

for their sakes

    a. (guess) _____

    b. (dictionary) _____

obligingly

    a. (guess) _____

    b. (dictionary) _____

keep them company

    a. (guess) _____

    b. (dictionary) _____

3.9
Going Beyond the Words

Good writers choose their vocabulary carefully. Colorful and interesting words can create pictures in the reader's mind or convey a certain atmosphere. Well-chosen words and phrases also help the reader understand a character's personality, emotions, and inner thoughts.

The sentences in this exercise create images through the words Anne Tyler chooses. Think about the meaning of the italicized words and phrases. Then think beyond the words to the real meaning Anne Tyler wants to convey.

Work with your small group. First think about each person's mood or reaction. How does he or she feel inside? (e.g., happy, angry, pleased, excited, satisfied, hesitant, suffering, surprised, etc.) Then, use the questions as a springboard for discussing the deeper meaning of each statement. Refer back to the section in the reading for more context. (*Note*: Each statement may have more than one possible interpretation.)

1. "Ruth, I really, truly love you," he said. I'm *sick over* you. I can't even eat. Look at me. I've lost eleven pounds." (paragraph 3)

   a. Cody's mood or reaction: _____

   b. Is Cody really sick? What is Cody trying to explain to Ruth?

2. "Over me, you said. You must be *making fun*." (paragraph 9)

   a. Ruth's mood or reaction: _____

   b. Do you think Ruth is angry or pleased? How else does she feel? Does she believe what Cody is saying?

3. He accepted the spoon that she held out. He dipped it in the soup *reluctantly* and took a sip. (paragraph 21)

   a. Cody's mood or reaction: _____

   b. Pretend you are starring in the movie version of this book. Demonstrate to the others in your group how Cody tried the soup. How did he accept the spoon? What kind of expression did he probably have on his face?

4. "Eat up," she told him. "*Put some meat on your bones*." (paragraph 28)

   a. Ruth's mood or reaction: _____

   b. Why does Ruth want Cody to eat? What does this say about her feelings toward Cody?

5. Cody ate everything. *As long as* he ate, she watched him. (paragraph 30)

   a. Ruth's mood or reaction: _____

   b. Why does Ruth watch Cody? What is she probably thinking about?

6. When she brought him more butter for his rolls, she leaned close over him and he felt the warmth she *gave off*. (paragraph 30)

   a. Cody's mood or reaction: _____

   b. What is Cody feeling about Ruth at this point?

7. She ate little herself, often toyed with her food; and she implied some criticism of those who acted hungry or over-interested in what they were served . . . . And Cody himself was not much different, *when you came right down to it*. (paragraphs 32 and 33)

   a. Cody's mood or reaction: _____

   b. Cody is comparing himself to his mother. Is he happy with his conclusion?

8. But *above all* else, he was a feeder. He would set a dish before you and then stand there with his face expectant, his hands clasped tightly under his chin, his eyes following your fork. (paragraph 34)

   a. Ezra's mood or reaction: _____

   b. What does this say about Ezra's personality? How do you picture him?

3.10
Application, Critical Evaluation, and Synthesis

Choose one or two topics to discuss with your small group or write about.

1. "You are what you eat." What does this statement mean to you? Do you agree with it? Discuss your opinion by giving several reasons why you agree or disagree with this statement. You may want to explain what kinds of foods you think people should (or should not) eat, whether it makes a difference what kinds of foods you eat, or how different foods might affect you.

2. Cody thought it was strange to eat chicken feet. In a recent survey, most people in the United States said they would not eat insects, brains, octopus, or snake. Make a list of several foods that you think are strange, and explain why you would not eat them. Next, describe some foods that you thought were strange and then discovered you liked after you tried them. What did you think these foods would be like before you tried them and how did your ideas change after you tried them? Compare your opinions with the other people in your small group.

3. Do you think Ezra would serve genetically altered foods in his restaurant? Would Ruth want to cook such foods? Would Cody eat them? What about Cody and Ezra's mother? Think about what each person says and does in the selection you just read. Then list several characteristics that would describe how he or she would probably react to genetically altered foods. Make a chart like the one below to help you organize your thinking.

WHO WOULD USE GENETICALLY ALTERED FOODS?		
Person	**Yes/No**	**Characteristics**

4. This reading described different people's attitudes toward food. Think about one or two of the following topics. Explain your opinions and give several examples.

   a. Cody didn't care about food. A woman told him that this was a sign of some flaw—a lack of ability to enjoy himself. Do you agree or disagree with her idea?

   b. Ezra got pleasure from feeding other people. Do you know anyone who is like Ezra? How does this person act when people eat (or don't eat) the food she or he prepares?

   c. Can you classify a person purely by examining his or her attitude toward food? Do you know any feeders, nonfeeders, gourmets, or picky eaters? Do you think there is any connection between their attitude towards food and their behavior?

5. Write a story and include the following sentence in it: "_____ is the secret ingredient," she said.

6. From your own reading of newspapers and magazines, discuss a recent article that you have seen concerning nutrition or food. What issues does the article examine (e.g., health, agriculture, medical benefits or problems)? Who is affected (e.g., everyone, children, older adults, pregnant women, food manufacturers)? Are any experiments or scientific studies described; are any specialists quoted? What is the conclusion of the article?

AT THE END OF EVERY UNIT YOU ARE INVITED TO TURN TO THE EXPANSION SECTION BEGINNING ON PAGE 233. THIS SECTION CONCENTRATES ON THE FUNDAMENTALS OF LIBRARY RESEARCH AND REPORT WRITING.

Vocabulary Games

Here is a chance to review some of the vocabulary you have encountered in this unit. After you finish the game quizzes on your own, discuss your answers with your group members. You may use your dictionary to look up items to resolve disagreements. Scoring: 5 points for each correct answer.

Synonyms

Read each passage carefully and then draw a circle around the word or phrase that means the same thing (or almost the same thing) as the italicized word or phrase. If a word or phrase has more than one meaning, choose the meaning that fits the context in the passage.

Example: The food we eat is *converted* into nutrients for our bodies.
a. changed   b. improved   c. inserted

Passage One

Eat a variety of foods to help keep your body *fit* and healthy. *Handle* and cook foods in ways that *retain* the most nutrients. Look for vitamin pills that have a reliable *dosage* of each vitamin, since certain vitamins accumulate in the body and may eventually cause damage. For example, too much Vitamin A can cause *blurred* vision.

1. *fit*
   a. the correct size   b. in good condition   c. well-nourished

2. *handle*
   a. deal with   b. hold   c. clean

3. *retain*
   a. preserve   b. remove   c. create

4. *dosage*
   a. source   b. quality   c. amount

5. *blurred*
   a. distinct   b. unclear   c. blind

Passage Two

Two high school honor students who are sophisticated computer users were arrested last month for *tampering* with the library's computer. They *altered* the library's recordkeeping system by *inserting* a code that converted newly checked-out books to "overdue" status. The punishment was *unconventional*. They will do volunteer work in the library for one year to help them understand the *consequences* of their actions.

6. *tampering*
   a. playing   b. searching   c. interfering

7. *altered*
   a. exposed   b. destroyed   c. modified

8. *inserting*
   a. putting in   b. taking out   c. looking through

9. *unconventional*
   a. common   b. severe   c. unusual

10. *consequences*
    a. damages   b. results   c. importance

Antonyms

Antonyms are words that have opposite meanings, e.g., cold-hot; tall-short; dark-light. Read the next passage carefully and then draw a circle around the word or phrase that means the opposite (or almost the opposite) of the italicized word or phrase. If a word or phrase has more than one meaning, choose the meaning that fits the context in the passage.

Example: She *reluctantly* took a bite of the strange food.

a. quickly   b. hesitantly   c. enthusiastically

[*Enthusiastically* is the opposite of *reluctantly* .]

Passage Three

The delivery people knocked on the door. A man in *rumpled* clothes reluctantly let them in, and they carried the new exercise equipment to a corner. "Not there," said the man *irritably*, "*set* it here." They *obligingly* moved the equipment again. "You understand," the man said with *distaste*, "I don't want to exercise, but my doctor says I have to."

11. *rumpled*
    a. dirty   b. neat   c. stylish

12. *irritably*
    a. pleasantly   b. sorrowfully   c. quietly

13. *set*
a. leave   b. drop   c. remove

14. *obligingly*
a. rudely   b. cheerfully   c. forcefully

15. *distaste*
a. regret   b. sourness   c. pleasure

Logical Relationships

Look at the first pair of words, determine the relationship between them (are they synonyms or antonyms?). Then circle the word or phrase that fills in the blank to logically make a similar type of relationship.

    Example: make fun of : insult = accumulate : _____

        a. throw away   (b. collect)   c. carry

        [*Make fun of* is related to *insult* (synonyms) in the same way *accumulate* is related to *collect*.]

16. nutritious : healthful = precious : _____
a. worthless   b. ordinary   c. valuable

17. demonstrating : showing = imposing : _____
a. filling   b. requiring   c. desiring

18. imagine : definitely know = convert : _____
a. keep apart   b. be changed   c. remain the same
[*Hint: imagine* and *definitely know* are antonyms.]

19. compromise : disagreement = accuracy : _____
a. error   b. correctness   c. satisfaction

20. collaborate : cooperate = persuade : _____
a. disagree   b. convince   c. associate

SCORE: Number of correct answers _____ × **5 =** _____

Why Do People Behave the Way They Do?

It has been said that human beings are shaped partly by nature (what we are born with) and partly by nurture (what we learn as we grow up). Where do we learn our values and how to act toward others? Why do most people like to conform? Should schools have a role in teaching children how to behave in society? Do violent images in the media play a role in shaping the way people are today? These are some of the questions that will be considered in this unit.

Discussion

Before you begin reading, think about the following questions and discuss your answers. *Note:* You may wish to choose two or three questions to explore in detail with a small group of students from your class.

1. What is a lottery? Do you enjoy participating in lotteries? Why? Have you ever won a lottery? If yes, what did you win and how did you feel?

2. Why do people enjoy ghost stories, horror movies, and murder mystery novels?

3. Why do people follow fads—in clothing, style, and behavior, for example? What are some fads or fashions that you have participated in? Is it important to you to do what "everyone else" is doing?

4. What does it mean to be "a good citizen"? How do children learn to be good citizens?

5. What are some of the values that you were taught in school (such as conformity, independence, helpfulness, competitiveness)? What would happen if a child acted differently, i.e., if he or she didn't conform to the accepted group behavior?

The Lottery

This story by Shirley Jackson is about the people in a small town. It was first published in June 1948 in *The New Yorker* magazine and has become a classic, reprinted in many anthologies. When "The Lottery" was first published, many people said they could not understand what the story meant; it still has different meanings to different people. As you read, think about the things that happen and what the townspeople say and do. Reprinted by permission of Farrar, Strauss and Giroux, Inc.

1.1

First Reading

Read the story and try to understand what happens. Do *not* stop to look up words in your dictionary.

1 The morning of June 27th was clear and sunny, with the fresh warmth of a full-summer day; the flowers were blossoming profusely and the grass was richly green. The people of the village began to gather in the square, between the post office and the bank, around ten o'clock; in some towns there were so many people that the lottery took two days and had to be started on June 26th, but in this village, where there were only about three hundred people, the whole lottery took less than two hours, so it could begin at ten o'clock in the morning and still be through in time to allow the villagers to get home for noon dinner.

2 The children assembled first, of course. School was recently over for the summer, and the feeling of liberty sat uneasily on most of them; they tended to gather together quietly for a while before they broke into boisterous play, and their talk was still of the classroom and the teacher, of books and reprimands. Bobby Martin had already stuffed his pockets full of stones, and the other boys soon followed his example, selecting the smoothest and roundest stones; Bobby and Harry Jones and Dickie Delacroix—the villagers pronounced this name "Dellacroy"—eventually made a great pile of stones in one corner of the square and guarded it against the raids of the other boys. The girls stood aside, talking among themselves, looking over their shoulders at the boys, and the very small children rolled in the dust or clung to the hands of their older brothers or sisters.

3 Soon the men began to gather, surveying their own children, speaking of planting and rain, tractors and taxes. They stood together, away from the pile of stones in the corner, and their jokes were quiet and they smiled rather

than laughed. The women, wearing faded house dresses and sweaters, came shortly after their menfolk. They greeted one another and exchanged bits of gossip as they went to join their husbands. Soon the women, standing by their husbands, began to call to their children, and the children came reluctantly, having to be called four or five times. Bobby Martin ducked under his mother's grasping hand and ran, laughing, back to the pile of stones. His father spoke up sharply, and Bobby came quickly and took his place between his father and his oldest brother.

4 The lottery was conducted—as were the square dances, the teen-age club, the Halloween program—by Mr. Summers, who had time and energy to devote to civic activities. He was a round-faced, jovial man and he ran the coal business, and people were sorry for him, because he had no children and his wife was a scold. When he arrived in the square, carrying the black wooden box, there was a murmur of conversation among the villagers, and he waved and called, "Little late today, folks." The postmaster, Mr. Graves, followed him, carrying a three-legged stool, and the stool was put in the center of the square and Mr. Summers set the black box down on it. The villagers kept their distance, leaving a space between themselves and the stool, and when Mr. Summers said, "Some of you fellows want to give me a hand?" there was a hesitation before two men, Mr. Martin and his oldest son, Baxter, came forward to hold the box steady on the stool while Mr. Summers stirred up the papers inside it.

5 The original paraphernalia for the lottery had been lost long ago, and the black box now resting on the stool had been put into use even before Old Man Warner, the oldest man in town, was born. Mr. Summers spoke frequently to the villagers about making a new box, but no one liked to upset even as much tradition as was represented by the black box. There was a story that the present box had been made with some pieces of the box that had preceded it, the one that had been constructed when the first people settled down to make a village here. Every year, after the lottery, Mr. Summers began talking again about a new box, but every year the subject was allowed to fade off without anything's being done. The black box grew shabbier each year; by now it was no longer completely black but splintered badly along one side to show the original wood color, and in some places faded or stained.

6 Mr. Martin and his oldest son, Baxter, held the black box securely on the stool until Mr. Summers had stirred the papers thoroughly with his hand. Because so much of the ritual had been forgotten or discarded, Mr. Summers had been successful in having slips of paper substituted for the chips of wood that had been used for generations. Chips of wood, Mr. Summers had argued, had been all very well when the village was tiny, but now that the population was more than three hundred and likely to keep on growing, it was necessary to use something that would fit more easily into the black box. The night before the lottery, Mr. Summers and Mr. Graves made up the slips of paper and put them in the box, and it was then taken to the safe of Mr. Summers' coal company and locked up until Mr. Summers was ready to take it to the square next morning. The rest of the year, the box was put away, sometimes one place, some-

times another; it had spent one year in Mr Graves's barn and another year under foot in the post office, and sometimes it was set on a shelf in the Martin grocery and left there.

7 There was a great deal of fussing to be done before Mr. Summers declared the lottery open. There were the lists to make up—of heads of families, heads of households in each family, members of each household in each family, there was the proper swearing-in of Mr. Summers by the postmaster as the official of the lottery; at one time, some people remembered, there had been a recital of some sort, performed by the official of the lottery, a perfunctory, tuneless chant that had been rattled off duly each year[1]; some people believed that the official of the lottery used to stand just so when he said or sang it, others believed that he was supposed to walk among the people, but years and years ago this part of the ritual had been allowed to lapse. There had been, also, a ritual salute, which the official of the lottery had had to use in addressing each person who came up to draw from the box, but this also had changed with time, until now it was felt necessary only for the official to speak to each person approaching. Mr. Summers was very good at all this; in his clean white shirt and blue jeans, with one hand resting carelessly on the black box, he seemed very proper and important as he talked interminably to Mr. Graves and the Martins.

8 Just as Mr. Summers finally left off talking and turned to the assembled villagers, Mrs. Hutchinson came hurriedly along the path to the square, her sweater thrown over her shoulders, and slid into place in the back of the crowd. "Clean forgot what day it was," she said to Mrs. Delacroix, who stood next to her, and they both laughed softly. "Thought my old man was out back stacking wood," Mrs. Hutchinson went on, "and then I looked out the window and the kids was gone, and then I remembered it was the twenty-seventh and came a-running." She dried her hands on her apron, and Mrs. Delacroix said, "You're in time, though. They're still talking away up there."

9 Mrs. Hutchinson craned her neck to see through the crowd and found her husband and children standing near the front. She tapped Mrs. Delacroix on the arm as a farewell and began to make her way through the crowd. The people separated good-humoredly to let her through; two or three people said, in voices just loud enough to be heard across the crowd, "Here comes your Missus, Hutchinson," and "Bill, she made it after all." Mrs. Hutchinson reached her husband, and Mr. Summers, who had been waiting, said cheerfully, "Thought we were going to have to get on without you, Tessie." Mrs. Hutchinson said, grinning, "Wouldn't have me leave m'dishes in the sink, now, would you, Joe?," and soft laughter ran through the crowd as the people stirred back into position after Mrs. Hutchinson's arrival.

10 "Well, now," Mr. Summers said soberly, "guess we better get started, get this over with, so's we can go back to work. Anybody ain't here?"

11 "Dunbar," several people said. "Dunbar, Dunbar."

---

1. This means that, in the old days, the person who conducted the lottery would recite a short, simple statement in a very disinterested way.

12   Mr. Summers consulted his list. "Clyde Dunbar," he said. "That's right. He's broke his leg, hasn't he? Who's drawing for him?"

13   "Me, I guess," a woman said, and Mr. Summers said, "Don't you have a grown boy to do it for you, Janey?" Although Mr. Summers and everyone else in the village knew the answer perfectly well, it was the business of the official of the lottery to ask such questions formally. Mr. Summers waited with an expression of polite interest while Mrs. Dunbar answered.

14   "Horace's not but sixteen yet," Mrs. Dunbar said regretfully. "Guess I gotta fill in for the old man this year."

15   "Right," Mr. Summers said. He made a note on the list he was holding. Then he asked, "Watson boy drawing this year?"

16   A tall boy in the crowd raised his hand. "Here," he said. "I'm drawing for m'mother and me." He blinked his eyes nervously and ducked his head as several voices in the crowd said things like "Good fellow, Jack," and "Glad to see your mother's got a man to do it."

17   "Well," Mr. Summers said, "guess that's everyone. Old Man Warner make it?"

18   "Here," a voice said, and Mr. Summers nodded.

19   A sudden hush fell on the crowd as Mr. Summers cleared his throat and looked at the list. "All ready?" he called. "Now, I'll read the names—heads of families first—and the men come up and take a paper out of the box. Keep the paper folded in your hand without looking at it until everyone has had a turn. Everything clear?"

Review

1. How do the townspeople seem to feel as the lottery drawing begins?

Prediction

2. What do you think the prize might be?

---

20   The people had done it so many times that they only half listened to the directions; most of them were quiet, wetting their lips, not looking around. Then Mr. Summers raised one hand high and said, "Adams." A man disengaged himself from the crowd and came forward. "Hi, Steve," Mr. Summers said, and Mr. Adams said, "Hi, Joe." They grinned at one another humorlessly and nervously. Then Mr. Adams reached into the black box and took out a folded paper. He held it firmly by one corner as he turned and went hastily back to his place in the crowd, where he stood a little apart from his family, not looking down at his hand.

21   "Allen," Mr. Summers said. "Anderson. . . . Bentham."

22   "Seems like there's no time at all between lotteries any more," Mrs. Delacroix said to Mrs. Graves in the back row. "Seems like we got through with the last one only last week."

23   "Time sure goes fast," Mrs. Graves said.

24 "Clark . . . Delacroix."

25 "There goes my old man," Mrs. Delacroix said. She held her breath while her husband went forward.

26 "Dunbar," Mr. Summers said, and Mrs. Dunbar went steadily to the box while one of the women said, "Go on, Janey," and another said, "There she goes."

27 "We're next," Mrs. Graves said. She watched while Mr. Graves came around from the side of the box, greeted Mr. Summers gravely, and selected a slip of paper from the box. By now, all through the crowd there were men holding the small folded papers in their large hands, turning them over and over nervously. Mrs. Dunbar and her two sons stood together, Mrs. Dunbar holding the slip of paper.

28 "Harburt . . . Hutchinson."

29 "Get up there, Bill," Mrs. Hutchinson said, and the people near her laughed.

30 "Jones."

31 "They do say," Mr. Adams said to Old Man Warner, who stood next to him, "that over in the north village they're talking of giving up the lottery."

32 Old Man Warner snorted. "Pack of crazy fools," he said. "Listening to the young folks, nothing's good enough for them. Next thing you know, they'll be wanting to go back to living in caves, nobody work any more, live *that* way for a while. Used to be a saying about 'Lottery in June, corn be heavy soon.' First thing you know, we'd all be eating stewed chickweed and acorns. There's *always* been a lottery," he added petulantly. "Bad enough to see young Joe Summers up there joking with everybody."

33 "Some places have already quit lotteries," Mrs. Adams said.

34 "Nothing but trouble in *that*," Old Man Warner said stoutly. "Pack of young fools."

35 "Martin." And Bobby Martin watched his father go forward. "Overdyke . . . Percy."

36 "I wish they'd hurry," Mrs. Dunbar said to her older son. "I wished they'd hurry."

37 "They're almost through," her son said.

38 "You get ready to run tell Dad," Mrs. Dunbar said.

39 Mr. Summers called his own name and then stepped forward precisely and selected a slip from the box. Then he called, "Warner."

40 "Seventy-seventh year I been in the lottery," Old Man Warner said as he went through the crowd. "Seventy-seventh time."

41 "Watson." The tall boy came awkwardly through the crowd. Someone said, "Don't be nervous, Jack," and Mr. Summers said, "Take your time, son."

42 "Zanini."

43 After that, there was a long pause, a breathless pause, until Mr. Summers, holding his slip of paper in the air, said, "All right, fellows." For a minute, no one moved, and then all the slips of paper were opened. Suddenly, all

the women began to speak at once, saying, "Who is it?," "Who's got it?," "Is it the Dunbars?," "Is it the Watsons?" Then the voices began to say, "It's Hutchinson. It's Bill," "Bill Hutchinson's got it."

44 "Go tell your father," Mrs. Dunbar said to her older son.

45 People began to look around to see the Hutchinsons. Bill Hutchinson was standing quiet, staring down at the paper in his hand. Suddenly, Tessie Hutchinson shouted to Mr. Summers, "You didn't give him time enough to take any paper he wanted. I saw you. It wasn't fair!"

46 "Be a good sport, Tessie," Mrs. Delacroix called, and Mrs. Graves said, "All of us took the same chance."

47 "Shut up, Tessie," Bill Hutchinson said.

48 "Well, everyone," Mr. Summers said, "that was done pretty fast, and now we've got to be hurrying a little more to get done in time." He consulted his next list. "Bill," he said, "you draw for the Hutchinson family. You got any other households in the Hutchinsons?"

49 "There's Don and Eva," Mrs. Hutchinson yelled. "Make *them* take their chance!"

50 "Daughters draw with their husbands' families, Tessie," Mr. Summers said gently. "You know that as well as anyone else."

51 "It wasn't *fair*," Tessie said.

52 "I guess not, Joe," Bill Hutchinson said regretfully. "My daughter draws with her husband's family, that's only fair. And I've got no other family except the kids."

53 "Then, as far as drawing for families is concerned, it's you," Mr. Summers said in explanation, "and as far as drawing for households is concerned, that's you, too. Right?"

54 "Right," Bill Hutchinson said.

55 "How many kids, Bill?" Mr. Summers asked formally.

56 "Three," Bill Hutchinson said. "There's Bill, Jr., and Nancy, and little Dave. And Tessie and me."

57 "All right, then," Mr. Summers said. "Harry, you got their tickets back?"

58 Mr. Graves nodded and held up the slips of paper. "Put them in the box, then," Mr. Summers directed. "Take Bill's and put it in."

59 "I think we ought to start over," Mrs Hutchinson said, as quietly as she could. "I tell you it wasn't *fair*. You didn't give him time enough to choose. *Everybody* saw that."

60 Mr. Graves had selected the five slips and put them in the box, and he dropped all the papers but those onto the ground, where the breeze caught them and lifted them off.

61 "Listen, everybody," Mrs. Hutchinson was saying to the people around her.

62 "Ready, Bill?" Mr. Summers asked, and Bill Hutchinson, with one quick glance around at his wife and children, nodded.

63 "Remember," Mr. Summers said, "take the slips and keep them folded until

each person has taken one. Harry, you help little Dave." Mr. Graves took the hand of the little boy, who came willingly with him up to the box. "Take a paper out of the box, Davy," Mr. Summers said. Davy put his hand into the box and laughed. "Take just *one* paper," Mr. Summers said. "Harry, you hold it for him." Mr. Graves took the child's hand and removed the folded paper from the tight fist and held it while little Dave stood next to him and looked up at him wonderingly.

64 "Nancy next," Mr. Summers said. Nancy was twelve, and her school friends breathed heavily as she went forward, switching her skirt, and took a slip daintily from the box. "Bill, Jr.," Mr. Summers said, and Billy, his face red and his feet over-large, nearly knocked the box over as he got a paper out. "Tessie," Mr. Summers said. She hesitated for a minute, looking around defiantly, and then set her lips and went up to the box. She snatched a paper out and held it behind her.

65 "Bill," Mr. Summers said, and Bill Hutchinson reached into the box and felt around, bringing his hand out at last with the slip of paper in it.

66 The crowd was quiet. A girl whispered, "I hope it's not Nancy," and the sound of the whisper reached the edges of the crowd.

67 "It's not the way it used to be," Old Man Warner said clearly. "People ain't the way they used to be."

68 "All right," Mr. Summers said. "Open the papers. Harry, you open little Dave's."

69 Mr. Graves opened the slip of paper and there was a general sigh through the crowd as he held it up and everyone could see that it was blank. Nancy and Bill, Jr., opened theirs at the same time, and both beamed and laughed, turning around to the crowd and holding their slips of paper above their heads.

70 "Tessie," Mr. Summers said. There was a pause, and then Mr. Summers looked at Bill Hutchinson, and Bill unfolded his paper and showed it. It was blank.

71 "It's Tessie," Mr. Summers said, and his voice was hushed. "Show us her paper, Bill."

72 Bill Hutchinson went over to his wife and forced the slip of paper out of her hand. It had a black spot on it, the black spot Mr. Summers had made the night before with the heavy pencil in the coal-company office. Bill Hutchinson held it up, and there was a stir in the crowd.

73 "All right, folks," Mr. Summers said. "Let's finish quickly."

74 Although the villagers had forgotten the ritual and lost the original black box, they still remembered to use stones. The pile of stones the boys had made earlier was ready; there were stones on the ground with the blowing scraps of paper that had come out of the box. Mrs. Delacroix selected a stone so large she had to pick it up with both hands and turned to Mrs. Dunbar. "Come on," she said. "Hurry up."

75 Mrs. Dunbar had small stones in both hands, and she said, gasping for breath, "I can't run at all. You'll have to go ahead and I'll catch up with you."

76 The children had stones already, and someone gave little Davy Hutchinson a few pebbles.

77 Tessie Hutchinson was in the center of a cleared space by now, and she held her hands out desperately as the villagers moved in on her. "It isn't fair," she said. A stone hit her on the side of the head.

78 Old Man Warner was saying, "Come on, come on, everyone." Steve Adams was in the front of the crowd of villagers, with Mrs. Graves beside him.

79 "It isn't fair, it isn't right," Mrs. Hutchinson screamed, and then they were upon her.

Number of words: 3,372

Reading Times		**Reading Speed**
1st reading _____ minutes		20 minutes = 169 wpm
3rd reading _____ minutes		17 mintues = 198 wpm
		15 minutes = 225 wpm
		12 minutes = 281 wpm
		10 minutes = 337 wpm

1.2
Second Reading

Go back and read the selection again. Take as much time as you need. Look up some of the unfamiliar words in the glossary at the end of this book or in your dictionary if you wish.

1.3
Third Reading

Read the selection quickly a third time. Concentrate on understanding the main ideas and the meanings of new vocabulary words in the contexts in which they appear.

1.4
Reader Response

In order to explore your response to this reading, write for 15 minutes about anything that interested you in the selection. You may wish to write about a personal experience this reading reminded you of—or you may wish to agree or disagree with something in the reading. Try to explore *your own thoughts and feelings* as much as possible. Do *not* merely summarize or restate the ideas in the selection.

1.5
Response Sharing

Read your response to two or three other people in your class. Listen carefully to what the others have written. After you have discussed each other's responses, talk about other points of interest in the selection.

1.6
Identifying Main Ideas

Working with the same small group, make a list of the main ideas in this selection. Be sure to state the main ideas in your own words. Don't just copy sentences directly from the text. Think carefully about what the writer is trying to tell you.

1.7
Analyzing the Text

Work with your group members on this exercise. Discuss the answers carefully, particularly if there are disagreements among members of your group. In some cases there may be more than one possible interpretation.

1. Explain the history of the lottery in the town. When did it begin? What were the rules? What changes have occurred over the years? What do the people think of it now?

2. In which paragraphs did you begin to suspect that something strange was happening? What are some of the clues that made you think this?

3. Why did the town keep the lottery?

4. What do you know about the black box? What does the information at the end of paragraph 6 tell you about how the townspeople felt about the black box?

5. Why did Mr. Hutchinson have to force the paper out of Tessie Hutchinson's hand? What happened to Tessie Hutchinson at the end of the story? Why did this happen? How did you feel about what happened?

1.8
Vocabulary Study

Study the italicized words and phrases in their contexts and guess their meanings. Write your guess on the first line. Then look up the word or phrase in your dictionary and write the definition on the second line.

1, 2, and **3.** (paragraph 2) The children *assembled* first, of course. School was recently over for the summer, and the feeling of *liberty* sat uneasily on most of them; they tended to gather together quietly for a while before they broke into *boisterous* play.

assembled

a. (guess) _____

b. (dictionary) _____

liberty

a. (guess) _____

b. (dictionary) _____

boisterous

a. (guess) _____

b. (dictionary) _____

4, 5, and **6.** (paragraph 3) They greeted one another and exchanged *bits* of *gossip* as they went to join their husbands. Soon the women, standing by their husbands, began to call their children, and the children came *reluctantly*, having to be called four or five times.

bits

a. (guess) _____

b. (dictionary) _____

gossip

a. (guess) _____

b. (dictionary) _____

reluctantly

a. (guess) _____

b. (dictionary) _____

7 and **8.** (paragraph 5) There was a story that the present box had been made with some pieces of the box that had *preceded* it, the one that had been *constructed* when the first people settled down to make a village here.

preceded

a. (guess) _____

b. (dictionary) _____

constructed

a. (guess) _____

b. (dictionary) _____

9 and **10.** (paragraph 64) She hesitated for a minute, looking around *defiantly*, and then set her lips and went up to the box. She *snatched* a paper out and held it behind her.

defiantly

a. (guess) _____

b. (dictionary) _____

snatched

a. (guess) _____

b. (dictionary) _____

1.9
Understanding the Story:
Imagination and Conclusions

"The Lottery" is a strange and disturbing story. It is simple and straightforward, but with a horrifying ending. The story makes most people feel uncomfortable because so many questions are left unanswered. You have to use your imagination to picture some things, and you must draw your own conclusions about some events. As you do this exercise, discuss your answers with your small group. Which things do you agree on? Which do you disagree on?

Using Your Imagination

In "The Lottery" Shirley Jackson describes the lottery itself in great detail, but she gives us almost no description of the town or the people in it. As readers, we have to see things in our minds that are not explained to fully understand the story. Using your imagination, explain how you visualize the following people and places. *Note:* As you discuss your answers with your group, remember that there are no correct or incorrect answers here. You will all imagine different things although there may be some areas of general agreement.

1. How do you picture the town? Where do you imagine the town is located?

2. What do you think the townspeople look like? What do Mr. Warner, Tessie, and Mr. Summers look like?

3. How do you think the townspeople get along with each other? What kind of relationships do you think they have with each other?

4. How do you picture the black box? How big is it?

5. Who is describing this event? Do you think the narrator is from this town? Explain your answer.

Drawing Conclusions

The author describes some things about the town and the lottery in an indirect way. She gives a number of clues (examples) and you have to draw your own conclusions. This means that you have to decide for yourself. For the items below, find several clues *in the reading* that would lead you to the conclusion that is given.

6. **Conclusion**: The lottery is a normal, accepted annual event to the townspeople.

   Clues:

   Example: Mr. Warner says he has been participating in the lottery for 77 years. (Give as many other clues as you can.)

7. **Conclusion**: The town (except for the lottery) is an ordinary, contemporary small town.

   Clues:

1.10
Application, Critical Evaluation, and Synthesis

Choose one or two of these topics to discuss in your small group or to write about.

1. Stories often have a lesson or moral that is not directly stated. We, the readers, have to infer it from the events and from what the characters do and say. Some readers interpret "The Lottery" as a description of the destructive side of human nature. Other readers feel "The Lottery" represents the dangers of the "crowd mentality," where people in a group may do something that they would never do as individuals. What do you think the author is trying to tell us about people and society in this story? Why does the town really hold the lottery? Why do you think the author doesn't tell us much about the town or the people? Support your answers with examples from the story. (*Note:* Different people have different explanations for this story. There is no "correct" meaning.)

2. A scapegoat is a victim chosen by a crowd of people who use the scapegoat to rid themselves of their unhappy feelings, anger, or fear.

   a. What is the purpose of the scapegoat in "The Lottery"? How do you think the lottery affected the people who took part in it?

b. Describe some examples from history or from current events in which people turned against a person, a group, or an idea and made it a scapegoat. Can you think of some examples of how contemporary society might sacrifice its citizens—or of groups that turn against a person or another group? What do you think are the reasons for such actions? Who was the scapegoat? Why did society need a scapegoat? What happened to the scapegoat? Was there any change to the society after the scapegoat was sacrificed? Explain and give examples.

c. Do you think it is easy to convince people to turn against someone or some idea? Why do you think so? What kind of conditions might cause this to happen (e.g., worries about the future, fear of another culture)? Do you think modern technology, such as television and computers, makes it easier — or more difficult — for people to develop a crowd mentality and carry out a scapegoat sacrifice? Please give some reasons to explain your answer.

3. What do you think happens after the end of "The Lottery" (to the townspeople, to the members of the Hutchinson family)?

4. The narrator of "The Lottery" tells the story like a newspaper reporter, very neutrally, just reporting the facts. The story could have been told in a different way if one of the townspeople had been the narrator. Rewrite "The Lottery" from the perspective of Mr. Hutchinson, Tessie Hutchinson, Mr. Warner, or any other person in the story who interests you.

5. When "The Lottery" was first published, many readers were upset because it made them uncomfortable, and they weren't really certain what it meant. The author said "This is just a story I wrote; it doesn't mean anything in particular." Does "The Lottery" make you feel uncomfortable? Why? Do you think "it doesn't mean anything in particular"? Why?

Social Influence:
Conformity, Compliance,
and Obedience to Power

This reading is excerpted from Chapter 8 of *Social Psychology*, a college textbook by David O. Sears, Letitia Anne Peplau, and Shelley E. Taylor. The chapter examines how our behavior is influenced by other people and groups. Reprinted by permission of Prentice-Hall. Seventh edition, 1991.

2.1

First Reading

Read the selection quickly for the main ideas. Pay attention to the title and the text headings as you read. Do *not* stop to look up words in your dictionary.

1 Consider these illustrations of social influence:
   In the 1950s, American college men were virtually all clean shaven, with short hair; only farmers wore blue jeans as everyday clothing; and college women almost invariably had short hair and dressed in blouses and skirts, with hemlines well below the knee. By the late 1960s, college students of both sexes grew their hair long and wore blue jeans regularly. How would you describe fashion trends at your college today? Why do so many students tend to dress so similarly?

2 As you hurry into the local supermarket, a young woman stops you and asks you to sign a petition urging the city to build a new shelter for homeless families. You somewhat reluctantly read and sign the petition. Next the woman asks you to donate $5 to a campaign to help the homeless. You give her a dollar and duck into the market. Why did you comply, at least partially, with her requests?

3 In Nazi Germany during World War II, Adolf Hitler commanded his troops into battle—a common practice for heads of state during war-time. But he also ordered the construction of concentration camps where millions of civilians were put to death. Why did so many people obey Hitler's extraordinary orders to kill children and unarmed civilians?

4 Social psychologists have long been interested in how our behavior is influenced by other people and groups. Indeed, Elliot Aronson (1984, p. 6) has defined the core topic of social psychology as "the influences that people have

upon the beliefs or behaviors of others." We have already explored some aspects of social influence in our analysis of the processes of attitude change. This chapter examines three types of social influence: conformity, compliance, and obedience to authority.

5 When someone voluntarily performs an act because others are doing it, we call it *conformity*. College students are presumably free to pick their own clothes and hairstyles. But students often prefer to dress like others in their social group, thus conforming to current standards of fashion on campus. What factors affect conformity to group pressures?

6 When people do what they are asked to do, even though they might prefer not to, we call it *compliance*. The distinguishing feature of compliance is that we are responding to a request from another individual or group. Compliance can occur in many settings—when a friend asks us for a ride to the airport, or a group of Halloween trick-or-treaters ask for candy, or a Red Cross volunteer asks for donations.

7 In some social situations, we perceive one person or group as having the *legitimate authority* to influence our behavior. The government has a right to ask us to pay taxes, parents have a right to ask their children to wash the dinner dishes, and medical personnel have the right to ask us to take off our clothes for a physical exam. In these cases, social norms permit those in authority to make requests. Although authorities often make reasonable and appropriate requests, their power can be abused. During World War II, Nazi military leaders ordered the mass murder of millions of civilians. After the war, when individuals such as Adolf Eichmann were put on trial for carrying out these orders, they often attempted to excuse their behavior by saying they were "just following orders" from those in command. . . .

Conformity

8 People often conform—even when doing so means contradicting their own perceptions of the world. In many cases, individuals continue to believe that their private judgments are correct and that the group is wrong. Nevertheless, when asked to respond publicly, they give the same incorrect responses that the others give. This is what we mean by conformity.

Why Do People Conform?

9 Basically, people conform for two major reasons—to be right and to be liked (Campbell & Fairey, 1989). . . . Similarly, people are more likely to conform to group behaviors when they think the group members are right and when they want to be liked by the group.

10 **Informational Influence: The Desire to be Right.** One reason for conformity is that the behavior of other people often provides useful information. A thirsty traveler at an oasis in the Sahara Desert who sees [local people] drinking from one well and avoiding another well would be smart to copy their behavior. By drinking from the popular well, the traveler may avoid drinking

contaminated water. The tendency to conform based on informational influence depends on two aspects of the situation: how well-informed we believe the group is and how confident we are in our own independent judgment.

11   The more we trust the group's information and value their opinions in a situation, the more likely we are to go along with the group. . . . Balanced against the individual's confidence in the group is the individual's confidence in his or her own views. Early studies found that the more ambiguous or difficult the [situation], the more likely people were to conform (Coleman, Blake, & Mouton, 1958), presumably because they were less certain of their own judgment. . . .

Normative Influence: The Desire to Be Liked.

12   A second major reason for conformity is to gain the approval, or avoid the disapproval, of other people. We often want others to accept us, like us, and treat us well. In growing up, people often learn that one way to get along with a group is to go along with group standards. In deciding how to dress for the senior prom, we may try to wear the "right" clothes so that we will fit in, give a good impression, and avoid disapproval. We may not really like wearing formal clothes, but do it anyway because it's socially appropriate for the occasion. When we're with our weight-conscious friends, we may eat salads and "health foods" even though we don't especially like them; when we're alone, we're more likely to follow our personal preferences by eating hamburgers and fries. In such situations, conformity leads to an outward change in public behavior, but not necessarily to a change in the individual's private opinions.

Individuals feel freer to disagree when even one other person does not go along with the group.

13 This fear of being deviant is justified by the group's response to deviance. When someone does not go along with a group, that person becomes the target of efforts to bring them in line and may ultimately risk rejection. . . .

14 A group can also apply punishment. [In a research experiment conducted at one factory, a group of workers developed their own standards of how much work they should do each day.] Anyone who worked harder would make the others look bad and might cause management to increase its expectation of work output. The group exerted intense pressure on its members to conform to the group standard for productivity. People who worked too much [were criticized by the others. Group members also enforced their standards by] giving the deviate a sharp blow on the upper arm. Not only did this hurt, but it was a symbolic punishment for going against the group. Any group member could deliver the punishment, and the person who was [hit] could not fight back. The punishment had to be accepted and with it, the disapproval it indicated. This is a dramatic example of the kinds of pressure present in all groups that cause members to conform to accepted opinions, values, and behavior. In many cases, just being aware of the potential costs of nonconformity and the benefits of conformity leads people to follow group standards. When this fails, groups use persuasion, threats of ostracism, direct punishment, and offers of rewards to pressure individuals to conform.

15 In summary, the motivation to conform stems from a desire to be right and a desire to be liked by the group. The strength of these two motives varies considerably depending on the situation.

When Do People Conform?

16 Several important features of the group situation that can affect conformity are commitment, group size, and unanimity. Research also shows that there are individual differences in the desire for individuation or uniqueness.

17 **Commitment to the Group.** Conformity is affected by the strength of the bonds between individuals and the group (Forsyth, 1983). *Commitment* refers to all the forces, positive and negative, that act to keep an individual in a relationship or group. Positive forces attracting an individual to a group might include liking other group members, believing the group accomplishes important goals, feeling that the group works well together, expecting to gain from belonging to the group, and identifying with group values. Another important factor is the individual's sense of identification with the group (Hogg & Turner, 1987).

18 Negative forces keeping an individual from leaving a group also increase commitment. These include such barriers as having few alternatives or having made large investments in the group that would be costly to give up. Regardless of the sources of commitment, the more committed a person is to a group, the greater the pressures for conformity.

19 We use the term *cohesiveness* to describe the extent to which group members as a whole are strongly or weakly committed to the group. In general, the more highly cohesive a group, the greater the potential pressures to-

ward conformity. Groups with high morale, where members enjoy working together and believe they function well as a team, are more vulnerable to conformity pressures than are less cohesive groups. . . .

20 **Group Unanimity.** An extremely important factor in producing conformity is the unanimity of the group opinion. A person faced with a unanimous group decision is under great pressure to conform. If, however, a group is not united, there is a striking decrease in the amount of conformity. When even one other person does not go along with the rest of the group, conformity drops to about one-fourth the usual level. This is true when the group is small, and it also appears to hold with up to 15 people. One of the most impressive things about this phenomenon is that it does not seem to matter who the nonconforming person is. Regardless of whether this dissenter is a high-prestige, expert figure or someone of low prestige who is not at all expert, conformity tends to drop to low levels (Asch, 1955; Morris & Miller, 1975). . . .

21 **The Desire for Individuation (Uniqueness).** People differ in their willingness to do things that publicly differentiate them from others. Whereas some people are more comfortable blending in with a group and going along with group opinions, others prefer to stand out. . . .

Minority Influence: Innovation in Groups

22 Conformity to majority patterns is a basic aspect of social life. But our emphasis on the power of the majority should not blind us to the importance of m*inority influence*. Sometimes a forceful minority with a new idea or unique perspective can effectively change the position of the majority. . . .

Review

1. What is conformity?
2. Why do people like to conform?
3. Do you ever conform to something even if you don't want to? Why?

Compliance

23 One of the most basic ways we influence other people is to ask them directly to do something. Think of some of the requests you might make of a friend—to water your plants while you are on vacation, to borrow some money for a few days, to refrain from smoking in your car, to tell you what they really think of your new haircut, to join the volunteer group you're organizing, and so on. How might you present these requests to increase the chances that your friend will comply? Research on compliance has attempted to understand some of the processes that lead people to comply (or refuse to comply) with requests.

24   Sometimes we seem to comply with requests for no reason at all. In one study, researchers approached people using a photocopying machine and asked to go first in line because "I have to make copies" (Langer, Blank, & Chanowitz, 1978). This so-called explanation actually gave no real justification for going out of turn. But many subjects went along with the request, apparently not paying much attention to the content of the explanation. Ellen Langer refers to this behavior as *mindlessness* because people respond without thinking seriously about their behavior. Perhaps out of habit, we have learned that when someone asks for something, especially something trivial, and gives a reason (even a meaningless reason), we should go along. We spare ourselves the mental effort of thinking about the situation and simply comply with the request. Mindlessness may not explain most instances of compliance, but it is a fascinating aspect of human behavior.

Six Bases of Social Power

25   When David Kipnis (1984, p. 186) asked managers in business organizations how they try to influence their co-workers to do something, they said things like: "I simply order him to do what I ask," "I act very humble while making my request," or "I explain the reasons for my request." In contrast, when he asked dating couples how they influence their partners, they said things like: "I get angry and demand he give in," "I act so nice that she cannot refuse when I ask," or "We talk about why we don't agree." Social psychologists have studied the diverse ways people try to get others to comply with their wishes.

26   A useful way to classify influence strategies is provided in a model developed by Bertram Raven and his colleagues (French & Raven, 1959; Raven, 1988). They identify six major bases of power, each reflecting a different type of resource a person might use to influence someone. [These six bases are: rewards, coercion, expertise, information, referent power, and legitimate authority. A person may convince others to comply with his or her requests by giving rewards, by forcing someone to do something (coercion), by offering special knowledge or training (expertise), or by giving or withholding information. The final two bases, referent power and legitimate authority, are described below.]

27   **Referent power.** A basis of influence with special relevance to personal relationships and groups is referent power. This exists when we admire or identify with a person or group and want to be like them. In such cases, we may voluntarily copy their behavior or do what they ask because we want to become similar to them. In everyday life we may not think of identification as a type of influence, but it can be very effective. A young child who looks up to an older brother, tries to imitate his mannerisms, and adopts his interests is one illustration. A young man who drinks a particular brand of beer because he identifies with the "macho" image of the sportsmen promoting the product in TV commercials is also being influenced by referent power. Recently, Raven (1988) has discussed the possibility of "negative referent

power," which occurs when we want to separate ourself from a disliked or unappealing person or group. To avoid being identified with the unattractive other, we may deliberately avoid copying their behavior.

28 **Legitimate Authority.** Sometimes one person has the right or authority to ask another person to act a certain way. The manager who "simply orders" a subordinate to do what she wants or the general who orders his troops into battle are likely to be exercising legitimate authority. Similarly, in most families, parents feel they have the right to tell young children when to go to bed, and children usually feel obligated to comply. Children may try to renegotiate bedtime rules or ask to make an exception for a special occasion, but they usually accept their parents' authority to make rules.

29 Social roles such as parent-child, teacher-student, or supervisor-employee often dictate the legitimate rights and responsibilities of people in a relationship. Even very young children seem to sense that the requests of physicians and dentists should be obeyed. When someone deviates from agreed-upon rules, we feel we have the right to remind them of their obligations. A prerequisite for effective legitimate authority is that all parties agree about the norms in their relationship. . . .

30 A summary of the key features of the six major bases of power is provided in Table 8-1 on p. 122.

Obedience to Authority

31 In this final section we take a closer look at one of the six bases of power identified by Raven: obedience to legitimate authority. In any social group, organization, or society, it is important that people obey orders from those who have legitimate authority. In wartime, generals expect soldiers to obey orders and severely punish disobedience. We expect drivers to follow the orders of police directing traffic. Most people believe that public health officials have the right to require vaccinations against polio and other communicable diseases for school children. Obedience is based on the belief the authorities have the right to make requests. In many cases, we agree with the policies of those in charge, and obey orders willingly.

32 But what about situations in which the demands of the authorities conflict with our own beliefs and values? How do parents respond if they believe that a new vaccination required for public schools is potentially hazardous to their children? How do soldiers and citizens react if they believe their government is pursuing a misguided or immoral policy?

33 Herbert Kelman and Lee Hamilton (1989) have used the term "crimes of obedience" to describe immoral or illegal acts that are committed in response to orders from an authority. Kelman and Hamilton reject the idea that crimes of obedience are things of the past, committed only in Nazi Germany or by fanatical cults. Rather, they suggest that crimes of obedience continue to occur in our society. For example, crimes of obedience occur when employees carry out orders from corporate executives that violate the

law or harm public welfare, when political leaders order their subordinates to engage in shady campaign practices, or when soldiers and guerilla fighters obey orders to torture or kill unarmed civilians. . . .

34   In this chapter, you have learned a great deal about conformity, compliance, and obedience to authority. Knowledge of influence techniques can sometimes help people to resist social pressures and to follow their individual beliefs. What personal lessons do you draw from the social psychological research on social influence presented in this chapter?

Number of words: 3,010

Reading Times	Reading Speed
1st reading _____ minutes	16 minutes = 188 wpm
3rd reading _____ minutes	14 minutes = 215 wpm
	12 minutes = 250 wpm
	10 minutes = 301 wpm
	8 minutes = 376 wpm

2.2
Second Reading

Go back and read the selection again. Take as much time as you need. Look up some of the unfamiliar words in the glossary at the end of this book or in your dictionary if you wish.

2.3
Third Reading

Read the selection quickly a third time. Concentrate on understanding the main ideas and the meanings of new vocabulary words in the contexts in which they appear.

2.4
Reader Response

In order to explore your response to this reading, write for 15 minutes about anything that interested you in the selection. You may wish to write about a personal experience this reading reminded you of—or you may wish to agree or disagree with something in the reading. Try to explore *your own thoughts and feelings* as much as possible. Do *not* merely summarize or restate the ideas in the selection.

2.5
Response Sharing

Read your response to two or three other people in your class. Listen carefully to what the others have written. After you have discussed each other's responses, talk about other points of interest in the selection.

2.6
Understanding Citations

When writers use information from books and magazine articles, it is important for them to tell where they found their information. These references are called *citations*. Citations are listed in the footnotes and the bibliography. (For more information about footnotes and bibliographies, see Expansion section page 249.)

Why are citations important? First, the writer must never present someone else's information as if it were his or her own. Second, the reader may want to refer to the source to get more information on the topic. A citation always includes the author's name, the title of the book or article, the publisher, and the date of publication. For magazine or journal articles, the citation also includes the issue or volume number followed by the page numbers (for example, 7:146 or 6, 184-195). If the citation is for a book, the title is printed in *italics*. If the citation is for an article or chapter in a book, the article name is shown in regular type and the name of the book or journal follows in italics. If more than one work is cited for an author, the reading will indicate which one is being referred to.

Using the bibliography on pp. 122–123, answer the following.

1. Find one example of a book citation. _____

2. Find one example of a journal article and indicate the volume and pages.

_____

3. Find one example of a publisher and a date of publication.

_____

In this textbook selection, references to other books are shown in parentheses, for example (Hogg & Turner, 1987). Using the bibliography and Table 8-1 on p. 122, work with your small group to answer the following questions about citations. Refer to the paragraph in the selection as you answer each question.

4. In paragraph 4, what is the title of Elliot Aronson's book and who published it? How can you tell which of the three citations is the correct one?

5. Does the Hogg & Turner citation in paragraph 17 refer to a book or a journal? What clue in the citation helps you decide?

6. In which issue of the journal will you find the article by Morris & Miller cited in paragraph 20? What pages is the article on?

7. Which one of Raven's works is cited in paragraph 27?

8. Where is Table 8-1, "The Six Bases of Power," adapted from? Is the citation for Table 8-1 a book or a journal article? When was it published?

2.7
Analyzing the Text

Work with your group members on this exercise. Discuss the answers carefully, particularly if there are disagreements among members of your group. In some cases there may be more than one possible interpretation.

1. What is the difference between conformity and compliance? Give several examples to explain your answer.

2. What are the two major reasons why people conform? Explain each reason in detail and give examples.

3. List the forces, both positive and negative, that contribute to commitment.

4. What is group unanimity? What happens to unanimity if there is disagreement by even one person?

5. Explain the six bases of social power and give an example of each.

2.8
Vocabulary Study

Study the italicized words and phrases in their contexts and guess their meanings. Write your guess on the first line. Then look up the word or phrase in your dictionary and write the definition on the second line.

1, 2, and **3.** (paragraph 5) College students are *presumably* free to *pick* their own clothes and hairstyles. But students often prefer to dress like others in their social group, thus *conforming* to current standards of fashion on campus.

presumably

a. (guess) _____

b. (dictionary) _____

pick

a. (guess) _____

b. (dictionary) _____

conforming

a. (guess) _____

b. (dictionary) _____

4 and 5. (paragraph 19) Groups with high *morale*, where members enjoy working together and believe they function well as a team, are more vulnerable to conformity pressures than are less *cohesive* groups.

morale

a. (guess) _____

b. (dictionary) _____

cohesive

a. (guess) _____

b. (dictionary) _____

6, 7, and 8. (paragraph 21) Whereas some people are more comfortable *blending in* with a group and *going along with* group opinions, others prefer to *stand out*.

blending in

a. (guess) _____

b. (dictionary) _____

going along with

a. (guess) _____

b. (dictionary) _____

stand out

a. (guess) _____

b. (dictionary) _____

9 and 10. (paragraph 24) Perhaps out of habit, we have learned that when someone asks for something, especially something *trivial*, and gives a reason (even a *meaningless* reason), we should go along.

trivial

a. (guess) _____

b. (dictionary) _____

meaningless

a. (guess) _____

b. (dictionary) _____

11 and 12. (paragraph 29) When someone *deviates* from agreed-upon rules, we feel we have the right to remind them of their *obligations*.

deviates

a. (guess) _____

b. (dictionary) _____

obligations

a. (guess) _____

b. (dictionary) _____

2.9
Dictionary Skills Review

A dictionary has many uses in addition to helping you understand the meanings of words. It can help you with spelling, pronunciation, stress, the division of words into syllables, the meaning of phrases and idiomatic expressions, and the relationship of words to each other. Look at this page from the *Oxford American Dictionary* (1980) and answer the questions. Discuss your answers with your small group.

1. a. The guide words at the top of the page (**pres. part.** and **prettify**) show the first and last words on that page. By looking only at the guide words you can quickly tell which words will appear on that page. Circle the words that would appear on a page with **pres. part./prettify** for guide words.

    pretentious   preserve   pressurized   president   priceless   prevail

    b. If the guide words were **wilderness** and **wind**, which words would appear on the page?

    wildlife   windpipe   wink   wince   wiggle   willingly

2. On this dictionary page look at the word **pressurize**. The word is separated into three syllables: pres-sur-ize. Indicate how **pressurization** is divided into syllables.

    _____

3. Look up the following words in your dictionary and rewrite them to show how they are divided into syllables. (*Note:* If you need to divide a word at the end of a line, always divide it between syllables.)

    impression _____   whereas _____

    communicable _____   reluctantly _____

    imitate_____   trivial_____

    unanimous_____   situation _____

process of presoaking. **presoak** v. to soak beforehand.

pres. part. abbr. present participle.

press[1] (pres) v. 1. to apply weight or force steadily to (a thing). 2. to squeeze juice etc. from. 3. to make by pressing. 4. to flatten or smooth, to iron (clothes etc.). 5. to exert pressure on (an enemy etc.), to oppress. 6. to urge or entreat, to demand insistently, *press for a 35-hour week.* 7. to force the acceptance of, *they pressed candy upon us.* 8. to insist upon, *don't press that point.* 9. to throng closely. 10. to push one's way. **press** n. 1. pressing, *give it a slight press.* 2. crowding, a throng of people. 3. hurry, pressure of affairs, *the press of modern life.* 4. an instrument or machinery for compressing or flattening or shaping something. 5. a printing press, a printing or publishing firm. 6. newspapers and periodicals, the people involved in writing or producing these, *a press photographer.* □**be pressed for,** to have barely enough of, *we are pressed for time.* **press agent,** a person employed to take care of publicity. **press box,** a reporters' enclosure, especially at a sports event. **press clipping,** a cutting from a newspaper. **press conference,** an interview given to journalists by a person who wishes to make an announcement or answer questions. **press gallery,** a gallery for reporters, especially in a legislative assembly. **press release,** a news release, written information given to the press for publication.

press[2] v. (old use) to force to serve in the army or navy. □**press into service,** to bring into use as a makeshift.

press·ing (pres-ing) adj. 1. urgent, *a pressing need.* 2. urging something strongly, *a pressing invitation.* **pressing** n. a thing made by pressing, a phonograph record or series of these made at one time.

press·man (pres-măn) n. (pl. **-men**, pr. -měn) the operator of a printing press.

press·room (pres-room) n. 1. the room in a printing factory where the presses are kept. 2. a room set aside for reporters and journalists.

pres·sure (presh-ŭr) n. 1. the exertion of continuous force upon something. 2. the force exerted, that of the atmosphere, *pressure is high in eastern areas.* 3. a compelling or oppressive influence, *is under pressure to vote against it; the pressures of business life.* **pressure** v. (**pres·sured, pres·sur·ing**) to try to compel (a person) into some action. □**pressure center,** (in meteorology) a condition of the atmosphere with pressure above or below average. **pressure cooker,** a pot in which things can be cooked quickly by steam under high pressure. **pressure gauge,** a device for showing the pressure of air, steam, etc. **pressure group,** an organized group seeking to influence policy by concerted action and intensive propaganda. **pressure point,** a sensitive point on the skin; a part of the body which when pressed arrests the flow of blood through an artery lying close to the surface. **pressure suit,** a pressurized suit.

pres·sur·ize (presh-ŭ-rız) v. (**pres·sur·ized, pres·sur·iz·ing**) to keep (a closed compartment, such as an aircraft cabin) at a constant atmospheric pressure. **pres·sur·i·za·tion** (presh-ŭ-ri-zay-shŏn) n. □**pressurized cabin,** an aircraft cabin in which normal atmospheric pressure is maintained. **pressurized suit,** an inflatable suit designed to protect the body from

low pressure when flying at a high altitude.

pres·ti·dig·i·ta·tion (pres-ti-dij-i-tay-shŏn) n. sleight of hand. **pres·ti·dig·i·ta·tor** (pres-ti-dij-i-tay-tŏr) n.

pres·tige (pre-steezh, -steej) n. respect for a person resulting from his good reputation, past achievements, etc.

pres·ti·gious (pre-stij-ŭs) adj. having or bringing prestige. **pres·ti'gious·ly** n.

pres·to (pres-toh) adv. (especially in music) quickly. **presto!** interj. a conjurer's word used at a moment of sudden change.

pre·stressed (pree-strest) adj. (of concrete) strengthened by means of stretched wires within it.

pre·sum·a·ble (pri-zoo-mă-běl) adj. able to be presumed. **pre·sum'a·bly** adv.

pre·sume (pri-zoom) v. (**pre·sumed, pre·sum·ing**) 1. to take for granted, to suppose to be true. 2. to take the liberty of doing something, to venture, *may we presume to advise you?* 3. to be presumptuous. □**presume on,** to take unwarranted liberties because of, *they are presuming on her good nature.* ▷See the note under **assume.**

pre·sump·tion (pri-zump-shŏn) n. 1. presuming a thing to be true, something presumed. 2. presumptuous behavior.

pre·sump·tive (pri-zump-tiv) adj. giving grounds for presumption. □**heir presumptive, see heir.** ▷ Do not confuse *presumptive* with *presumptuous.*

pre·sump·tu·ous (pri-zump-choo-ŭs) adj. behaving with impudent boldness, acting without authority. **pre·sump'tu·ous·ly** adv. **pre·sump'tu·ous·ness** n. ▷ Do not confuse *presumptuous* with *presumptive.*

pre·sup·pose (pree-sŭ-pohz) v. (**pre·sup·posed, pre·sup·pos·ing**) 1. to take for granted. 2. to require as a prior condition, *effects presuppose causes.* **pre·sup·po·si·tion** (pree-sup-ŏ-zish-ŏn) n.

pre·tax (pree-taks) adj. existing before taxes are deducted, *pretax earnings.*

pre·teen (pree-teen) n. a child who has not yet become a teenager. **preteen** adj.

pre·tend (pri-tend) v. 1. to create a false appearance of something, either in play or so as to deceive others. 2. to claim falsely that one has or is something. 3. to lay claim, *he pretended to the title; pretended to exact knowledge,* claimed to have this. **pre·tend'ed·ly** adv.

pre·tend·er (pri-ten-děr) n. 1. a person who pretends. 2. a person who claims a throne or title etc.

pre·tense (pree-tens, pri-tens) n. 1. pretending, make-believe. 2. claim to merit or knowledge etc. 3. pretentiousness.

pre·ten·sion (pri-ten-shŏn) n. 1. the assertion of a claim to something. 2. pretentiousness.

pre·ten·tious (pri-ten-shŭs) adj. showy, pompous. **pre·ten'tious·ly** adv. **pre·ten'tious·ness** n.

pre·ter·mi·nal (pree-tur-mi-năl) adj. happening before death.

pre·ter·nat·u·ral (pree-těr-nach-ŭ-răl) adj. outside the ordinary course of nature, unusual. **pre·ter·nat'u·ral·ly** adv.

pre·test (pree-test) n. a preliminary test.

pre·text (pree-tekst) n. a reason put forward to conceal one's true reason.

Pre·to·ri·a (pri-tohr-i-ă) the administrative capital of the Republic of South Africa.

pret·ti·fy (prit-i-fı) v. (**pret·ti·fied, pret·ti·fy·**

4. The syllables give you clues to pronunciation, stress, and word division. Each dictionary has its own method for showing these things. On this dictionary page, where do you find the pronunciation of a word?

   a. It is placed in parentheses right after the word.

   b. It is indicated at the bottom of the page.

   c. It is placed at the end of each entry.

   How does your own dictionary show pronunciation?

5. This dictionary page indicates stress by

   a. using stress marks in the pronunciation guide.

   b. printing the stressed syllable in bold type in the original word entry.

   c. printing the stressed syllable in bold type in the pronunciation guide.

   How does your dictionary show stressed syllables?

6. Circle the stressed syllables in these words:

   (pres - ing)   (pres - ti - dij - i - tay - shon)   (pree - su - pohz)   (pree - taks)

7. Words may have more than one meaning.

   a. How many meanings are given for **press**-1 used as a verb? _____

   b. Which of the dictionary meanings is used here? "He **pressed** through the crowd to get to the front of the bus." Meaning number _____

   c. Which of the dictionary meanings is used here? "They *press* grapes to make wine." Meaning number _____

   d. The word **press**-2 is an *(old use)*. What does "old use" mean?

8. a. How many meanings are given for **pretend**? _____

   b. Write a sentence to illustrate meaning 1 of pretend.

   _____

9. Dictionaries show you the parts of speech of a word. Write the following forms:

   a. The adjective form of **prestige**: _____

   b. The past tense of **prettify**: _____

   c. The verb form of **pressure**: _____

10. In a dictionary, each major word is called an entry. Find:

    a. an entry for an abbreviation: _____

    b. the entry that means "quickly" in music: _____

    c. two entries that should not be confused with each other:

       1. _____   2. _____

    How does this dictionary alert you to special information like this?

11. Dictionary entries often include special phrases or idioms associated with the entry word.

    a. What are the special phrases listed under **pressurize**?

    _____

    b. Find two other special phrases or idioms on this dictionary page.

        1. _____   2. _____

    c. How are these idioms indicated (by a number; by italics; by a box)?

    d. In the entry **presume**, is "may we presume to advise you?" an idiom? If yes, why? If no, what is it?

12. Where can you find some other information about **presume**?

2.10
Application, Critical Evaluation, and Synthesis

Choose one or two topics to discuss in your small group or to write about.

1. Paragraph 1 of this selection describes how people are influenced by fashion trends. Why do you think many people like to dress in the latest style? Think of some fads or fashions in the past that you especially liked or disliked. What were those fashions or fads? Which groups of people wore them? Why did you like (or dislike) them? If you ever wore fashions that you disliked, explain why you wore them.

2. Develop a chart like the one in the table (page 122) showing how the six bases of power would be used in one of the following situations:

    a. Your teacher tells you when to turn in a term paper.

    b. Your boss tells you to finish a project in two days.

    c. You ask your noisy neighbor to stop playing music so loud.

    d. Any situation that you choose.

3. The townspeople in "The Lottery" (Chapter 1) follow a ritual so old that they have forgotten why they do it, but they feel that it is important to continue it. The Chapter 2 textbook excerpt contains information that might explain the townspeople's actions and behavior. Think about how conformity, compliance, or obedience to power are involved in the behavior of the people in "The Lottery." What are some examples of how the townspeople try to conform to each other? In what ways are they compliant regarding the lottery? Do you think there is a source of power that controls their actions? Describe the source(s) of power and give some examples from that story.

TABLE 8-1
The Six Bases of Power[a]

	Definition	Example
Reward	Power based on providing or promising a positive outcome	If you brush your teeth every night this week, I'll take you to the movies on Saturday.
Coercion	Power based on providing or promising a negative outcome	If you don't brush your teeth, you can't play Nintendo.
Expertise	Power based on special knowledge or ability	The dentist told you to brush twice a day and he knows best.
Information	Power based on the persuasive content of the message	If you don't brush your teeth, you'll get cavities that will hurt. And the dentist will have to drill holes in your teeth to fill the cavities.
Referent power	Power based on identifying with or wanting to be like another person or group	Your big brother Stan always brushes twice a day.
Legitimate authority	Power based on the influencer's right or authority to make a request	I'm your mother and I'm telling you to brush your teeth—now!

Source: Adapted from Raven and Rubin (1983).
[a]According to Bertram Raven and his associates, compliance can be based on six major bases of power. Here we consider how a parent might use each approach to persuade a child to brush her teeth.

Bibliography

Aronson, E. (1984). *The social animal*, 4th ed. New York: W. H. Freeman.

Aronson, E., Stephan, C., Sikes, J., Blaney, N., & Snapp, M. (1978). The Jigsaw Classroom. Beverly Hills, CA: Sage.

Aronson, E., & Osherow, N. (1980). Cooperation, social behavior, and academic performance: Experiments in the desegregated classroom. In L. Bickman (Ed.), *Applied social psychology annual* (Vol. 1). Beverly Hills, CA; Sage Publications.

Hogg, M. A., & Abrams. D. (1988). *Social Identifications: A social physchology of intergroup relations and group processes*. New York: Routledge.

Hogg, M. A., & Turner, J. C. (1987). Social identity and conformity: A theory of referent information influence. In W. Doise & S. Moscovici (Eds.), *Current issues in European social psychology* (Vol. 2, pp. 139–182). New York: Cambridge University Press.

Morris, W. N., & Miller, R. S. (1975). The effects of consensus-breaking and con-sensus-preempting partners on reduction in conformity. *Journal of Experimental Social Psychology.* 11, 215–223.

Raven, B. H. (1988, August). *French and Raven 30 years later: Power, interaction and interpersonal influence.* Paper presented at the International Congress of Psychology, Sydney, Australia.

Raven, B. H. (1988). Social power and compliance in health care. In S. Maes, C. D. Spielberger, P. B. Defares, & I. G. Sarason (Eds.), *Topics in health psychology* (pp. 229–244). New York: Wiley.

Raven, B. H. & Rubin, J. Z. (1983). *Social psychology,* 2nd ed. New York: Wiley.

Learning to Bow: Conformity in Japan

As a society, the Japanese people like to conform. Bruce Feiler, an American who speaks Japanese, spent a year teaching English in the junior high schools in Sano, a small city north of Tokyo. Mr. Feiler lived and worked in a typical Japanese environment and wrote a book about his observations and experiences. The following excerpts come from that book, *Learning to Bow: Inside the Heart of Japan*, published by Ticknor and Fields, 1991.

3.1
First Reading

Read the three selections quickly for the main ideas. As you read, think about how conformity in Japan compares to conformity in the United States or another country. You may also want to consider how the six bases of power (described in the previous chapter) are used in Japan. Do *not* stop to look up words in your dictionary.

Section I

1 Once during my early months in Sano, I wrote a letter to some Japanese friends while I was at my office. When I had finished, I put the letter into an envelope, copied the address of my friends on the front, and gave it to Arai-san, the affable "office lady" who daily gathered the mail.

2 Several days later, Mr. C approached my desk with my letter in hand. "Mr. Bruce," he said in a low voice, squatting beside my chair as he did when he had important matters to discuss, "I'm afraid we cannot mail this envelope."

3 "Why not?" I asked in a similar hushed tone. I assured him that the letter contained important office business.

4 "It's not the letter," he said, "it's the envelope. You have not prepared it correctly."

5 "But the address is accurate on the front," I protested, "and I wrote the return address of our office on the back. Can you not read my writing?"

6 "Oh no, your writing is very beautiful—more lovely than mine," he said in one of those fatuous compliments that usually warned of something harsh to come. "But you have forgotten a very important detail. You left out the

character for *sama* [a more formal, written version of the honorific *san*]. I'm sorry, but we cannot mail this letter without it."

7   Was this a joke, I wondered—a parody, perhaps, of the Japanese obsession with detail? Would the authorities in this office really not mail my letter without the Japanese equivalent of "Mr." or "Mrs." scripted on the front? Did they really check every letter that passed through the mail bag to make sure that all the names were anointed and all the *kanji* were crossed?[1] The truth, I realized, was that this was no joke. The senior secretary of the Ansoku Education Office of the Tochigi Prefectural Board of Education had delivered my mislabeled letter to her section chief, who had conveyed it in turn to *my* section chief, who had passed it finally to my boss, who had dutifully come to inform me that the Japanese government refused to spend sixty yen to mail any envelope that did not contain the proper appellation of respect.

8   I thanked Mr. C for his advice, apologized for the inconvenience, and told him I would solve the problem. But instead of just adding the missing character, as any humble civil servant would have done, I vowed to prove that my officemates had grossly overreacted. I took the errant letter to the post office, purchased a stamp, and mailed the envelope myself—*sans sama*. Any friend of mine, I thought, would not be offended by this trivial lapse of etiquette.

9   The next time I visited these friends—a middle-aged couple in Osaka whom I had known for some time—I related this story to them, expecting us all to share a hearty laugh. But when I reached the end of my story, my friends didn't laugh. They didn't even titter.

10 "Mr. Bruce," they said with utter sincerity, "your boss was right. We always know when we get a letter from you, because you never address an envelope in the proper way. Form is very important, you know."

11 Envelopes, as I learned the hard way, are more than mere packaging in Japan. They are more than simple wrappers that protect a private letter and are later thrown away. As a school uniform defines a student or knickers a mountain hiker, an envelope actually becomes a part of the message itself. "In Japan, the package is a thought," wrote the philosopher Roland Barthes. Within minutes of reprimanding my poor form, my friends led me to a special drawer in their home which they reserved exclusively for new envelopes. Inside they kept containers for every occasion—from births to deaths, from New Year's gifts to mortgage payments. Some were wrapped in ribbons of red, while others were garnished with silk cherry blossoms. They even had a special envelope for the tooth fairy.[2]

12 The last, and most elaborate, package they drew from their drawer actually consisted of two wrappers in one. On the inside was a white sheet of paper,

---

1. Everything was done properly, without any errors.
2. It is customary in some countries to give a little gift to children each time a "baby" tooth falls out. The "tooth fairy" leaves the gift under the child's pillow while the child is sleeping.

folded twice to conceal its secret contents, and on top of this slid a thicker slip of paper which was sheathed in red and white twine, knotted around the midsection, and adorned with sprigs of pine.

13 "This is the most precious kind of envelope in Japan," my friends said as they handed me this paper bouquet that seemed more suited for framing and hanging than licking and stamping. "We put a crisp yen note in the inner fold, tuck this into the outer sheet, wrap both sheets inside a silk handkerchief, and give it to a bride and groom on their wedding day. This is our Japanese custom."

Section II

[Mr. Feiler hurt his ankle badly while playing tennis with his colleague, Mogi-sensei. He was taken to the emergency room of Sano Kosei Hospital, where his leg was x-rayed.]

14 The black and white picture of my leg showed no splinters in the bone, but there was a small black pocket where white ligament should have been. Momentarily the doctor arrived, a young, disheveled man with heavy side-burns, tennis shoes, and a slight, worried smile. As he entered the room, the nurses took two steps back, bowed deeply, and asked for his gracious protection. Turning toward me, he began his diagnosis in Japanese. But after realizing I was having difficulty understanding his technical language, he took a deep breath and started again, this time in English.

15 "Ligament. Rupture. Cast . . . Shall we?"[3]

16 He breathed an audible sigh of relief and gestured for the nurses to prepare the plaster.

17 "Excuse me," I interrupted, moving back into Japanese, "can't we discuss this a little more?"

18 Stunned, he sank back into a chair.

19 What followed was a rather arduous conversation as he repeated the same finding. "Ligament. Rupture. Cast . . . Understand?" I had the uneasy feeling that he knew about six words of English and was adjusting his diagnosis to fit his vocabulary. . . . Soon he stopped talking altogether, pulled on his plastic gloves, and declared, "Let's go."

20 "Yes, let's," the nurses cheered, lifting me to the table.

21 "But wait," I pleaded, "aren't there any other options?"

22 All the people around me—the doctor, nurses, and Mogi-sensei—were convinced that they should go ahead and wrap my leg in a cast. But I felt uneasy, mostly because the diagnosis had been so brief. (Later I learned that the Japanese have a special word for such diagnoses, *sanpun-kan shindan*, the three-minute treatment.) Should I submit to the will of everyone

---

3. The **ligament** connects bones or muscles to each other. A **cast** is made of **gauze** (thin cloth) and **plaster** (a white powder that hardens when wet); it is the hard white shell that prevents a broken bone or injured body part from moving.

around me or follow my instincts and ask to speak to another doctor who I knew could speak English? Ironically, here I found myself inside the circle of a Japanese group, and all I wanted was to get out.

23 "Excuse me," I whispered to Mogi-sensei, opting for prudence over harmony, "perhaps we could call Dr. Endo."

24 Dr. Endo, the head of the Sano Public Health Department, was an elder statesman in the local medical community. I had met him on my first round of greetings in August and since that time had visited his home several times. He speaks fluent English, having lived and worked in the Philippines, Malaysia, and the United States, and has an affable charm that cuts through the formality of even the stiffest situation. But none of this seemed to matter at the time. To the people gathered at the hospital, Dr. Endo was first and foremost just another doctor.

25 "Why do you want to call Dr. Endo?" Mogi-sensei whispered back. "After all, this doctor is a bone specialist."

26 "But don't you agree. . .," I said with a resolute smile. . . .

27 Without meaning to, I had violated the sanctity of the teacher-pupil relationship by appearing to question the wisdom of the doctor. In most cases, the doctor decides and the patient accepts. Realizing that I had disturbed not only the doctor but also my hosts, I hastened to mend the rift. "In my country," I tried to explain, "we often seek the advice of two doctors." For good measure I added that Dr. Endo was not just any doctor but a friend of mine, and that I had been to his house for dinner just the previous week. Perhaps if they did not understand the need for a second opinion, they would see that Dr. Endo was part of my extended family.

28 A tense moment followed as they looked pleadingly at me to rescind the request, but I remained quiet, trying to convince myself that this was a time to withstand the pressure. . . . Eventually the circle relaxed, and I was allowed to make the call. . . .

29 Dr. Endo arrived promptly at the hospital, bowed to the teacher, used honorific speech toward the doctor, joked with the nurses, and generally loosened a tense situation. After conferring with the doctor he assured me that the cast was necessary. Then he smiled and relayed the doctor's recommendation that I be admitted to the hospital.

30 "The hospital," I gasped, "for a sprained ankle?"

31 "Yes," Dr. Endo answered. "You'll be unable to walk on your cast."

32 "Unable to walk?"

33 "Yes," the other doctor added, "but only for a week. Then I'll give you another cast."

34 Despite protestations, I knew I was trapped. Having placed all of my hopes with Dr. Endo, I could hardly have convinced my doctor and my colleagues that a third opinion was in order. Within seconds they had pulled a cotton sock above my knee and wrapped my leg in plaster strips. When they finished, I was allowed one telephone call, sent home, and told to return post-haste with a towel, a change of clothes, and a pair of chopsticks.

Section III

(Here Mr. Feiler describes a special school event, Trash Day, which teaches children the importance of keeping their environment clean.)

35 In every school across the country, students are assigned to a homeroom class, or *kumi*. The word *kumi*, which is rooted in the Japanese character for thread, was first used several hundred years ago to describe small bands of samurai warriors attached to a feudal lord. Like these faithful fighters of the past, students learn today that duty and honor begin with dedication to this group. . . .

36 [At 2:30 every afternoon when classes end, the students clean their homeroom. They mop the floor, throw out the trash, wash the chalkboard, and clean the erasers. Their teacher, Mrs. Negishi, helps with the cleaning.] She taught by example. "If I don't clean, the students don't clean," she told me. "It's part of my responsibility." This is one of the main tenets of the *kumi* system: a partnership between students and teachers. Together they work to promote the welfare of the community and foster the hygiene of its mem-

bers. Students and teachers have clear roles, but the success of each depends on the cooperation of the other. At times the teacher plays disciplinarian, at times counselor, at times trusted friend. It is no wonder that students who grow up in this nurturing and protective environment learn to be dependent on those around them for everything from answering questions in English to deciding when to leave the hospital. From here students need only make a short leap of faith to transfer their trust in the *kumi* to reliance on their corporate co-workers later in life.

37   Beyond their commitment to the homeroom, however, students also learn to be aware of the higher structure that allows their *kumi* to prosper. Once a week students deferred tidying their own rooms to clean the entire school. They emptied the ashtrays in the teachers' room, scrubbed the toilets in the bathrooms, and pulled weeds from the garden in the parking lot. Before the *undo-kai* [sports festival] in October, students even clipped the grass on the playing field with classroom scissors. But the ultimate lesson for students is that they must look beyond their homeroom and their schoolyard to fulfill their obligation to the community as a whole. For this purpose, schools developed Trash Day.

38   "EVERY DAY WE ARE AWAKENING TO OUR OWN NEIGHBORHOOD," screamed the headline atop the student handout. "LET'S FRESHEN OUR CITY TODAY." At an outdoor rally just after lunch, each student received a mimeographed map, marked with a route for his or her *kumi* to follow, and two empty plastic bags: one for paper, the other for aluminum cans. After the guidelines had been explained, the principal took to the pitcher's mound and reiterated the theme of progress. "This year we want to press toward greater cleanliness," he yelled. "This year we want to achieve a new order. Let's go out and make our city proud!"

39   After the pep talk, the members of Class 9-1 headed west out the back gate, toward the span of factories and small plants that lined the outer fields of Sano. Like other events during the school day, this seemingly burdensome activity was carried out with great verve and enthusiasm. The students raced in and out of muddy ditches as well as up and down trees in search of unsightly debris. The local newspaper sent a photographer; shopkeepers and mill workers emerged from their buildings to cheer the students on. The whole experience felt like a holiday parade. My students were so spirited that they even carried their class flag on the hunt, a red and white banner with a caricature of Mrs. Negishi, emblazoned with the slogan "9-1 IS NUMBER 1."

40   As I limped along with the students, I decided to teach them an American game, I Spy.

41   "I spy something red," I would cry, and the students raced to retrieve the prize. Eventually I began giving points for every item I spied that students named in English.

42   "A box."

43   "One point."

44 "A bottle."

45 "One point."

46 "A potato chip bag."

47 "Two points."

48 This little diversion occupied the students for most of an hour, especially after they realized that I would give extra points for complete sentences. "This is a pen" earned four, and "I see a tire" earned five. But the biggest awards of the day went to objects so extraordinary that they needed no verb. I gave a ten-point bonus for a Georgia Coffee can and a five-point *penalty* for an "adult magazine." This phrase was Living English, all right, but not what the government had in mind.

49 Compared with the normal drone of classes, events like this were thrilling for the students, and they reinforced the message that community service can be fun when performed in a group. Trash Day was a painless way to teach students that their rights as students go hand in hand with their responsibilities to the nation. The only problem in the course of the afternoon was that the students felt they had not met this year's goal of greater cleanliness.

50 "I was embarrassed by how much trash we found this year," one of the girls in 9-1 complained at the end of the day as she dumped her cans into a recycling bin. "Our city should be ashamed."

51 "Our school should be ashamed as well," her friend added. "The streets around here are just a mess. I think we should ask the PTA to help us with this problem."

52 "But what can they do?" the first girl asked.

53 "Maybe they can go with us," her friend answered. "We could pick up trash together."

54 The first girl thought about this idea and agreed that it was worth a try. "If our parents don't care about this problem," she declared, "then we should show them how."

55 Students learn the importance of working with a group and serving their community. In short, they learn to be good citizens. . . . [However,] the exhaustive emphasis on group training in Japan also has negative side effects, especially on students who for one reason or another feel left out of their *kumi*. In my early months as a teacher, no one mentioned to me that students who live abroad for a while are often shunned by their classmates when they return to Japan. No one told me that the country still suffers from the legacy of a four-hundred-year-old feudal class system that was officially outlawed over a century ago. And no one warned me that certain students are ostracized by their peers because they come from families that are still tainted by this past. In Sano, all of these problems would boil to the surface in the course of my year as a teacher, and one would end in tragedy.

56 While the *kumi* network has definite drawbacks, the system triumphs in one of its primary goals: to develop a community ethic among most stu-

dents. Through repetition and eventually habit, students learn that they should spend a part of their day, indeed a part of themselves, tending the world around them. What begins in the homeroom at school later becomes the spirit of cooperation in many companies which so many Westerners admire. The lesson from the *kumi* is that this spirit is not mysteriously passed down through management seminars or religious rituals but is systematically and deliberately taught in schools. For students who pass through this system, a simple axiom serves as their personal pledge of allegiance: This above all, to thy *kumi* be true.

Number of Words: 2,906

Reading Times	**Reading Speed**
1st reading _____ minutes	16 minutes = 182 wpm
3rd reading _____ minutes	14 minutes = 208 wpm
	12 minutes = 242 wpm
	10 minutes = 291 wpm

3.2
Second Reading

Go back and read the selection again. Take as much time as you need. Look up some of the unfamiliar words in the glossary at the end of this book or in your dictionary if you wish.

3.3
Third Reading

Read the selection quickly a third time. Concentrate on understanding the main ideas and the meanings of new vocabulary words in the contexts in which they appear.

3.4
Reader Response

In order to explore your response to this reading, write for 15 minutes about anything that interested you in the selection. You may wish to write about a personal experience this reading reminded you of—or you may wish to agree or disagree with something in the reading. Try to explore *your own thoughts and feelings* as much as possible. Do *not* merely summarize or restate the ideas in the selection.

3.5
Response Sharing

Read your response to two or three other people in your class. Listen carefully to what the others have written. After you have discussed each other's responses, talk about other points of interest in the selection.

3.6
Identifying Main Ideas

Working with the same small group, make a list of the main ideas in this selection. Be sure to state the main ideas in your own words. Don't just copy sentences directly from the text. Think carefully about what the writer is trying to tell you.

3.7
Analyzing the Text

Work with your group members on this exercise. Discuss the answers carefully, particularly if there are disagreements among members of your group. In some cases there may be more than one possible interpretation.

1. In paragraph 8, Mr. Feiler says "Any friend of mine, I thought, would not be offended by this trivial lapse of etiquette." Were his friends offended? Why did they react that way? Why do they keep so many kinds of envelopes? Why is the last envelope they showed him more suited for framing and hanging?

2. In paragraph 28, why did the hospital staff want Mr. Feiler to rescind his request for a second opinion? Why did Mr. Feiler decide to withstand the pressure?

3. The three episodes in this reading describe types of desirable behavior in Japan. Match each behavior with the episode that describes it. Then find an example of that behavior in the reading. (*Note*: Some behaviors are described in more than one episode.)

   Episode: 1. Envelopes   2. Hospital   3. *Kumi* classroom

Behavior	*Example*

   __3__ a. duty _____students clean the entire school once a week_____

   _____ b. respect for authority _____

   _____ c. attention to detail _____

   _____ d. cooperation _____

   _____ e. correct form _____

   _____ f. dependency _____

   _____ g. submit to will of group _____

   _____ h. dedication to the group _____

4. What is a *kumi*? Why is it important to the Japanese school system and social system?

5. Give examples of how Japanese students learn to conform and how this influences their future as citizens of Japan.

3.8
Vocabulary Study

Study the italicized words and phrases in their contexts and guess their meanings. Write your guess on the first line. Then look up the word or phrase in your dictionary and write the definition on the second line.

1, 2, and **3.** (paragraph 7) The senior secretary . . . had delivered my *mislabeled* letter to her section chief, who had *conveyed* it in turn to my section chief, who had passed it finally to my boss, who had *dutifully* come to inform me that the Japanese government refused to spend sixty yen to mail any envelope that did not contain the proper appellation of respect.

mislabeled

a. (guess) _____

b. (dictionary) _____

conveyed

a. (guess) _____

b. (dictionary) _____

dutifully

a. (guess) _____

b. (dictionary) _____

4, 5, and **6.** (paragraph 11) Within minutes of *reprimanding* my poor form, my friends led me to a special drawer in their home which they *reserved exclusively* for new envelopes.

reprimanding

a. (guess) _____

b. (dictionary) _____

reserved

a. (guess) _____

b. (dictionary) _____

exclusively

a. (guess) _____

b. (dictionary) _____

7. (paragraph 27) Without meaning to, I had violated the *sanctity* of the teacher-pupil relationship by appearing to question the wisdom of the doctor.

a. (guess) _____

b. (dictionary) _____

8, 9, and **10.**　(paragraph 39) Like other events during the school day, this *seemingly* burdensome activity was *carried out* with great *verve* and enthusiasm.

seemingly

a. (guess) _____

b. (dictionary) _____

carried out

a. (guess) _____

b. (dictionary) _____

verve

a. (guess) _____

b. (dictionary) _____

11, 12, and **13.** (paragraph 56) While the *kumi* network has definite *drawbacks*, the system *triumphs* in one of its primary goals: to develop a community ethic among most students. Through repetition and eventually habit, students learn that they should spend a part of their day, indeed a part of themselves, *tending* the world around them.

drawbacks

a. (guess) _____

b. (dictionary) _____

triumphs

a. (guess) _____

b. (dictionary) _____

tending

a. (guess) _____

b. (dictionary) _____

3.9

Drawing Inferences and Implications

Sometimes when people speak or write, they do not directly say what they mean. We often have to "read between the lines" and think about the topic in order to understand the deeper meaning. Some of the most important information about a topic may come from *inferences*, ideas that are implied but not directly stated. In the situations below, choose the answer that best describes what the person really means. Then explain why you chose your answers.

1. Read paragraphs 7 and 8. By taking the letter to the post office himself, Mr. Feiler implies, but does not directly say, that

   a. he was embarrassed that he had made an error and wanted to correct it.

   b. he thought the concern for the missing character was silly and really not necessary.

   c. he knew his friends very well and realized they wouldn't care.

   Explain your answer.

2. Read paragraph 11. "As a school uniform defines a student or knickers a mountain hiker, an envelope actually becomes a part of the message itself." What can you infer from this statement?

   a. Envelopes are probably expensive in Japan.

   b. Students and mountain hikers must wear specific clothing.

   c. The Japanese are very concerned about proper form.

3. Read paragraph 18. "Stunned, he sank back into his chair" implies that the doctor

   a. was surprised that Mr. Feiler, his patient, spoke Japanese.

   b. was in a hurry to put a cast on his patient's leg and didn't want to wait.

   c. couldn't believe that his patient was questioning his diagnosis and decision.

4. Even though it is not said directly, you can infer from the reading that Mr. Feiler

   a. taught in Japan because he had to.

   b. enjoyed living and teaching in Japan.

   c. disliked his experience in Japan.

   How do you know? Find several examples to support your answer.

Here is a chance for you to read between the lines yourself and draw your own inferences. What do the following statements imply about the situations, even though they do not directly say it?

5. In paragraph 14, as the doctor entered the room, the nurses took two steps back, bowed deeply, and asked for his gracious protection. What might you infer about how the nurses feel about the doctor?

6. Read paragraph 35. What is implied by using the word *kumi* for a homeroom class?

7. Read paragraph 48. "I gave . . . a five-point penalty for an 'adult magazine.'" Why did Mr. Feiler give a penalty? Why was the phrase not what the government had in mind?

8. Read paragraphs 50 to 54. Do the two girls think Trash Day is important? Why or why not? What can you infer from their conversation?

9. How does Mr. Feiler feel about the *kumi* system? From what information in the reading did you infer this?

3.10
Application, Critical Evaluation, and Synthesis

Choose one or two topics to discuss in your small group or to write about.

1. In the episode about the misaddressed envelope, the author's friends say, "Form is very important, you know." According to this reading, why is form important in Japan? What would you have said in the same situation? Why? Explain your answer and give some reasons.

2. Mr. Feiler points out that Japanese schools develop social guidelines among the children that will make them better citizens (for example, feelings of social responsibility, commitment to the group, individuality, the difference between right and wrong). What sort of social guidelines were you taught in the schools that you went to as a child? How did the teachers teach those guidelines? Describe and give examples.

3. Reread paragraph 55. Mr. Feiler discusses some negative side effects of group training. Can you guess how the students mentioned in paragraph 55 might be treated? Why might they be shunned? What might their futures be like?

4. Look back at Chapter 2 (Conformity and Compliance). Using the information in that chapter, discuss why the Japanese like to conform. What are some reasons why people, in general, like to conform? Give specific examples from this Japan chapter to support those reasons. What are the reasons why people like to comply? Explain by giving several examples from the Japan chapter. Why is group unanimity so important in Japan? How important do you think minority influence is in Japan?

5. Read the section on the six bases of power in Chapter 2 (pages 112–113). Which of the six bases do you think the Japanese prefer to use to influence someone? Why do you think they prefer that one? Give reasons and examples from the Japan reading, if possible. (*Note:* You may choose more than one.) Which of the six do you think the Japanese dislike using? Why? Give reasons and examples.

AT THE END OF EVERY UNIT YOU ARE INVITED TO TURN TO THE EXPANSION SECTION BEGINNING ON PAGE 233. THIS SECTION CONCENTRATES ON THE FUNDAMENTALS OF LIBRARY RESEARCH AND REPORT WRITING.

Vocabulary Games

Here is a chance to review some of the vocabulary you have encountered in this unit. After you finish the game quizzes on your own, discuss your answers with your group members. You may use your dictionary to look up items to resolve disagreements. Scoring: 5 points for each correct answer.

Synonyms

Read each passage carefully and then draw a circle around the word or phrase that means the same thing (or almost the same thing) as the italicized word or phrase. If a word or phrase has more than one meaning, choose the meaning that fits the context in the passage.

> **Example:** The crowd *assembled* in the arena to watch the basketball game.
>
> a. struggled   (b. gathered)   c. played

Passage One

With just five seconds remaining, the basketball star *snatched* the ball and *defiantly* threw it into the basket, winning the game. The *boisterous* fans roared their approval. The opposing team slowly walked back to the locker room, *hushed* and defeated, carrying their *paraphernalia* with them.

1. *snatched*

   a. grabbed   b. dropped   c. maneuvered

2. *defiantly*

   a. hastily   b. daintily   c. boldly

3. *boisterous*

   a. noisy   b. devoted   c. respectful

4. *hushed*

   a. screaming   b. silent   c. exhausted

5. *paraphernalia*

   a. vitality   b. equipment   c. banner

138

Passage Two

In the mid-1990's, it was fashionable for teenagers to dye their hair in *striking* colors, such as green or orange. *Presumably* these teenagers were deliberately *deviating* from community standards. However, in their attempts *to stand out*, they formed a *cohesive* group of their own, conforming to their own standards of fashion.

6. *striking*

   a. noticeable   b. dreadful   c. bright

7. *presumably*

   a. we can suppose   b. we know definitely   c. we have no idea if

8. *deviating*

   a. rejecting   b. differing (from)   c. complying (with)

9. *to stand out*

   a. to look unappealing   b. to be prominent   c. to raise morale

10. *cohesive*

   a. influential   b. diverse   c. unified

Antonyms

Antonyms are words that have opposite meanings, e.g., cold-hot; tall-short; dark-light. Read the next passage carefully and then draw a circle around the word or phrase that means the opposite (or almost the opposite) of the italicized word or phrase. If a word or phrase has more than one meaning, choose the meaning that fits the context in the passage.

   Example: She *carries out* her work competently.

       a. performs   b. retrieves   (c. neglects)

       [*Neglects* is the opposite of *carries out* in this context.]

Passage Three

Anna Rampal carries out her job with great *verve* and dedication. However, there are a few *drawbacks* that disrupt the *harmony* of her work environment. She has to work a lot of overtime, and her boss (who *seemingly* is a pleasant person) *reprimands* the staff over trivial matters.

11. *verve*

   a. enthusiasm   b. weariness   c. precision

12. *drawbacks*

   a. methods   b. adventures   c. advantages

13. *harmony*

   a. dissent   b. agreement   c. quality

14. *seemingly*

   a. questionably   b. evidently   c. dutifully

15. *reprimands*

   a. overreacts to   b. shuns   c. praises

Logical Relationships

Look at the first pair of words, determine the relationship between them (are they synonyms or antonyms?). Then circle the word or phrase that fills in the blank to logically make a similar type of relationship.

   Example: assembled : gathered = constructed : _____

   (a. built)   b. demolished   c. dedicated

   [*Assembled* is related to *gathered* (a synonym) in the same way that *constructed* is related to *built*.]

16. exclusively : generally = deliberately : _____

   a. legitimately   b. accidentally   c. elaborately
   [Hint: *exclusively* and *generally* are antonyms.]

17. compliance : agreement = pause : _____

   a. hesitation   b. unanimity   c. commitment

18. sanctify : special recognition = triumph : _____

   a. failure   b. obligation   c. victory

19. blended in : combined = reserved : _____

   a. withstood   b. saved   c. reiterated

20. retrieve : lose = shun: _____

   a. acknowledge   b. disregard   c. convey

SCORE: Number of correct answers _____ × **5 =** _____

The Human Brain and How It Works

S cientists are learning more and more about how the human brain developed and how it works. They have figured out some of the ways the brain has adapted to meet environmental needs more effectively and to insure survival. Interesting research is currently being conducted on differences between male and female brains. In this unit, you will have the opportunity to explore some of the areas of research currently being conducted on the human brain.

Discussion

Before you begin reading, think about the following questions and discuss your answers. *Note:* You may wish to choose one or two questions to explore in detail either on your own or with a small group of students from your class.

1. What do you know about the human brain? Name as many parts of the brain as you can.

2. Do you think there are differences between male and female brains? Why? Or why not? Do you think men and women behave differently because of the way their brains function or because of the way they have been brought up—or both? Explain your reasoning with examples.

3. What are some questions you have about the human brain? Make a list of these questions and compare it with the lists of others in your group.

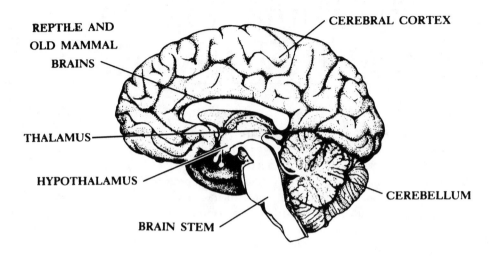

REPTILE AND
OLD MAMMAL
BRAINS

CEREBRAL CORTEX

THALAMUS

HYPOTHALAMUS

CEREBELLUM

BRAIN STEM

The Old Brain and the New

R obert Jastrow is the author of *The Enchanted Loom: Mind in the Universe* (The Reader's Library, a division of Simon & Schuster, 1981), the book from which the following selection comes. Professor Jastrow has taught at Dartmouth College and Columbia University, and he has written extensively about the human brain—what it looks like, how it developed, and how it works. In the following passage Jastrow explains how and why the brain evolved over time from the primitive reptilian brain to the much larger and more complicated human brain. Reprinted by permission.

1.1
First Reading

Read this passage quickly for the main ideas. Pay attention to the title and text headings as you read. Examine the illustrations of the brain closely. Do *not* stop to look up words in your dictionary.

1 The human brain consists of several different regions that evolved at different times. As each new section of the brain grew in our ancestors, nature generally did not discard the old parts; instead, they were retained and the latest section was built on top of them. Today the cerebral cortex, the newest and most important region in the human brain, folds around and smothers the older and more primitive regions. Yet these regions have not been completely overpowered. They remain underneath, no longer in undisputed command of the body, but still active. These primitive parts of the human brain continue to operate in accordance with a stereotyped and unthinking set of programs that go back to the mammals on the forest floor, and back farther still to the brutish reptiles who spawned the mammal tribe. Experiments have shown that much of the human repertoire of behavior originates in deeply buried regions of the brain that once directed the business of life for our ancestors.

2 The brains of our reptile forebears were divided cleanly into three compartments: a front compartment for smell, a middle compartment for vision, and a rear compartment for balance and coordination. All three compartments grew out of the brain stem, a still more ancient collection of neurons at the top of the spinal column.

3 These arrangements were inherited from the simple brain of the fishes. The receptors for vision and smell were coordinated in a region between the smell brain and the vision brain, which was a command post called the

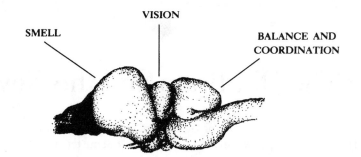

Figure 1   THE THREE-COMPARTMENT BRAIN OF THE REPTILE. This brain contains compartments for smell, vision, and balance. It is a simple brain, wired from birth with the programs or patterns of behavior needed for the reptile's survival. Remembering and learning play little role in the life of a reptile. Newly hatched snapping turtles, for example, find their way to the water by instinct and at once begin to catch insects and small fish without parental instruction.

diencephalon.[1] Here, the inputs from the different senses were compared and put together for a program of action. The basic instincts of survival—sexual desire, the search for food and the aggression responses of "fight-or-flight"—were wired into this region of the reptile's brain. Responses to the sex object, food, or the dangerous predator were automatic and programmed; the cerebral cortex, with its circuits for weighing options and selecting a course of action, did not exist.

4 When the mammals evolved out of the reptiles, their brains began to change. First, they developed a new package of instincts, related to the reptilian instincts for sex and procreation, but modified for the special needs of a mammalian lifestyle. Chief among these was the instinct for parental care of the young. Here was a revolutionary advance over the behavior of reptile parents, for whom the newly hatched young provided a tasty snack if they could catch them. But the reptile young were prepared to fight for their lives; they came into the world with all the needed programs of action wired into their brains. These hatchlings were miniature adults from the moment of birth. In the population of the mammals, on the other hand, the young arrived in a helpless and vulnerable state, and parental affection was essential for their survival. In these circumstances the mammal that lacked an instinct for the care of its young left few descendants. In the course of many generations, the traits of the indifferent parents were pruned from the stock of the mammals, and every mammal that remained was an attentive parent, and descended from a long line of attentive parents.

5 The new instincts of the mammals for parental care did not replace the older reptilian instincts; they augmented them. The ancient programs of the reptile brain—the search for food, the pursuit of a mate, and flight from

---

1. The *diencephalon* is also called the *thalamencephalon*, from the Latin meaning "the couch on which the brain rests." In more advanced brains the diencephalon became the site of the thalamus and the hypothalamus.

the predator—were still essential to survival. As a result, the command post in the brain that controlled instinctive behavior grew larger. Its responsibilities now included parental care, in addition to its other burdens.

6 The brains of the mammals changed in another important way that was related to their nocturnal lifestyle. As these animals passed into their 100-million-year time of darkness, the vision brain diminished in importance and the smell brain expanded. Two bulbous swellings grew out of the smell brain, one on each side, packed with circuitry for comparing the input from the sense of smell with information yielded by the other senses. These swellings and their circuits had been present in the reptile's brain, but they did not dominate that brain. In the early mammal, for whom the sense of smell was more valuable than any other, the expanding globes of the smell brain gradually took over the functions of the main command post, and the older, reptilian centers of the brain diminished in importance.

7 The two swellings in the smell brain were the cerebral hemispheres. In the beginning, when smell was the main function of the cerebral hemispheres, these parts of the brain were modest in size and could be fitted into the cranium of the mammal without wrinkling or folding. Later, when the ruling reptiles disappeared and the mammals began to move about by day and rely on the sense of vision as well as smell, more circuits had to be added to the brain to receive the new information from the eyes and analyze it. The added circuits for vision were in the cerebral hemispheres, which swelled to an even larger size as a result.

8 A heightened sense of vision placed additional demands on the memory capacity of the mammal's brain. The circuits for this function also were located in the cerebral hemispheres. The hemispheres now grew at an even faster rate. Their surfaces, crammed into skulls of limited size, began to acquire the wrinkled appearance characteristic of a very brainy animal. The cerebral hemispheres also acquired a new name in the terminology of the brain. Being nearly all surface, these regions of the brain became known as the cerebral cortex, from the Latin word for the rind of a fruit.

9 The rate of growth of the cerebral hemisphere—now the cerebral cortex—was greatest in the monkey and the ape. The growth of the cerebral cortex accelerated further in man's immediate ancestors, and reached explosive proportions in the last million years of human history, culminating in the appearance of Homo sapiens.

10 The primitive region in the brain that held the circuits for the instinctive behavior of the reptile and the old mammal was now completely enveloped by and buried within the human cerebral cortex. Yet this ancient command post, relic of our distant past, is still active within us; it still vies with the cerebral cortex for control of the body, pitting the inherited programs of the old brain against the flexible responses of the new one.

11 Experiments suggest that parental feelings, source of some of the finest human emotions, still spring from these primitive, programmed areas of the brain that go back to the time of the old mammal, more than 100 million years ago. In

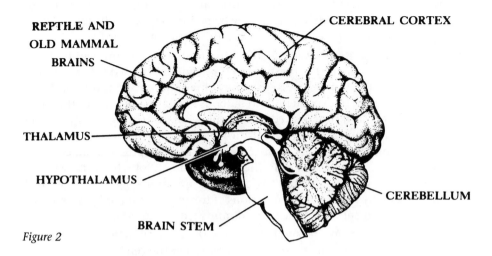

REPTILE AND
OLD MAMMAL
BRAINS

CEREBRAL CORTEX

THALAMUS

HYPOTHALAMUS

CEREBELLUM

BRAIN STEM

Figure 2

Figures 2, 3, 4   THE OLD BRAIN AND THE NEW. The views of the human brain illustrated here show the brain stem, the most ancient part of the brain. The brain stem lies under the cerebral cortex and carries messages into and out of the brain from the remainder of the body. The brain stem goes back at least 400 million years and is a remnant of the first centralized nervous system in the history of life.

The cerebral cortex, which covers the brain stem, is the newest and largest region in the human brain and makes up 90 per cent of its mass. The cerebral cortex is the seat of memory, learning, and abstract thinking.

Lying under the smothering masses of the cerebral hemispheres, at the top of the brain stem, are the reptile brain and the brain of the old mammal [Figure 2], which contain the basic survival programs related to flight from danger, hunger, thirst, procreation and parental care. These parts of the human brain evolved between 100 million and 300 million years ago. At the rear of the cerebral cortex is the cerebellum, or little brain, which coordinates the muscles of the body in complex maneuvers like waltzing or driving a car that involves the teamwork of dozens of muscles. When the body is learning a complicated sequence of movements, the brain has to think about each step in the sequence. After the sequence has been learned, the instructions to the body for executing it are stored in the cerebellum. They reside there permanently, like steps in a computer program, available for subsequent use without conscious thought. If, for example, the cerebral cortex decides to turn left at the next traffic light, it sends a command to the cerebellum, which takes over and executes the maneuver smoothly without further engaging the conscious mind. Of all parts of the brain, the cerebellum is closest to an automatic computer.

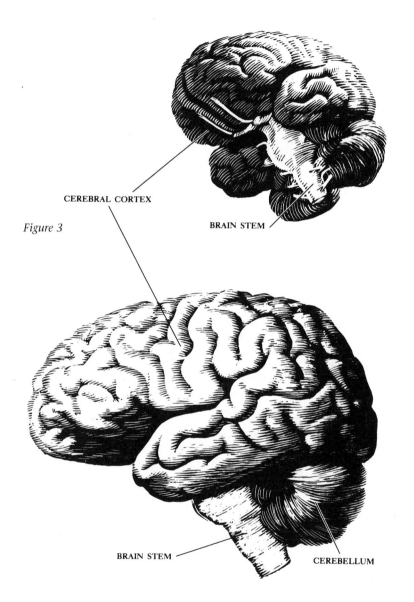

Figure 3

CEREBRAL CORTEX

BRAIN STEM

Figure 4

BRAIN STEM

CEREBELLUM

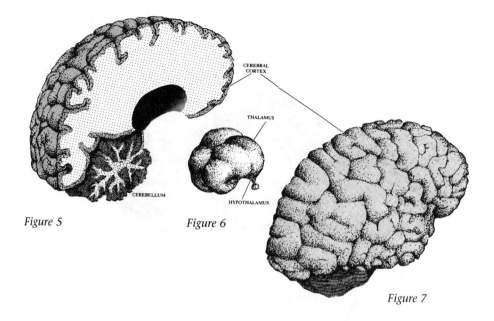

Figure 5   *Figure 6*

Figure 7

Figures 5, 6, and 7   ONE BRAIN WITHIN ANOTHER. This exploded view of the human brain shows the cavity deep within the cerebral cortex that holds the reptile and old mammal parts of the brain. Much of the cavity is filled by the thalamus—twin masses of grey matter the size of robin's eggs. The thalamus acts as a reception center for messages from all senses except the sense of smell, sending some signals on to the higher centers in the cerebral cortex, and taking immediate actions on others. Messages from the nose pass directly to the cerebral cortex in an arrangement that goes back to the early days of the mammals more than 100 million years ago when the cerebral hemispheres were first evolving out of the smell brains.

Under the thalamus lies the hypothalamus, a particularly important part of the old brain because it rouses the body and prepares it for actions appropriate to an emotional state. In times of stress, it is the hypothalamus that sends messages to the heart to quicken the pulse and messages to the stomach to cease digestion and release valuable blood to the muscles for flight.

one experiment, the cerebral cortex was removed from the brain of a female hamster, leaving only the reptile and old-mammal centers of instinctive behavior. Yet the hamster matured normally, showed an interest in male hamsters, gave birth to a litter, and was a good mother. In another experiment, when the cerebral hemispheres were left intact but the old-mammal centers of instinct were removed, the hamster lost all interest in its newborn young.

12 One part of the old brain, called the hypothalamus, is only the size of a walnut in the human brain, and yet a minute electrical stimulus applied to this region in the brain can create the emotional states of anger, anxiety or acute fear. The stimulation of nearby regions, only a few tenths of an inch away, produces sexual desire, or a craving for food or water.

13 The hypothalamus also appears to contain centers for aggression, killing, and fight-or-flight responses. A rat that will normally kill a mouse placed

in its cage no longer does so after these centers are removed. The action of the hypothalamus has a strong effect on personality. If a small electrical stimulus is applied to a particular part of the hypothalamus, an affectionate cat will turn into a biting, snarling animal, furious with the world; but its rage collapses instantly on cessation of the electrical current.

14 These experiments indicate that states of anger and aggression are created by electrical signals originating in the hypothalamus. The hypothalamus behaves as though it contains a gate that can open to let out a display of anger or bad temper. Normally, this gate is kept closed, but now and then the animal's senses tell its brain that its rights are endangered; a mate is lured away, food is stolen, or threat signals are received; and then the package of brain survival programs called "the emotions" comes into play, and an electrical signal to open the gate comes from some ancient center of instinct deep within the brain. Inhibiting signals for the cerebral cortex—the seat of reason—may quell the electrical disturbance in the old brain and keep the gate closed; but if the perceived threat is very great, the electrical signals arriving at the gate are overwhelming, and the gate opens. And if these electrical signals are introduced artificially by the discharge of an electrode implanted in the brain, as in the experiments on the cat, the gate can open without provocation.

15 It is as if two mentalities resided in the same body. One mentality is ruled by emotional states that have evolved as a part of age-old programs for survival, and the seat of this mentality is in the old-mammal centers of the brain beneath the cerebral cortex. The other mentality is ruled by reason and resides in the cerebral cortex. A person who loses his temper sometimes becomes aware of the two mentalities within him; he feels he is outside himself, watching the display of anger and wishing that it would cease, but powerless to end it. In these moments, the centers of reason in the cortex lose control over the primitive circuits buried in the brain and stand by watching as these circuits take over the body. It is not without cause that people will speak of a person in such a case as having "lost his reason" or being "beside himself."

16 In man, the cerebral cortex, or new brain, is usually master over the old brain; its instructions can override the strongest instincts towards eating, procreation or flight from danger. But the reptile and the old mammal still lie within us; sometimes they work with the highest centers of the brain and sometimes against them; and now and then, when there is competition between the two mentalities and the discipline of reason momentarily weakens, they spring out and take command.

17 These properties of the human brain lead to a prediction regarding the life that will follow man. As nature built the new brain on top of the old in our ancestors, so too, in the next stage of evolution after man, we can expect that a still newer and greater brain will join the "old" cerebral cortex, to work in concert with the cerebral cortex in directing the behavior of a form of life as superior to man as he is to the ancient forest mammal.

Number of words: 2,604

Reading Times	**Reading Speed**
1st reading _____ minutes	18 minutes = 145 wpm
3rd reading _____ minutes	16 minutes = 163 wpm
	14 minutes = 186 wpm
	12 minutes = 217 wpm
	10 minutes = 260 wpm

1.2
Second Reading

Go back and read the passage again. Take as much time as you need. Look up some of the unfamiliar words in the glossary at the end of the book or in your dictionary if you wish.

1.3
Third Reading

Read the passage quickly a third time. Concentrate on understanding the main ideas of the passage and the meanings of new vocabulary words in the contexts in which they appear.

1.4
Reader Response

In order to explore your response to this reading, write for 15 minutes about any-thing that interested you in this article. You may wish to write about your reactions to some of the ideas presented here. Try to explore *your own thoughts and feelings* as much as possible. Do *not* merely summarize or restate the ideas in this passage.

1.5
Response Sharing

Read your response to two or three other people in your class. Listen carefully to what the others have written. After you have discussed each other's responses, talk about other points of interest in the passage.

1.6
Identifying Main Ideas

Working with the same small group, make a list of the main ideas in this passage. Be sure to state the main ideas in your own words. Don't just copy sentences di-rectly from the text. Think carefully about what the writer is trying to tell you.

1.7
Analyzing the Text

Work with your group members on this exercise. Discuss the answers carefully, particularly if there are disagreements among members of your group. In some cases there may be more than one possible interpretation.

1. How does the title relate to the article? Does the title fit the article? Explain and give examples.

2. Name two differences between the early mammalian brain and the reptilian brain.

3. Read each statement carefully, decide if it is true or false according to this article, and then write *T* (true) or *F* (false) on the line in front of the statement.

   a. _____ Reptiles have highly developed parenting instincts.

   b. _____ The early mammalian brain was more complex than the reptilian brain.

   c. _____ Mammalian young were more vulnerable at birth than reptilian young, and they needed more parental care.

   d. _____ The cerebral cortex is the region where complex reasoning occurs, and it is part of the "new" brain.

   e. _____ As new parts of the brain developed, the old parts disappeared.

4. Name two differences in mammalian and reptilian lifestyles. How did these differences affect the development of their brains?

5. Look at one of the illustrations in this chapter and explain in some detail what it signifies.

1.8
Vocabulary Study

Study the italicized words and phrases in their contexts and guess at their meanings. Write your guess in the first blank. Then look up the word or phrase in your dictionary and write the definition in the second blank.

1. (paragraph 1) The human brain consists of several different regions that *evolved* at different times.

   a. (guess) _____

   b. (dictionary) _____

2. (paragraph 4) In the population of the mammals, on the other hand, the young arrived in a helpless and *vulnerable* state, and parental affection was essential for their survival.

   a. (guess) _____

   b. (dictionary) _____

3, 4, 5, and **6.** (paragraph 4) In the course of many generations, the *traits* of the *indifferent* parents were *pruned* from the stock of the mammals, and every mammal that remained was an *attentive* parent, and descended from a long line of attentive parents.

traits

a. (guess) _____

b. (dictionary) _____

indifferent

a. (guess) _____

b. (dictionary) _____

pruned

a. (guess) _____

b. (dictionary) _____

attentive

a. (guess) _____

b. (dictionary) _____

7. (paragraph 5) The new instincts of the mammals for parental care did not replace the older reptilian instincts; they *augmented* them.

a. (guess) _____

b. (dictionary) _____

8 and **9.**   (paragraph 6) The brains of the mammals changed in another important way that was related to their *nocturnal* lifestyle. As these animals passed into their 100-million-year time of darkness, the vision brain *diminished* in importance and the smell brain expanded.

nocturnal

a. (guess) _____

b. (dictionary) _____

diminished

a. (guess) _____

b. (dictionary) _____

10. (paragraph 10) Yet this ancient command post, relic of our distant past, is still active within us; it still *vies* with the cerebral cortex for control of the body, pitting the inherited programs of the old brain against the flexible responses of the new one.

a. (guess) _____

b. (dictionary) _____

1.9
Paragraph Organization and Development

It is important in both reading and writing to understand how information is presented in a well-organized and developed paragraph. Study the example below. How can you figure out what order the sentences follow? Look at both syntactic (structure) and semantic (meaning) clues.

Example:

a. __*2*__ First, they developed a new package of instincts related to the reptilian instincts for sex and procreation, but modified for the special needs of a mammalian lifestyle.

b. __*3*__ Chief among these was the instinct for parental care of the young.

c. __*1*__ When the mammals evolved out of the reptiles, their brains began to change.

d. __*4*__ Here was a revolutionary advance over the behavior of reptile parents for whom the newly hatched young provided a tasty snack if they could catch them.

Look at the sentences below and put them in the logical order. Take a pencil and lightly mark every word or punctuation mark that gave you a clue.

e. _____ it still vies with the cerebral cortex for control of the body, pitting the inherited programs of the old brain against the flexible responses of the new one.

f. _____ Yet this ancient command post, relic of our distant past, is still active within us;

g. _____ The primitive region in the brain that held the circuits for the instinctive behavior of the reptile and the old mammal was now completely enveloped by and buried within the human cerebral cortex.

Again, look at the sentences below and figure out how they should be ordered. Take a pencil and lightly mark anything that gave you a clue.

h. _____ Experiments suggest that parental feelings, source of some of the finest human emotions, still spring from these primitive, programmed areas of the brain that go back to the time of the old mammal, more than 100 million years ago.

i. _____ Yet the hamster matured normally, showed an interest in male hamsters, gave birth to a litter, and was a good mother.

j. _____ In one experiment, the cerebral cortex was removed from the brain of a female hamster, leaving only the reptile and old-mammal centers of instinctive behavior.

k. _____ In another experiment, when the cerebral hemispheres were left intact but the old-mammal centers of instinct were re-moved, the hamster lost all interest in its newborn young.

1.10
Application, Critical Evaluation, and Synthesis

Choose one or more topics to discuss with your small group or to write about.

1. Discuss the importance of parenting instincts in mammals and how and why they developed. Compare parenting instincts in reptiles and mammals. How are they different and why?

2. The human brain has been compared to an archeological dig: the deeper you go, the older the brain. What is meant by the *old brain* and the *new brain*? Explain the development of the brain and give examples. Refer to the brain areas by specific name. You may find it helpful to refer to the brain illustrations in this chapter.

3. Go to a library and look up recent articles on the brain (see Expansion section, pp. 243–246 on doing library research.) Write a one-paragraph summary of each of the articles. Be sure to explain both the subject and the main idea of each article clearly enough so that other people would understand the focus of the article.

4. Go to a library and look up information on the brain in an encyclopedia, preferably a medical or science encyclopedia. Write a brief report in which you combine information from the encyclopedia selection with information from this article. You may wish to concentrate on a particular region of the brain, e.g., the cerebral cortex or the cerebellum. Draw a picture of the brain (perhaps using figures from this chapter as a guide) to accompany your report.

Gray Matters

Men and women don't think the same way. They see the world differently. We all know that, we've always known it, and now science knows it too. Recent studies, in fact, show that men and women, for whatever reasons, use their brains quite differently when they are thinking, feeling, or remembering. New imaging technologies are able to capture these differences in pictures. The following article by Sharon Begley, with Andrew Murr and Adam Rogers, appeared in *Newsweek* (March 27, 1995). It is reprinted by permission.

2.1

First Reading

Read this article quickly for the main ideas. Pay attention to the headings (in boldface type). Do *not* stop to look up words in your dictionary.

1 Of course men and women are different. *Boy*, are they different. In every sphere of life, it seems, the sexes act, react or perform differently. Toys? A little girl daintily sets up her dolls, plastic cups and saucers, while her brother assembles his Legos into a gun—and ambushes the tea party. Navigating? The female tourist turns her map every which way but right, trying to find the way back to that charming bistro, while her boyfriend charges ahead, remembering every tricky turn without fail. Relationships? With spooky intuition, women's acute senses pick up subtle tones of voice and facial expressions; men are insensitive clods who can't tell a sad face until it drenches them in tears. Cognition? Females excel at language, like finding just the right words to make their husbands feel like worms; males can't verbalize even one good excuse for stumbling home at 2 a.m.

2 Stereotypes? Maybe—but as generalizations they have a large enough kernel of truth that scientists, like everyone else, suspect there's *something* going on here. As Simon LeVay, the Salk Institute neuroscientist who in 1991 discovered structural differences between the brains of gay and straight men, put it recently, "There are differences in the mental lives of men and women."

3 The mind, of course, is just what the brain does for a living. So if LeVay is right, those mental differences must arise from differences in that gelatinous three-pound blob. For a decade neuroscientists have been discovering evidence of differences. Although the findings are tentative and ambiguous, at the end of the day, relaxing over beers at a neuroscience conclave, most specialists agree that women's and men's brains differ slightly in structure. But the studies have been frustratingly silent on whether the anatomical

differences in their brains make men and women think differently. But now—drumroll, please—thanks to an array of new imaging machines that are revolutionizing neuroscience, researchers are beginning to glimpse differences in how men's and women's brains actually function.

4   With new technologies like functional magnetic resonance imaging (FMRI) and positron emission tomography (PET), researchers catch brains in the very act of cogitating, feeling or remembering. Already this year researchers have reported that men and women use different clumps of neurons when they take a first step toward reading when their brains are "idling." And, coming soon to a research journal near you, provocative studies will report that women engage more of their brains than men when they think sad thoughts—but, possibly, less of their brains when they solve SAT math problems. "Now that we actually have functional brain data, we're getting lots of new insights," says Richard Haier, professor of pediatrics and neurology at the University of California, Irvine, and leader of the SAT study. "Even at this early point we have data to support the idea that men and women in general have brains that work differently." The latest studies:

Review

1. In one sentence, state the main point of the article so far.

Prediction

2. What do you think "the latest studies" are going to demonstrate?

5   • **Make your mind a blank:** To compare male and female brains at work, subjects were instructed to think of . . . nothing. In January scientists led by Ruben Gur of the University of Pennsylvania reported a PET study of 37 men and 24 women, mostly recruited by ads in local papers. Each volunteer got an injection of radioactive glucose. Glucose is brain food; active regions of the brain use more glucose than quiescent areas and so emit radioactivity, which PET detects. For 30 minutes a volunteer lay in a quiet, dimly lit room with eyes open and head in a tunnel with detectors embedded in the walls. Each volunteer was told to relax, without "exerting mental effort"—while PET read his or her mind.

6   In men's idling brains, the action was in the temporal-limbic system. This primitive region controls highly unsubtle expressions of emotion, such as fighting. It is often dubbed the "reptilian" brain. In most of the women's supposedly idling brains, the neurons were buzzing in the posterior cingulate gyrus, an evolutionarily newer addition to mammals' brains. Not even the researchers are sure what all of this shows. For one thing, 13 men and four women showed activity more like the other sex's. But the real problem is that "thinking of nothing" is nearly impossible. Volunteer (and coresearcher) Lyn Mozley admits that "some of the time I was probably thinking, 'When is this going to be over?'" What the PET scans may actu-

ally be showing is that, when told to think of nothing, men fixate on sex and football, while women weave together strings of words. But if, in men, the pilot light is always on in neurons that control aggression and action, it may explain why they're more violence-prone than women.

7 • **I say tomahto . . . :** Last month researchers announced that men and women use different parts of their brains to figure out rhymes. Sally Shaywitz, her husband, Bennett Shaywitz, and colleagues at Yale University weren't looking for the brain's poetry center; rather, sounding out is the first step in reading, so rhyming was meant as a proxy for that skill. The 19 men and 19 women volunteers had to determine whether pairs of nonsense words (lete and jete, loke and jote), when flashed on a screen, rhymed. A volunteer lay in an FMRI machine, which is a four-foot-long tube containing a detector that pinpoints active brain regions.

8 In all 19 men, one region in the left inferior frontal gyrus (that's behind the left eyebrow) lit up like Las Vegas. So far, so good: for more than a century scientists have known that the left brain controls language. But in 11 of the 19 women, that area *plus* one behind the right eyebrow lit up. The right side of the brain is the seat of emotion. Perhaps women are more felicitous with language because they draw on feelings (right brain) as well as reason (left brain) when they use words. The Yale team made one more intriguing find. In eight of the women—42 percent—the brain worked like the men's. "That some of the women's brains looked like the men's is true of all these sex studies," says neuropsychologist Melissa Hines of UCLA. "Girls play with

boys' toys more than boys play with girls', for instance. Males for whatever reason are more exclusively channeled into one way of behaving"—and, possibly, thinking.

9 • **Let X be an integer . . . :** At Irvine, Haier PET-scanned 22 male and 22 female student volunteers while they did SAT math problems. Half the men and half the women had SAT math scores above 700; the other half scored 540 or so. According to his unpublished results, which he previewed at a science meeting last summer, in gifted men the temporal lobes were on overdrive compared with the average men. (The temporal lobes are behind the ears.) Ability seemed to correlate with effort. But in the 700-club women, the temporal lobes showed little activity, and there was a hint that the women didn't use their brain any more intensely than the average women. "There was a suggestion that women who did better [in math] might be using their brain more efficiently than women who did average," says Haier. "The men and women performed equally well. They just seemed to use the brain differently to do it." "Different," in other words, does not mean "better."

10 • **No hard feelings:** Last year Penn's Ruben Gur and his wife, neuroscientist Raquel Gur, enlisted PET in the aid of an old stereotype: that men can't read emotions on people's faces. (The pair got into the field of sex differences when they were struck by their own temperamental differences. He is more intrigued by numbers and details, she likes to work with people; he reacts to a setback by taking a deep breath and moving on, she analyzes it.) They and their colleagues asked volunteers to judge whether male and female faces showed happiness or sadness. Both sexes were almost infallible at recognizing happiness. But sadness was a different story. Women picked out a sad face 90 percent of the time on men and women, but men had more trouble. They recognized sadness on men's faces 90 percent of the time—that is, they did as well as the women—but were right only 70 percent of the time when judging sadness on women's faces.

11 Well, of course. Evolutionarily speaking, it makes sense that a man would have to be hypervigilant about men's faces; otherwise he would miss the first hint that another guy is going to punch him. Being oblivious to a woman's emotions won't get him much worse than a night on the sofa. The Gurs may even have stumbled on why women can't understand why men find it so hard to be sensitive to emotions. According to the PET scans, women's brains didn't have to work as hard to excel at judging emotion. Women's limbic system, the part of the brain that controls emotion, was *less* active than the limbic system of men doing worse. That is, the men's brains were working overtime to figure out the faces. But the extra effort didn't do them much good.

12 • **Sad, so sad:** The little boy in black standing at his father's funeral, the happily married woman hearing her husband demand a divorce . . . 10 women and 10 men called up these and other sad memories while psychiatrist Mark George of the National Institute of Mental Health and colleagues PET-scanned them. In both sexes, the front of the limbic system glowed with activity. But

in women, the active area was eight times as big as it was in the men. That difference in intensity might explain why women are twice as likely as men to suffer major depression, say the scientists. In depression, the limbic system is unresponsive and almost lethargic; "perhaps hyperactivity during normal bouts of sadness" made these circuits unresponsive, George speculates.

Review

1. Finish the sentence: These studies indicate that _____
_____

Prediction

2. Do you think the evidence suggesting that men's and women's brains function differently hurts or helps women to achieve equal rights with men? Why?
3. The subject of physical differences between male and female brains will be discussed later in this article. What do you think the article will suggest on this point?

---

13 The brain-imaging studies are the latest, and the highest-tech, periscope into sex differences in the brain. Yet no matter how "scientific" it gets, this research serves as ammunition in society's endless gender wars. When Raquel Gur gave a talk to M.D.-Ph.D. students in Illinois about sex differences in brains, a group of women asked her to stop publicizing the work; they were afraid women would lose 20 years of gains if word got out that the sexes aren't the same. They had good reason to worry. Among the choicer passages from recent pop-science books: Male brains "are not so easily distracted by superfluous information." "A woman may be less able to separate emotion from reason." And "the male brain is a tidier affair," as Anne Moir and David Jessel write in their 1991 book "Brain Sex." The subject of sex differences in the brain attracts almost as much inflammatory rhetoric as the "science" of racial differences in IQ.

14 Even before scientists caught images of the brain thinking or emoting, there were hints that men's brains and women's differed. As long ago as 1880, English surgeon James Crichton-Browne reported slight differences in the brain anatomy of men and women—a slightly larger gaggle of neurons *here* in one sex, and *there* in the other. But by far the most frequent finding through the years has been that the bundle of nerve cells through which the left side of the brain talks and listens to the right—it's called the corpus callosum—is larger in women than in men. In perhaps the best study of this kind, in 1991 UCLA neuroendocrinologists Roger Gorski and Laura Allen examined 146 brains from cadavers and found that the back part of women's callosum is up to 23 percent bigger than men's.

15 This brought neuroscientists as close as they ever get to jumping up and down in public. It fit their cherished idea that, in male brains, the right and the left side barely know what the other is doing, while in women there's

practically nonstop left-right neural chitchat. If women's brains are paragons of holism, while men's are a house divided, it could explain findings both serious and curious. Women's language ability better survives a left-brain stroke—perhaps because they tap the language capacity of the right brain. Women tend to have better language skills—perhaps because the emotional right brain enriches their left-brain vocabulary. And women have better intuition—perhaps because they are in touch with the left brain's rationality and the right's emotions simultaneously.

16 There is just one problem with these tidy explanations. A bigger corpus callosum matters only if it has more neurons, the cells that carry communications. After all, fat phone cables carry more conversations only if they contain more wires. But despite years of searching, scientists cannot say for sure that women's corpus callosum has more neurons.

17 The quest for other anatomical differences has been only a little more successful. In rats, biologists have found 15 regions that differ in size between males and females. Finding such differences in humans has been much tougher. But in November, at the annual meeting of the Society for Neuroscience, Sandra Witelson of McMaster University in Ontario reported results from a study of nine autopsied brains. (She gets them from people with terminal cancer who bequeath their brains to science.) Women, despite having smaller brains (on average) than men because their whole bodies are smaller, have more neurons. The extra 11 percent are all crammed into two layers of the cerebral cortex whose job is to understand language and recognize melodies and tone of voice.

18 Neuroscientists know of only one force that can prune and stimulate, kill and nourish the brain's gaggles of neurons: sex hormones. Before birth, a fetus's brain is bathed in sex hormones—different ones, in different amounts, depending on whether the fetus is male or female. Ethics prevents scientists from experimenting to see how a fetus's brain would change if its hormone exposure changed. But nature has no such compunctions. Girls with a rare birth defect called CAH, which made them churn out high levels of the male hormone testosterone as fetuses, score better than the average female on spatial tests. (The extra testosterone exposure also masculinizes their genitals.) As girls, they prefer cars and trucks and other toys that boys usually grab. Other girls were exposed to male-like levels of testosterone before birth when their mothers took the hormone DES to prevent miscarriages. As children, the DES girls did better than their normal sisters on rotating a figure in space and other tasks at which boys outdo girls. Finally, boys with a syndrome that makes them insensitive to testosterone are better at language than their unaffected brothers. But they are less adept at spatial tasks—the typical female intellectual pattern. Hormonal effects, wrote psychologist Doreen Kimura of the University of Western Ontario in 1992, "appear to extend to all known behaviors in which males and females differ . . . [such as] problem solving, aggression and the tendency to engage in rough-and-tumble play."

19 Are these hormonal effects present at birth, or do they result from how a child is raised? The feminized boys (whose cognitive abilities resemble women's) and the CAH girls (minds like boys) are not physically normal. Their parents know they are different, and likely treat them differently from their sisters and brothers. Perhaps even more crucial, the hormonally abnormal girls might identify, psychologically, not with girls but with boys, aping their behavior and preferences. Similarly, the feminized boys might identify with girls. So if the girls play like tomboys and do better in math than normal girls, and the boys have superior language tasks compared with their normal brothers, it is impossible to tell whether the reason is hormones alone or life's experiences, too. Only Hines's DES girls are pure products of pre-birth hormones; they looked like ordinary little girls, so people treated them as girls and they saw themselves as female. Their male-like cognitive function is the only one ever found that can't be easily explained away as the result of nurture.

20 Hines's work has been seized as proof that biology is destiny, but other research undermines that dogma. For one thing, the overlap between men's and women's scores on just about every psychological test is huge. Any randomly chosen woman might do better at a "male" skill than a man, and vice versa. "This [overlap] is also true of brain structures," says UCLA's Gorski. More important, the nature-nurture dichotomy is simplistic. Nurture affects nature; experience, that is, affects biology. The brain is so malleable that rats raised in a cage filled with toys and mazes grow more connections between their neurons than rats raised in a bare cage. Also in rats, mothers sense their sons' testosterone and lick them more than daughters; that causes more nerve cells at the base of the tail to grow. The human brain is malleable, too: in people whose hands were amputated, scientists reported last year, the part of the brain that once registered feelings from the missing hand vanishes.

21 Is it farfetched to wonder whether parts of girls' brains grow or shrink, while different parts of boys' expand or shrivel, because they were told not to worry their pretty heads about math, or because they started amassing Legos from birth, or because . . . well, because of the vastly different experiences boys and girls have? "Surely the more complex social interactions among humans also sculpt the developing nervous system," argues psychologist Marc Breedlove of UC, Berkeley. "The studies provide no evidence favoring either nature or nurture." But, he adds, "there's one thing I know that testosterone does to masculinize [men's] brains. It causes them to be born with a penis. And everybody treats the baby differently [than they do a girl]. I'm sure that affects the development of the brain. Is that a biological effect or a social effect? It's both."

22 The recent PET scans and FMRIs are silent "on *how* the brains of men and women get to be different," says Irvine's Richard Haier. The scans probe adults, whose brains are the products of years of living, feeling, thinking and experiencing. Children have not yet been scanned in the service of sci-

ence. But in studies of fetal brains (from miscarriages) and newborns' (from stillbirths), "none of the sex differences in [the brain] have been reliably detected," says Breedlove.

23 The powerful new techniques of brain imaging are just beginning to be trained on the age-old question of what makes the sexes different. As the answers trickle in, they will surely challenge our cherished notions of what makes us think, act and feel as we do—and as members of the opposite sex do not. But if the first tantalizing findings are any clue, the research will show that our identities as men and women are creations of both nature and nurture. And that no matter what nature deals us, it is we—our choices, our sense of identity, our experiences in life—who make ourselves what we are.

Number of Words: 3,319
Reading Times
1st reading _____ minutes
3rd reading _____ minutes

Reading Speed
20 minutes = 166 wpm
18 minutes = 184 wpm
15 minutes = 221 wpm
13 minutes = 255 wpm
10 minutes = 332 wpm

2.2
Second Reading

Go back and read the article again. Take as much time as you need. Look up some of the unfamiliar words in the glossary at the end of the book or in your dictionary.

2.3
Third Reading

Read the article quickly a third time. Concentrate on understanding the main ideas of the article and the meanings of new vocabulary words in the contexts in which they appear.

2.4
Reader Response

In order to explore your response to this reading, write for 15 minutes about anything that interested you in this article. You may wish to write about your reactions to some of the ideas presented here—or you may wish to disagree with something in the article. Try to explore *your own thoughts and feelings* as much as possible. Do *not* merely summarize or restate the ideas in this article.

2.5
Response Sharing

Read your response to two or three other people in your class. Listen carefully to what the others have written. After you have discussed each other's responses, talk about other points of interest in the article.

2.6
Citing Scientific Evidence

Part One

It is very important to know how to organize and present scientific evidence so that your reader or listener will understand the study. You must be able to give the following information clearly and concisely.

1. *Who* conducted the study and *where* and *when* was it conducted?

   Ruben Gur and Raquel Gur at the University of Pennsylvania (Penn) in 1994

   Sally Shaywitz and Bennett Shaywitz at Yale University in 1995

2. *What* was the study? You give a description of the subjects and a step-by-step description of the experiment in chronological order. Present the facts, but do not interpret them.
   - Subjects: 37 men and 24 women, mostly recruited by ads in local papers
   - Step one: each volunteer received an injection of radioactive glucose
   - Step two: each volunteer was told to relax and to not make any mental effort
   - Step three: for 30 minutes the volunteer lay in a quiet, dimly lit room with eyes open and head in a tunnel with detectors embedded in the walls
   - Step four: PET (positron emission tomography) read the mind of each volunteer (i.e., showed in pictures how each brain functioned, which areas were active, and which areas were quiet)

3. *What happened?* After you give the facts of how the study was set up and conducted, then give a factual description of the results. Do not explain or interpret the results at this point.
   - Men had action in the temporal-limbic system, the primitive part of the brain that controls fighting and aggression;
   - Women had action in the posterior cingulate gyrus, a newer part of the brain;
   - Seventeen men and four women showed patterns more like the other sex's (i.e., the 17 men had brain patterns more like the women's patterns, and four of the women had patterns like the men's).

4. *What do the results mean?* At this point, interpret the results (i.e., explain what the results mean—or could mean).

   • It may not be possible to "think of nothing," so the study may not have been valid.

   • Men and women may think of different things when they are told to "think about nothing." Men may be thinking about sex and sports, while women may be thinking about words, or at least about something very different from the subjects men think about.

   • If men's brains are always active in the area that controls aggression and action, this may explain why men tend to be more violent than women.

   (Notice the frequent use of "may" in interpreting the results.)

Part Two

Look at the Richard Haier study on how men and women solve math problems (paragraph 9). Explain this study following the format presented in Part One above.

1. *Who* conducted the study and *where* and *when* was it conducted?
   (*Hint*: Look at the end of paragraph 4.)

2. *What* was the study? Describe the subjects and then give a step-by-step factual description of the experiment in chronological order. Do not interpret the facts. Use as many steps as you need.

   • subjects:

   • step one:

   • step two:

   • step three:

   • step four:

3. *What happened?* After you list the facts of how the study was set up and conducted, you then give a factual description of the results. You do not explain or interpret the results at this point.

4. *What do the results mean?* Finally you interpret the results, i.e., you explain what the results mean—or could mean.

2.7
Analyzing the Text

Work with your group members on this exercise. Discuss the answers carefully, particularly if there are disagreements among members of your group. In some cases, there may be more than one possible interpretation.

1. *Gray matter* is another term for *brain*. The title of this article, *Gray Matters*, has two meanings. What are these meanings? How does the title relate to the article? Explain and give examples from the text.

2. An acronym is a new word made up of the first letter of each word in a succession of words.

   Example: Scholastic Aptitude Test = SAT

   Study this example and then write the acronyms for the following word groups. (Acronyms are written entirely in capital letters: SAT.)

   a. Positron emission tomography = _____

   b. Functional magnetic resonance imaging = _____

   c. Writing assessment test = _____

   d. Foreign language aptitude test = _____

   e. Alcoholics Anonymous = _____

   What do you think the main reasons for using acronyms are?

3. Scientists start off with a clear purpose when they begin their research. Before they begin, they state a research hypothesis—they make an educated guess about how they think the research will turn out.

   Example: Richard Haier hypothesized that men and women would use different areas of their brains to do the same tasks.

   The purpose of a scientific study is to test the hypothesis to see if the scientist's guess is correct or not. In the Haier study (paragraph 9), was Haier's hypothesis correct or not? Use examples from the study.

4. Raquel Gur said that a group of women asked her to stop publicizing her work about the differences between the brain functions of men and women. Reread paragraph 13 and explain why the women were worried. Did they have a reason to be worried? If so, why?

5. The conclusion of the writers of this article about why men and women think, act and feel differently is that

   a. nature (biological inheritance and genetics) is primarily responsible.

   b. nurture (experience) is primarily responsible.

   c. a combination of nature and nurture is responsible.

   Explain by referring to paragraph 23.

2.8
Vocabulary Study

Study the italicized words and phrases in their contexts and guess at their meanings. Write your guess in the first blank. Then look up the word or phrase in your dictionary and write the definition in the second blank.

1 and **2.** (paragraph 3) Although the findings are *tentative* and *ambiguous* . . . most specialists agree that women's and men's brains differ slightly in structure.

tentative

a. (guess) _____

b. (dictionary) _____

ambiguous

a. (guess) _____

b. (dictionary) _____

3 and **4.** (paragraph 3) But now . . . thanks to an *array* of new imaging machines that are *revolutionizing* neuroscience, researchers are beginning to glimpse differences in how men's and women's brains actually function.

array

a. (guess) _____

b. (dictionary) _____

revolutionizing

a. (guess) _____

b. (dictionary) _____

5 and **6.** (paragraph 5) Glucose is brain food; active regions of the brain use more glucose than *quiescent* areas and so *emit* radioactivity, which PET detects.

quiescent

a. (guess) _____

b. (dictionary) _____

emit

a. (guess) _____

b. (dictionary) _____

7. (paragraph 10) Both sexes were almost *infallible* at recognizing happiness.

a. (guess) _____

b. (dictionary) _____

8 and **9.** (paragraph 11) Evolutionarily speaking, it makes sense that a man would have to be *hypervigilant* about men's faces; otherwise he would miss the first hint that another guy is going to punch him. Being *oblivious* to a woman's emotions won't get him much worse than a night on the sofa.

hypervigilant

a. (guess) _____

b. (dictionary) _____

oblivious

a. (guess) _____

b. (dictionary) _____

10. (paragraph 18) Ethics prevents scientists from experimenting to see how a fetus's brain would change if its hormone exposure changed. But nature has no such *compunctions*.

a. (guess) _____

b. (dictionary) _____

11. (paragraph 18) Finally, boys with a syndrome that makes them insensitive to testosterone are better at language than their unaffected brothers. But they are less *adept* at spatial tasks—the typical female intellectual pattern.

a. (guess) _____

b. (dictionary) _____

12 and **13.** (paragraph 19) Their parents know they are different, and likely treat them differently from their sisters and brothers. Perhaps even more *crucial*, the hormonally abnormal girls might identify, psychologically, not with girls but with boys, *aping* their behavior and preferences.

crucial

a. (guess) _____

b. (dictionary) _____

aping

a. (guess) _____

b. (dictionary) _____

14 and **15.** (paragraph 20) Hines's work has been *seized* as proof that biology is destiny, but other research undermines that *dogma.*

seized

a. (guess) _____

b. (dictionary) _____

dogma

a. (guess) _____

b. (dictionary) _____

2.9
Drawing Inferences

It is important to be able to draw inferences—that is, to read between the lines to understand the deeper meaning of a passage. To draw an inference you must first read the passage carefully, think about the context and the facts that are given, and then make a decision about the underlying meaning that is implied but not stated. To practice this reading skill, study the following passages and explain deeper meanings you can infer from the underlined sentences.

1. Evolutionarily speaking, it makes sense that a man would have to be hypervigilant about men's faces; otherwise he would miss the first hint that another guy is going to punch him. Being oblivious to a woman's emotions won't get him much worse than a night on the sofa. (paragraph 11)

2. When Raquel Gur gave a talk to M.D.-Ph.D. students in Illinois about sex differences in brains, a group of women asked her to stop publicizing the work; they were afraid women would lose 20 years of gains if word got out that the sexes aren't the same. They had good reason to worry. Among the choicer passages from recent pop-science books: Male brains "are not so easily distracted by superfluous information." "A woman may be less able to separate emotion from reason." And "the male brain is a tidier affair," as Anne Moir and David Jessel write in their 1991 book "Brain Sex." (paragraph 13)

3. The subject of sex differences in the brain attracts almost as much inflammatory rhetoric as the "science" of racial differences in IQ. (paragraph 13)

4. In perhaps the best study of this kind, in 1991 UCLA neuroendocrinologists Roger Gorski and Laura Allen examined 146 brains from cadavers and found that the back part of women's callosum is up to 23 percent bigger than men's. This brought neuroscientists as close as they ever get to jumping up and down in public. It fit their cherished idea that, in male brains, the right and the left side barely know what the other is doing, while in women there's practically nonstop left-right neural chitchat. (paragraphs 14 and 15)

5. The recent PET scans and FMRIs are silent "on *how* the brains of men and women get to be different," says Irvine's Richard Haier. The scans probe adults, whose brains are the products of years of living, feeling, thinking and experiencing. Children have not yet been scanned in the service of science. But in studies of fetal brains (from miscarriages) and newborns' (from stillbirths), "none of the sex differences in [the brain] have been reliably detected," says Breedlove. (paragraph 22)

2.10
Application, Critical Evaluation, and Synthesis

Choose one or more topics to discuss with your small group or to write about.

1. *Men and women see the world differently.* Do you agree that men and women see the world differently? Why or why not? Explain your reasons and give examples to support them. If possible, give examples from your own experience, from your reading, or from what you have heard on the radio or seen on television. Be as specific as possible.

2. Boys generally do better than girls do in math and girls do better than boys do in language. What are some explanations for these gender differences? How much is biology and how much is cultural experience, perhaps differences in the education boys and girls receive or the encouragement and discouragement they receive from society? Do you think society encourages these gender differences? If so, why and how? Explain your answer and give examples to support your answer.

3. Have you ever had a misunderstanding with a member of the opposite sex that clearly showed the two of you saw the world differently? Explain the misunderstanding, how it occurred, what your view was, and what the other person's view was. Does this misunderstanding say anything about differences in male and female world views? How do you think some of the scientists in this study might interpret your misunderstanding?

4. *Biology is destiny.* What does this statement mean? Do you agree with it? completely? partially? not at all? Explain your position and give reasons to support your position, as well as examples to support your reasons.

5. Most cultures have stereotypes of "typical" male and female behavior. Many people in every culture, however, do not fit into the stereotype and, in fact, rebel against it. Do you know anyone in your culture who has rebelled against the cultural stereotype for his or her gender? If so, explain in detail. Who is this person? Why do you think the person rebelled? What form did the rebellion take? Give specific examples and details.

Dr. Vilayanus Ramachandran of the University of California at San Diego demonstrates the principle behind a mirrored device he has designed to help amputees deal with pain in a phantom limb.

CHAPTER THREE

Overcoming the Pain
in a Missing Limb

It is a strange fact that long after people lose an arm or a leg, they may continue to feel pain in that missing limb. Sometimes the pain is agonizing and completely debilitating. The problem is the brain plays tricks on the body, sending signals that the missing limb is still there and, thus, still able to feel pain. Now scientists are beginning to have some success in overcoming missing limb pain by deliberately tricking the brain back. The result can be relief from terrible pain. This article demonstrates the effective use of a technique for tricking the brain—through the use of mirrors. The following article by Sandra Blakeslee appeared in *The New York Times* (March 28, 1995). It is reprinted by permission.

3.1
First Reading

Read the article quickly for the main ideas. Pay attention to the headings (in boldface type). Do *not* stop to look up words in your dictionary.

1 The third time he lost his left arm, Derek Steen yelped with joy. He could not believe his good fortune. The problem began 10 years ago when Mr. Steen crashed his motorcycle, tearing all the nerves that attached his left arm to his spine. The arm was hopelessly paralyzed, bound in a sling. He lost his arm a second time, so to speak, one year later when, deemed useless and getting in the way, the limb was amputed.

2 But Mr. Steen, now a 28-year-old part-time worker in San Diego, continued to suffer. His phantom arm felt paralyzed, pressed against his body, and it ached horribly for 10 years.

3 Then, late last year Mr. Steen was cured. After a simple, three-week treatment involving mirrors, his paralyzed phantom arm suddenly vanished, as did the gnawing pain in his phantom elbow. In its place, Mr. Smith says, he has a much reduced phantom limb composed of his lower left palm and all five fingers, which he can now "wiggle" freely from the stump below his shoulder.

4 He is ecstatic, said Dr. Vilayanus S. Ramachandran, a professor of neuroscience at the University of California at San Diego, who devised the treatment. Mr. Steen's "body image," as he puts it, has been profoundly altered, he said, much for the better.

5 Dr. Ramachandran described the finding—a rare example of successful treatment for phantom limb pain—at the second annual meeting of the Cognitive Neuroscience Society being held in San Francisco. The three-day meeting [March 26–28, 1995] drew nearly 700 scientists who are engaged in basic research on the nervous system and how it leads to cognitive acts like learning, remembering, perceiving and consciousness.

6 Phantom limbs occur when the brain modifies its sensory maps after an amputation, he said. The brain region mapping an arm no longer gets input from the arm, but it continues to be constantly stimulated by inputs from adjacent body parts. These stimuli fool the brain into thinking the arm itself is still there.

7 But sometimes, as in Mr. Steen's case, a phantom limb can be paralyzed. "The arm is in a fixed position, as if frozen in cement," Dr. Ramachandran said. "The patient can't generate the slightest flicker of movement, even though he can feel all the parts. I started thinking why."

8 The answer lies in the feedback loops in the brain that integrate vision, senses, body movements, body image and motor commands, Dr. Ramachandran said. In the first few weeks after the accident, Mr. Steen would try to move his injured arm, to no avail. His brain sent signals to his arm, commanding motion, but though his eyes confirmed the arm was there, it did not move.

9 In time, Dr. Ramachandran said, Mr. Steen developed "learned paralysis."

10 "His brain constantly got information that his arm was not moving," even though it was still there, Dr. Ramachandran said. After the amputation, he still felt it was there.

11 "Now if it's true paralysis can be learned, can you unlearn it?" Dr. Ramachandran said. "And how do you do that if you don't really have an arm?"

12 Simple. With mirrors. Dr. Ramachandran constructed a simple box without a lid and front and placed a vertical mirror in the middle. By placing his right arm into the box, Mr. Steen could see a mirror image of his missing left arm.

13 "I asked him to make symmetric movements with both hands, as if he were conducting an orchestra," Dr. Ramachandran said. "He started jumping up and down and said," 'Oh, my God, my wrist is moving, my elbow is moving!' I asked him to close his eyes. He groaned, 'Oh no, it's frozen again,'" the scientist said. "The box cost only $5, so I told him to take it home and play around with it."

**When the brain plays tricks on the body,
the idea is to play tricks on the brain.**

---

14 Three weeks later, Dr. Ramachandran said, "he phones me, sounding agitated and excited." The conversation went like this:

15 "Doctor, it's gone!"

16   "What's gone?"

17   "My phantom arm is gone. "

18   . . . The reason the arm disappeared and the body image changed probably has to do with tremendous sensory conflict, Dr. Ramachandran said. "His vision was telling him that his arm had come back and was obeying his commands. But he was not getting feedback from the muscles in his arm. Faced with this type of conflict over a protracted period, the brain may simply gate the signals. It says, "This doesn't make sense. I won't have anything to do with it."

19   "In the process, the arm disappears and the elbow pain goes away," he said. "The reason the fingers survive and dangle from the shoulder is that they are overrepresented in the cortex, much more so than the rest of the arm. So there may be a kind of tip of the iceberg phenomenon going on here."

20   Dr. Ramachandran is now treating other kinds of phantom limb pain, including a clenching spasm of phantom hands. "People feel as if their fingernails are digging into their hands and say it is excruciatingly painful," he said. The mirror box has helped one such patient.

21   The new finding may also have relevance to stroke rehabilitation, Dr. Ramachandran said. In the early stages, some paralysis is due to swelling in the brain and learned paralysis could result. While destroyed tissue could not be revived, he said, other circuits might be reestablished with the use of mirrors.

**If paralysis can be learned,
perhaps it can be unlearned.**

---

22   These ideas remain highly speculative, Dr. Ramachandran said. Moreover, pain is notoriously susceptible to placebo effects, so it may be difficult to prove that these brain-based therapies are effective.

23   Nevertheless, striking results are being seen with some stroke patients who lose the ability to talk. At the University of Iowa, Dr. Antonio Damasio and his colleagues are teaching American Sign Language to patients whose primary language areas have been partly damaged but not destroyed. By learning a sign for a concept, he said, they are often able to reconnect with the word for that concept—and in this way can learn how to speak once again.

24   Such plasticity or adaptability in the adult brain may be more common than most people realize, said Dr. Michael Gazzaniga, a neuroscientist who is an expert on split brain patients at the University of California at Davis.

25   An effective treatment for severe epilepsy is to cut the bundle of fibers that connect the left and right brain hemispheres. Each half brain is conscious but does not know what the other half sees or does.

26   In such patients, the left brain "wakes up and starts talking," Dr. Gazzaniga said. The right brain usually shows no sign of language comprehension and it certainly has no ability to talk — until a patient named Joe stunned re-

searchers by learning how to talk with his right brain. Joe was like other split brain patients for 13 years, Dr. Gazzaniga said. Then his right brain started recognizing and saying words independently of the left brain. Now, 15 years after surgery, Joe can name 60 percent of the stimuli presented to his right brain, Dr. Gazzaniga said.

27 "It could be that new connections have been made, or that others have been unrepressed," Dr. Gazzaniga said. "At this point we have no idea how or why it happens." But answers, should they be found, might be used for helping people overcome all sorts of brain injuries and neuro-degenerative diseases.

Number of words: 1,501	
Reading Times	**Reading Speed**
1st reading _____ minutes	10 minutes = 150 wpm
3rd reading _____ minutes	8 minutes = 188 wpm
	6 minutes = 250 wpm
	4 minutes = 375 wpm

3.2
Second Reading

Go back and read the article again. Take as much time as you need. Look up some of the unfamiliar words in the glossary at the end of the book or in your dictionary if you wish.

3.3
Third Reading

Read the article quickly a third time. Concentrate on understanding the main ideas of the article and the meanings of new vocabulary words in the contexts in which they appear.

3.4
Reader Response

In order to explore your response to this reading, write for 15 minutes about anything that interested you in this article. You may wish to write about your reactions to some of the ideas presented here—or you may wish to disagree with something in the article. Try to explore *your own thoughts and feelings* as much as possible. Do *not* merely summarize or restate the ideas in this article.

3.5
Response Sharing

Read your response to two or three other people in your class. Listen carefully to what the others have written. After you have discussed each other's responses, talk about other points of interest in the article.

3.6
Understanding Main Ideas

Working with the same small group, make a list of the main ideas in this passage. Be sure to state the main ideas in your own words. Don't just copy sentences directly from the text. Think carefully about what the writer is trying to tell you.

3.7
Analyzing the Text

Work with your group members on this exercise. Discuss the answers carefully, particularly if there are disagreements among members of your group. In some cases there may be more than one possible interpretation.

1. What does the title of this article, *Overcoming the Pain in a Missing Limb*, mean and how does it relate to the article? Explain and give examples from the text.

2. *Irony* is the difference or gap between what is expected and reality. Explain why the following statement is ironic: The *third time he lost his left arm, Derek Steen yelped with joy.* What is the gap between what one would expect and reality? It may help you to read the first half of the sentence and then guess how you think the sentence would probably end. After that, read the second half of the sentence. Do the two halves fit together as you would have expected? If not, why not? What is the irony here?

3. This article begins The *third time he lost his left arm.* . . . How could a person lose an arm three times? What did the writer mean? What were the three times and the three types of loss? Do you think this is an effective way to begin an article? Why do you think the writer chose to begin this way?

4. What is the main idea of the article? Explain in detail.

5. What role did mirrors play in Dr. Ramachandran's discovery?

3.8
Vocabulary Study

Study the italicized words and phrases in their contexts and guess at their meanings. Write your guess in the first blank. Then look up the word or phrase in your dictionary and write the definition in the second blank.

1 and **2.** (paragraph 1) The third time he lost his left arm, Derek Steen *yelped* with joy. . . . He lost his arm a second time, so to speak, one year later when, *deemed* useless and getting in the way, the limb was amputated.

yelped

a. (guess) _____

b. (dictionary) _____

deemed

a. (guess) _____

b. (dictionary) _____

3 and **4.** (paragraph 3) After a simple, three-week treatment involving mirrors, his paralyzed *phantom* arm suddenly vanished, as did the *gnawing* pain in his phantom elbow.

phantom

a. (guess) _____

b. (dictionary) _____

gnawing

a. (guess) _____

b. (dictionary) _____

5 and **6.** (paragraph 4) He is *ecstatic* [because his] "body image" has been *profoundly* altered, much for the better.

ecstatic

a. (guess) _____

b. (dictionary) _____

profoundly

a. (guess) _____

b. (dictionary) _____

7. (paragraph 6) Phantom limbs occur when the brain *modifies* its sensory maps after an amputation, he said.

a. (guess) _____

b. (dictionary) _____

8 and 9. (paragraph 8) The answer lies in the feedback loops in the brain that *integrate* vision, senses, body movements, body image and motor commands. . . . In the first few weeks after the accident, Mr. Steen would try to move his injured arm, *to no avail.*

integrate

a. (guess) _____

b. (dictionary) _____

to no avail

a. (guess) _____

b. (dictionary) _____

10. (paragraph 13) "I asked him to make *symmetric* movements with both hands, as if he were conducting an orchestra," Dr. Ramachandran said.

a. (guess) _____

b. (dictionary) _____

11. (paragraph 21) The new finding may also have *relevance* to stroke rehabilitation, Dr. Ramachandran said.

a. (guess) _____

b. (dictionary) _____

12. (paragraph 26) A patient named Joe *stunned* researchers by learning how to talk with his right brain.

a. (guess) _____

b. (dictionary) _____

3.9
Narrative Reconstruction

It is important to learn how to reconstruct a narrative effectively. Think about the experiment reported in this article. Try to reconstruct this narrative. Think of the most important points and try to follow chronological order (i.e., what happened first, second, etc.) You may wish to make some notes to help you with your reconstruction. Report on your reconstruction in your group. (*Note*: This exercise may be done orally or in writing.)

3.10
Application, Critical Evaluation, and Synthesis

Choose one or more topics to discuss with your small group or to write about.

1. Phantom limb pain is an example of the brain playing a trick on the body. What is the trick? Why does it happen? What are the results? Use examples from the article in your explanation.

2. Dr. Ramachandran decided that the way to treat phantom limb pain was to play a trick on the brain and deliberately try to convince the brain that the missing limb is still there and that it can move freely. Explain his experiment. How did it work? What sensory information did the brain receive? What kind of confusion did this cause for the brain? What was the final result?

3. Derek Steen lost the use of an arm in an accident; later the arm was amputated. Each of these events was a devastating experience, and he probably thought that nothing worse could happen. In fact, however, the worst experience for Mr. Steen was later, when he had no arm and yet felt constant sensations of pain in his missing limb. All of us have had an experience in which the worst thing we could imagine turns out not to be as bad as something we have not imagined. Discuss an experience you have had in which your worst fear turned out not to be as bad as something else you had not imagined. Explain the situation clearly. What were you initially afraid of? What turned out to be worse? In Mr. Steen's case the situation was resolved. Was your situation resolved? Explain in as much detail as possible.

4. A placebo is a harmless medicine or treatment that has no medicinal value although a person's condition may improve while taking the placebo. For example, if you had a headache and you took a sugar pill that you thought was an aspirin, your headache might go away because you *believed* the pill would help you. The placebo effect occurs when your mind is convinced that the medicine or treatment is going to be effective. Have you ever had any experience with the placebo effect? If so, please explain in detail.

5. This unit contains three readings about the brain. Which reading did you find the most interesting and informative? Give specific examples of things you learned from the reading and explain why you found that interesting.

AT THE END OF EVERY UNIT YOU ARE INVITED TO TURN TO THE EXPANSION SECTION BEGINNING ON PAGE 233. THIS SECTION FOCUSES ON THE FUNDA-MENTALS OF LIBRARY RESEARCH AND REPORT WRITING.

Vocabulary Games

Here is a chance to review some of the vocabulary you have encountered in this unit. After you finish the game quizzes on your own, discuss your answers with your group members. You may use your dictionary to look up items to resolve disagreements. Scoring: 5 points for each correct answer.

Synonyms

Read each passage carefully and then draw a circle around the word or phrase that means the same thing (or almost the same thing) as the italicized word or phrase. If a word or phrase has more than one meaning, choose the meaning that fits the context in the passage.

Example: What are some of the important *traits* of good parents?

a. characteristics   b. habits   c. strengths

Passage One

Parenting skills are *critical* for mammals because their young are quite *vulnerable* when they are born. The parents need *to be attentive to* the needs of their newborns. If they are *indifferent,* it is possible that the babies will not survive. Even if they survive, they are not likely *to thrive.*

  1. *critical*

  a. negative   b. too judgmental   c. extremely important

  2. *vulnerable*

  a. helpless   b. small   c. self-sufficient

  3. *to be attentive to*

  a. to learn about   b. to pay close attention to   c. to ignore

  4. *indifferent*

  a. careful   b. careless   c. undistinguished

  5. *to thrive*

  a. to be healthy   b. to be active   c. to survive

Passage Two

Although some of the brain studies are *ambiguous,* the results seemed to suggest men's and women's brains may function differently. Men are often more *adept* at tasks involving spatial organization, whereas women are often more skilled in language-related activities. The research findings are certainly *tantalizing.* Scientists are asking whether sex differences in brain functioning are due to *nature* or *nurture.*

6. *ambiguous*

a. definite   b. related to the left and right brain   c. unclear

7. *adept*

a. adaptable   b. skillful   c. attracted (to)

8. *tantalizing*

a. fascinating   b. delicious   c. encouraging

9. *nature*

a. environmental influences   b. inborn characteristics
c. plants and animals

10. *nurture*

a. environmental influences   b. inborn characteristics
c. plants and animals

Antonyms

Antonyms are words that have opposite meanings, e.g., cold-hot; tall-short; dark-light. Read each passage carefully and then draw a circle around the word or phrase that means the opposite (or almost the opposite) of the italicized word or phrase. If a word or phrase has more than one meaning, choose the meaning that fits the context in the passage.

Example: It was a *complex* and unusual situation, and we weren't sure how to handle it.

a. complicated   (b. simple)   c. unclear

[*Simple* is the antonym of *complex* in this context.]

Passage Three

Derek Steen had severely *injured* his left arm in a motorcycle accident. Eventually he had the limb *amputated* because it was totally and permanently *paralyzed.* Mr. Steen continued to have terrible pain in his *phantom* left arm for 10 years because his brain did not recognize the fact that the limb was missing. He was *ecstatic* when his problem was solved after a short, simple treatment.

11. *injured*

a. hurt   b. repaired   c. destroyed

12. *amputated*

    a. surgically removed   b. surgically attached

    c. restored through physical therapy

13. *paralyzed*

    a. able to move   b. unable to move   c. slightly injured

14. *phantom*

    a. scary   b. invisible   c. visible

15. *ecstatic*

    a. deeply unhappy   b. overjoyed   c. satisfied

Logical Relationships

Look at the first pair of words, determine the relationship between them (are they synonyms or antonyms?). Then circle the word or phrase that fills in the blank to logically make a similar type of relationship.

Example:

women : men = girls : _____

    a. women   b. men   c. boys

[*Girls* is related to *boys* in the same way *women* is related to *men*.]

16. fix : restore = modify : _____

    a. fix   b. complete   c. change

[*Fix* is related to *restore* in the same way as *modify* is related to _____.]

17. small : insignificant = great : _____

    a. profound   b. beautiful   c. unimportant

18. different : same = sensitive : _____

    a. feeling   b. insensitive   c. caring

[*Hint: Different* and *same* are antonyms.]

19. originate : begin = oblivious : _____

    a. aware   b. unaware   c. against

20. noisy : quiescent = emit : _____

    a. quiet   b. exit   c. receive

SCORE: Number of correct answers _____ × **5 =** _____

Opening Up the Mind

The main point of education is to open up the mind and expand the world of the learner. In this unit you will read about how Helen Keller and Richard Wright were able to escape the constricting conditions of the world they were born into through education in general and reading in particular. In the third chapter, a famous Chinese writer/scholar, Lin Yu-T'ang, explains how reading enlarges, enriches and fundamentally changes the reader's world. Finally, in this unit, you will learn how you can escape the bonds of place and time through magic—the magic of reading.

Discussion

Before you begin reading, think about the following questions and discuss your answers. *Note:* You may wish to choose one or two questions to explore in detail either on your own or with a small group of students from your class.

1. Do you remember the first book you ever read? What was the title of the book and what was it about? How did you feel about being able to read? Describe your early reading experience in detail.

2. Did you ever overcome an obstacle that you thought you might not be able to overcome? What was the obstacle? How did you overcome it? How did you feel later? Explain in detail.

3. Do you think everyone should be required to read certain books in school or should all reading be entirely up to the individual? Explain your position in detail.

Helen Keller with her teacher, Anne Sullivan

CHAPTER ONE

Footsteps of My Life

Helen Keller (1880–1968) became blind and deaf as a very young child, and yet she was able to triumph over adversity to become a nationally known author and lecturer. She traveled all over the United States advocating the improvement of education and opportunity for physically disabled people. Keller was an inspiration not only for the disabled but for all people because of her courage and determination and her refusal to be limited by her disabilities. Keller was first taught at home by Anne Sullivan, who is mentioned in this passage. Later she went on to study at Radcliffe College from which she graduated cum laude. Keller wrote a number of highly acclaimed books and articles. The following selection comes from Keller's autobiography, *Story of My Life,* published by Doubleday in 1954. Reprinted by permission.

1.1
First Reading

Read this selection quickly for the main ideas. Do *not* stop to look up words in your dictionary.

1 The most important day I remember in all my life is the one on which my teacher, Anne Mansfield Sullivan, came to me. I am filled with wonder when I consider the immeasurable contrasts between the two lives which it connects. It was the third of March, 1887, three months before I was seven years old.

2 On the afternoon of that eventful day, I stood on the porch, dumb, expectant. I guessed vaguely from my mother's signs and from the hurrying to and fro in the house that something unusual was about to happen, so I went to the door and waited on the steps. The afternoon sun penetrated the mass of honeysuckle that covered the porch, and fell on my upturned face. My fingers lingered almost unconsciously on the familiar leaves and blossoms which had just come forth to greet the sweet southern spring. I did not know what the future held of marvel or surprise for me. Anger and bitterness had preyed upon me continually for weeks and a deep languor had succeeded this passionate struggle.

3 Have you ever been at sea in a dense fog, when it seemed as if a tangible white darkness shut you in, and the great ship, tense and anxious, groped her way toward the shore with plummet and sounding-line, and you waited with beating heart for something to happen? I was like that ship before my education began, only I was without compass or sounding-line, and had no

way of knowing how near the harbour was. "Light! give me light!" was the wordless cry of my soul, and the light of love shone on me in that very hour.

4   I felt approaching footsteps. I stretched out my hand as I supposed to my mother. Someone took it, and I was caught up and held close in the arms of her who had come to reveal all things to me, and, more than all things else, to love me.

5   The morning after my teacher came, she led me into her room and gave me a doll. The little blind children at the Perkins Institution had sent it and Laura Bridgman had dressed it; but I did not know this until afterward. When I had played with it a little while, Miss Sullivan slowly spelled into my hand the word "d-o-l-l." I was at once interested in this finger play and tried to imitate it. When I finally succeeded in making the letters correctly I was flushed with childish pleasure and pride. Running downstairs to my mother, I held up my hand and made the letters for doll. I did not know that I was spelling a word or even that words existed; I was simply making my fingers go in monkey-like imitation. In the days that followed I learned to spell in this uncomprehending way a great many words, among them *pin, hat, cup* and a few verbs like *sit, stand* and *walk*. But my teacher had been with me several weeks before I understood that everything has a name.

6   One day, while I was playing with my new doll, Miss Sullivan put my big rag doll into my lap also, spelled "d-o-l-l" and tried to make me understand that "d-o-l-l" applied to both. Earlier in the day we had had a tussle over the words "m-u-g" and "w-a-t-e-r." Miss Sullivan had tried to impress it upon me that "m-u-g" is *mug* and that "w-a-t-e-r" is *water*, but I persisted in confounding the two. In despair she had dropped the subject for the time, only to renew it at the first opportunity. I became impatient at her repeated attempts and, seizing the new doll, I dashed it upon the floor. I was keenly delighted when I felt the fragments of the broken doll at my feet. Neither sorrow nor regret followed my passionate outburst. I had not loved the doll. In the still, dark world in which I lived, there was no strong sentiment or tenderness. I felt my teacher sweep the fragments to one side of the hearth, and I had a sense of satisfaction that the cause of my discomfort was removed. She brought me my hat, and I knew I was going out into the warm sunshine. This thought, if a wordless sensation may be called a thought, made me hop and skip with pleasure.

7   We walked down the path to the well-house, attracted by the fragrance of the honeysuckle with which it was covered. Someone was drawing water and my teacher placed my hand under the spout. As the cool stream gushed over one hand, she spelled into the other the word water, first slowly, then rapidly. I stood still, my whole attention fixed upon the motions of her fingers. Suddenly I felt a misty consciousness as of something forgotten—a thrill of returning thought; and somehow the mystery of language was revealed to me. I knew then that "w-a-t-e-r" meant the wonderful cool something that was flowing over my hand. That living word awakened my soul, gave it light, hope, joy, set it free! There were barriers still, it is true, but barriers that could in time be swept away.

8   I left the well-house eager to learn. Everything had a name, and each name gave birth to a new thought. As we returned to the house, every object I touched seemed to quiver with life. That was because I saw everything with the strange, new sight that had come to me. On entering the door, I remembered the doll I had broken. I felt my way to the hearth and picked up the pieces. I tried vainly to put them together. Then my eyes filled with tears for I realized what I had done, and for the first time I felt repentance and sorrow.

9   I learned a great many new words that day. I do not remember what they all were, but I do know that *mother, father, sister, teacher* were among them—words that were to make the world blossom for me, "like Aaron's rod, with flowers." It would have been difficult to find a happier child than I was as I lay in my crib at the close of that eventful day and lived over the joys it had brought me, and for the first time I longed for a new day to come.

10 I had now the key to all language, and I was eager to learn to use it. Children who hear acquire language without any particular effort; the words that fall from others' lips they catch on the wing, as it were, delightedly, while the little deaf child must trap them by a slow and often painful process. But whatever the process, the result is wonderful. Gradually from naming an object, we advance step by step until we have traversed the vast distance between our first stammered syllable and the sweep of thought in a line of Shakespeare.

11 At first, when my teacher told me about a new thing, I asked very few questions. My ideas were vague, and my vocabulary was inadequate; but as my knowledge of things grew, and I learned more and more words, my field of inquiry broadened, and I would return again and again to the same subject, eager for further information. Sometimes a new word revived an image that some earlier experience had engraved on my brain.

12 I remember the morning that I first asked the meaning of the word "love." This was before I knew many words. I had found a few early violets in the garden and brought them to my teacher. She tried to kiss me, but at that time I did not like to have anyone kiss me except my mother. Miss Sullivan put her arm gently round me and spelled into my hand, "I love Helen."

13 "What is love?" I asked

14 She drew me closer to her and said, "It is here," pointing to my heart, whose beats I was conscious of for the first time. Her words puzzled me very much because I did not then understand anything unless I touched it

15 I smelt the violets in her hand and asked, half in words, half in signs, a question which meant, "Is love the sweetness of flowers?"

16 "No," said my teacher.

17 Again I thought. The warm sun was shining on us.

18 "Is this not love?" I asked, pointing in the direction from which the heat came. "Is this not love?"

19 It seemed to me there could be nothing more beautiful than the sun, whose warmth makes all things grow. But Miss Sullivan shook her head, and I was

greatly puzzled and disappointed. I thought it strange that my teacher could not show me love.

20 A day or two afterward, I was stringing beads of different sizes in symmetrical groups—two large beads, three small ones, and so on. I had made many mistakes, and Miss Sullivan had pointed them out again and again with gentle patience. Finally I noticed a very obvious error in the sequence and for an instant I concentrated my attention on the lesson and tried to think how I should have arranged the beads. Miss Sullivan touched my forehead and spelled with decided emphasis, "Think."

21 In a flash I knew that the word was the name of the process that was going on in my head. This was my first conscious perception of an abstract idea.

22 For a long time I was still—I was not thinking of the beads in my lap, but trying to find a meaning for "love" in the light of this new idea. The sun had been under a cloud all day, and there had been brief showers; but suddenly the sun broke forth in all its southern splendour.

23 Again I asked my teacher, "Is this not love?"

24 "Love is something like the clouds that were in the sky before the sun came out," she replied. Then in simpler words than these, which at that time I could not have understood, she explained: "You cannot touch the clouds, you know; but you feel the rain and know how glad the flowers and the thirsty earth are to have it after a hot day. You cannot touch love either; but you feel the sweetness that it pours into everything. Without love you would not be happy or want to play."

25 The beautiful truth burst upon my mind—I felt that there were invisible lines stretched between my spirit and the spirits of others.

26 From the beginning of my education, Miss Sullivan made it a practice to speak to me as she would speak to any hearing child; the only difference was that she spelled the sentences into my hand instead of speaking them. If I did not know the words and idioms necessary to express my thoughts, she supplied them, even suggesting conversation when I was unable to keep up my end of the dialogue.

27 This process was continued for several years; for the deaf child does not learn in a month, or even in two or three years, the numberless idioms and expressions used in the simplest daily intercourse. The little hearing child learns these from constant repetition and imitation. The conversation he hears in his home stimulates his mind and suggests topics and calls forth the spontaneous expression of his own thoughts. This natural exchange of ideas is denied to the deaf child. My teacher, realizing this, determined to supply the kinds of stimulus I lacked. This she did by repeating to me as far as possible, verbatim, what she heard, and by showing me how I could take part in the conversation. But it was a long time before I ventured to take the initiative, and still longer before I could find something appropriate to say at the right time.

28 The deaf and the blind find it very difficult to acquire the amenities of conversation. How much more this difficulty must be augmented in the case

of those who are both deaf and blind! They cannot distinguish the tone of the voice or, without assistance, go up and down the gamut of tones that give significance to words; nor can they watch the expression of the speaker's face, and a look is often the very soul of what one says.

29 The next important step in my education was learning to read.

30 A soon as I could spell a few words, my teacher gave me slips of cardboard on which were printed words in raised letters. I quickly learned that each printed word stood for an object, an act, or a quality. I had a frame in which I could arrange the words in little sentences; but before I ever put sentences in the frame, I used to make them in objects. I found the slips of paper which represented, for example, "doll," "is," "on," "bed," and placed each name on its object; then I put my doll on the bed with the words *is, on, bed* arranged beside the doll, thus making a sentence of the words, and at the same time carrying out the idea of the sentence with the things themselves.

31 One day, Miss Sullivan tells me, I pinned the word *girl* on my pinafore and stood in the wardrobe. On the shelf I arranged the words, *is, in, wardrobe*. Nothing delighted me so much as this game. My teacher and I played it for hours at a time. Often everything in the room was arranged in object sentences.

32 From the printed slip it was but a step to the printed book. I took my "Reader for Beginners" and hunted for the words I knew; when I found them, my joy was like that of a game of hide-and-seek. Thus I began to read. Of the time when I began to read connected stories I shall speak later.

33 For a long time I had no regular lessons. Even when I studied most earnestly, it seemed more like play than work. Everything Miss Sullivan taught me she illustrated by a beautiful story or a poem. Whenever anything delighted or interested me, she talked it over with me just as if she were a little girl herself. What many children think of with dread, as a painful plodding through grammar, hard sums and harder definitions, is today one of my most precious memories.

34 I cannot explain the peculiar sympathy Miss Sullivan had with my pleasures and desires. Perhaps it was the result of long association with the blind. Added to this she had a wonderful faculty for description. She went quickly over uninteresting details and never nagged me with questions to see if I remembered the day-before-yesterday's lesson. She introduced dry technicalities of science little by little, making every subject so real that I could not help remembering what she taught.

35 We read and studied out of doors, preferring the sunlit woods to the house. All my early lessons have in them the breath of the woods—the fine, resinous odour of pine needles, blended with the perfume of wild grapes. Seated in the gracious shade of a wild tulip tree, I learned to think that everything has a lesson and a suggestion. "The loveliness of things taught me all their use." Indeed, everything that could hum, or buzz, or sing, or bloom, had a part in my education—noisy-throated frogs, katydids and crickets held in my hand until, forgetting their embarrassment, they trilled their reedy note,

little downy chickens and wildflowers, the dogwood blossoms, meadow-violets and budding fruit trees. I felt the bursting cotton-bolls and fingered their soft fiber and fuzzy seeds; I felt the low soughing of the wind through the cornstalks, the silky rustling of the long leaves, and the indignant snort of my pony as we caught him in the pasture and put the bit in his mouth—ah me! how well I remember the spicy, clovery smell of his breath!

36   Sometimes I rose at dawn and stole into the garden while the heavy dew lay on the grass and flowers. Few know what joy it is to feel the roses pressing softly into the hand, or the beautiful motion of the lilies as they sway in the morning breeze. Sometimes I caught an insect in the flower I was plucking, and I felt the faint noise of a pair of wings rubbed together in a sudden terror, as the little creature became aware of a pressure from without.

37   Another favourite haunt of mine was the orchard, where the fruit ripened early in July. The large, downy peaches would reach themselves into my hand, and as the joyous breezes flew about the trees, the apples tumbled at my feet. Oh, the delight with which I gathered up the fruit in my pinafore, pressed my face against the smooth cheeks of the apples, still warm from the sun, and skipped back to the house!

38   Our favourite walk was to Keller's Landing, an old tumble-down lumber wharf on the Tennessee River, used during the Civil War to land soldiers. There we spent many happy hours and played at learning geography. I built dams of pebbles, made islands and lakes, and dug river-beds, all for fun, and never dreamed that I was learning a lesson. I listened with increasing wonder to Miss Sullivan's descriptions of the great round world with its burning mountains, buried cities, moving rivers of ice, and many other things as strange. She made raised maps in clay, so that I could feel the mountain ridges and valleys, and follow with my fingers the devious course of rivers. I liked this, too; but the division of the earth into zones and poles confused and teased my mind. The illustrative strings and the orange stick representing the poles seemed so real that even to this day, the mere mention of temperate zone suggests a series of twine circles; and I believe that if anyone should set about it, he could convince me that white bears actually climb the North Pole.

39   Arithmetic seems to have been the only study I did not like. From the first I was not interested in the science of numbers. Miss Sullivan tried to teach me to count by stringing beads in groups, and by arranging straws, I learned to add and subtract. I never had patience to arrange more than five or six groups at a time. When I had accomplished this, my conscience was at rest for the day, and I went out quickly to find my playmates.

40   In this same leisurely manner, I studied zoology and botany.

41   Once a gentleman whose name I have forgotten sent me a collection of fossils—tiny mollusk shells beautifully marked, and bits of sandstone with the print of birds' claws, and a lovely fern in bas-relief. These were the keys which unlocked the treasures of the antediluvian world for me. With trembling fingers I listened to Miss Sullivan's descriptions of the terrible beasts with uncouth, unpronounceable names which once went tramping through

the primeval forests, tearing down the branches of gigantic trees for food, and died in the dismal swamps of an unknown age. For a long time these strange creatures haunted my dreams, and this gloomy period formed a somber background to the joyous Now, filled with sunshine and roses and echoing with the gentle beat of my pony's hoof. . . .

42 Thus I learned from life itself. At the beginning I was only a little mass of possibilities. It was my teacher who unfolded and developed them. When she came, everything about me breathed of love and joy and was full of meaning. She has never since let pass an opportunity to point out the beauty that is in everything, nor has she ceased trying in thought and action and example to make my life sweet and useful.

43 It was my teacher's genius, her quick sympathy, her loving tact which made the first years of my education so beautiful. It was because she seized the right moment to impart knowledge that made it so pleasant and acceptable to me. She realized that a child's mind is like a shallow brook which ripples and dances merrily over the stony course of its education and reflects here a flower, there a bush, yonder a fleecy cloud; and she attempted to guide my mind on its way, knowing that like a brook, it should be fed by mountain streams and hidden springs, until it broadened out into a deep river, capable of reflecting in its placid surface, billowy hills, the luminous shadows of trees and the blue heavens, as well as the sweet face of a little flower.

44 Any teacher can take a child to the classroom, but not every teacher can make him learn. He will not work joyously unless he feels that liberty is his, whether he is busy or at rest; he must feel the flush of victory and the heart-sinking of disappointment before he takes with a will the tasks distasteful to him and resolves to dance his way bravely through a dull routine of textbooks.

45 My teacher is so near to me that I scarcely think of myself apart from her. How much of my delight in all beautiful things is innate and how much is due to her influence, I can never tell. I feel that her being is inseparable from my own, and that the footsteps of my life are in hers. All the best of me belongs to her—there is not a talent or an aspiration or a joy in me that has not been awakened by her loving touch.

Number of words: 3,818

Reading Times	**Reading Speed**
1st reading _____ minutes	17 minutes = 225 wpm
3rd reading _____ minutes	15 minutes = 255 wpm
	13 minutes = 294 wpm
	11 minutes = 347 wpm

1.2
Second Reading

Go back and read the passage again. Take as much time as you need. Look up some of the unfamiliar words in the glossary at the end of the book or in your dictionary if you wish.

1.3
Third Reading

Read the passage quickly a third time. Concentrate on understanding the main ideas of the story and the meanings of new vocabulary words in the contexts in which they appear.

1.4
Reader Response

In order to explore your response to this reading, write for 15 minutes about anything that interested you in this passage. You may wish to write about your reactions to some of the themes and ideas presented here—or you may wish to disagree with something in the selection. Try to explore your *own thoughts and feelings* as much as possible. Do *not* merely summarize or restate the ideas in this passage.

1.5
Response Sharing

Read your response to two or three other people in your class. Listen carefully to what the others have written. After you have discussed each other's responses, talk about other points of interest in the passage.

1.6
Identifying Main Ideas

Working with the same small group, make a list of the main ideas in this passage. Be sure to state the main ideas in your own words. Don't just copy sentences directly from the text. Think carefully about what the writer is trying to tell you.

1.7
Analyzing the Text

Work with your group members on this exercise. Discuss the answers carefully, particularly if there are disagreements among members of your group. In some cases there may be more than one possible interpretation.

1. How does the title relate to the passage? What point is Helen Keller trying to make with the title?

2. Helen Keller was deaf and blind, so she could not use her auditory and visual senses; yet her writing appeals strongly to other senses. Find examples of her appeal to other senses. What are these other senses?

3. Read each statement carefully, decide if it is true or false according to this article, and then write *T* (true) or *F* (false) on the line in front of the statement.

   a. _____ Helen could sense from her mother's actions that something unusual was going to happen the day Anne Sullivan came into her life.

   b. _____ Helen did not have the concept of words before Anne Sullivan became her teacher.

   c. _____ Helen immediately understood the meaning of the word *love*.

   d. _____ Helen was a reluctant student and did not enjoy learning.

   e. _____ Helen had enormous love and admiration for her teacher.

4. Helen Keller makes a distinction between "d-o-l-l" and *doll*. Why does she represent this word in two different ways? What does she mean by "d-o-l-l" and what does she mean by *doll*?

5. Education changes people's lives and it certainly changed Helen Keller's life radically. Name three ways her life changed and give examples from the passage.

1.8
Vocabulary Study

Study the italicized words and phrases in their contexts and guess at their meanings. Write your guess in the first blank. Then look up the word or phrase in your dictionary and write the definition in the second blank.

1, 2, and **3.** (paragraph 2) Anger and bitterness had *preyed* upon me continually for weeks and a deep *languor* had *succeeded* this passionate struggle.

preyed

a. (guess) _____

b. (dictionary) _____

languor

a. (guess) _____

b. (dictionary) _____

succeeded

a. (guess) _____

b. (dictionary) _____

4, 5, and **6.** (paragraph 3) Have you ever been at sea in a *dense* fog, when it seemed as if a *tangible* white darkness shut you in, and the great ship, tense and anxious, *groped* her way toward the shore. . . , and you waited with beating heart for something to happen?

dense

a. (guess) _____

b. (dictionary) _____

tangible

a. (guess) _____

b. (dictionary) _____

groped

a. (guess) _____

b. (dictionary) _____

7, 8, and **9.** (paragraph 6) Miss Sullivan had tried to *impress it upon me* that "m-u-g" is "mug" and that "w-a-t-e-r" is "water", but I *persisted* in *confounding* the two.

impress it upon me

a. (guess) _____

b. (dictionary) _____

persisted

a. (guess) _____

b. (dictionary) _____

confounding

a. (guess) _____

b. (dictionary) _____

10 and **11.** (paragraph 28) The deaf and the blind find it very difficult to acquire the *amenities* of conversation. How much more this difficulty must be *augmented* in the case of those who are both deaf and blind!

amenities

a. (guess) _____

b. (dictionary) _____

augmented

a. (guess) _____

b. (dictionary) _____

12. (paragraph 45) My teacher is so near to me that I scarcely think of myself apart from her. How much of my delight in all beautiful things is *innate* and how much is due to her influence, I can never tell. I feel that her being is inseparable from my own, and that the footsteps of my life are in hers.

a. (guess) _____

b. (dictionary) _____

1.9
Sequential Development

Helen Keller gives a step-by-step description of her intellectual development in the passage you have just read. Reread the passage and make a list of the steps in her development.

Example:
Helen Keller

1. copies the designs her teacher makes in her hand;
2. understands everything has a name;
3. realizes a word (e.g., *doll*) can stand for more than one object;

Continue this list by identifying as many steps as possible in Keller's intellectual development.

1.10
Application, Critical Evaluation, and Synthesis

Choose one or more topics to discuss with your small group or to write about.

1. Helen Keller begins by saying, "The most important day I remember in all my life is the one on which my teacher, Anne Mansfield Sullivan, came to me. I am filled with wonder when I consider the immeasurable contrasts between the two lives which it connects. It was the third of March, 1887, three months before I was seven years old." What is the most important day you remember in your life? Where were you? How old were you? What happened and how did your life change? How did this day connect your two lives and, in essence, make you into a new person?

2. Helen Keller tells us how her teacher, Anne Sullivan, changed her life and opened up the world for her. Write about a teacher who opened up your world in some way. Who was the teacher? How old were you? What was the subject? Why did this teacher make such a strong impression on you? How did your life change? Be as detailed and specific as possible.

3. Learning to read is an experience that changes most people's lives. Write about your experience of learning to read. How old were you? Where were you? What was the first book you read? Describe your thoughts and feelings in detail.

4. Helen Keller never allowed herself to be limited by her disabilities. She was blind and deaf and yet she graduated with high honors from a prestigious college and became a well-known writer and lecturer. Have you ever known or read about anyone who overcame personal adversity to achieve a goal others would have thought impossible? Who was this person? What adversities did he or she have to overcome? Be as detailed and as specific as possible.

Richard Wright, 1947

CHAPTER TWO

The Library Card

Richard Wright (1908–1960) is considered one of the leading Ameri-can writers of the twentieth century and, as an African American, he has strongly influenced other African American writers who followed him. Wright dramatically illustrated the devastating effects of poverty, violence, and racism on human lives, basing his writing, in part, on his own experiences. He grew up in rural Mississippi, the son of poor sharecroppers; later he experienced urban poverty in Chicago and New York, so he was intimately acquainted with the themes of his writing. The following selection comes from Wright's well-known autobiography, *Black Boy,* and it shows how he struggled against the crippling limitations of poverty and racism as a young man. This piece, copyrighted in 1937, is reprinted by permission of HarperCollins Publishers.

2.1
First Reading

Read the passage quickly for the main ideas. Pay attention to the title and the narrative; think about what the library card means to the young man telling the story. Why does he go to such lengths to get a library card? Why was it necessary for him to go to such lengths? Do *not* stop to look up words in your dictionary.

1 One morning I arrived early at work and went into the bank lobby where the Negro porter was mopping. I stood at a counter and picked up the Memphis *Commercial Appeal* and began my free reading of the press. I came finally to the editorial page and saw an article dealing with one H. L. Mencken. I knew by hearsay that he was the editor of the *American Mercury*, but aside from that I knew nothing about him. The article was a furious denunciation of Mencken, concluding with one, hot, short sentence: Mencken is a fool.

2 I wondered what on earth this Mencken had done to call down upon him the scorn of the South. The only people I had ever heard denounced in the South were Negroes, and this man was not a Negro. Then what ideas did Mencken hold that made a newspaper like the *Commercial Appeal* castigate him publicly? Undoubtedly he must be advocating ideas that the South did not like. Were there, then, people other than Negroes who criticized the South? I knew that during the Civil War the South had hated the northern whites, but I had not encountered such hate during my life. Knowing no more of Mencken than I did at that moment, I felt a vague sympathy for him. Had not the South, which had assigned me the role of a non-man, cast at him its hardest words?

3 Now, how could I find out about this Mencken? There was a huge library near the riverfront, but I knew that Negroes were not allowed to patronize its shelves any more than they were the parks and playgrounds of the city.[1] I had gone into the library several times to get books for the white men on the job. Which of them would now help me to get books? And how could I read them without causing concern to the white men with whom I worked? I had so far been successful in hiding my thoughts and feelings from them, but I knew that I would create hostility if I went about this business of reading in a clumsy way.

4 I weighed the personalities of the men on the job. There was Don, a Jew; but I distrusted him. His position was not much better than mine and I knew that he was uneasy and insecure; he had always treated me in an off-hand, bantering way that barely contained his contempt. I was afraid to ask him to help me to get books; his frantic desire to demonstrate a racial solidarity with the whites against Negroes might make him betray me.

5 Then how about the boss? No, he was a Baptist and I had the suspicion that he would not be quite able to comprehend why a black boy would want to read Mencken. There were other white men on the job whose attitudes showed clearly that they were Kluxers or sympathizers,[2] and they were out of the question.

6 There remained only one man whose attitude did not fit into an anti-Negro category, for I had heard the white men refer to him as a "Pope lover." He was an Irish Catholic and was hated by the white Southerners. I knew that he read books, because I had got him volumes from the library several times. Since he, too, was an object of hatred, I felt that he might refuse me but would hardly betray me. I hesitated, weighing and balancing the imponderable realities.

7 One morning I paused before the Catholic fellow's desk.

8 "I want to ask you a favor," I whispered to him.

9 "What is it?"

10 "I want to read. I can't get books from the library. I wonder if you'd let me use your card?"

11 He looked at me suspiciously.

12 "My card is full most of the time," he said.

13 "I see," I said and waited, posing my question silently.

14 "You're not trying to get me into trouble, are you, boy?" he asked, staring at me.

---

1. At the time Richard Wright was growing up in the South, most public places and public transportation were segregated. Therefore, as a Negro (now called an African-American), Wright was not allowed to use the public library.
2. **Kluxers** refers to members of the Ku Klux Klan (KKK), an organization of white supremicists who believe whites are superior to blacks. **Sympathizers** are people who support the KKK's belief in white racial superiority even though they are not formal members of the organization.

15 "Oh, no, sir."

16 "What book do you want?"

17 "A book by H. L. Mencken."

18 "Which one?"

19 "I don't know. Has he written more than one?"

20 "He has written several."

21 "I didn't know that."

22 "What makes you want to read Mencken?"

23 "Oh, I just saw his name in the newspaper," I said.

24 "It's good of you to want to read," he said. "But you ought to read the right things."

25 I said nothing. Would he want to supervise my reading?

26 "Let me think," he said. "I'll figure out something."

27 I turned from him and he called me back. He stared at me quizzically.

28 "Richard, don't mention this to the other white men," he said.

29 "I understand," I said. "I won't say a word."

30 A few days later he called me to him.

31 "I've got a card in my wife's name," he said. "Here's mine."

32 "Thank you, sir."

33 "Do you think you can manage it?"

34 "I'll manage fine," I said.

35 "If they suspect you, you'll get in trouble," he said.

36 "I'll write the same kind of notes to the library that you wrote when you sent me for books," I told him. "I'll sign your name."

37 He laughed.

38 "Go ahead. Let me see what you get," he said.

39 That afternoon I addressed myself to forging a note. Now, what were the names of books written by H. L. Mencken? I did not know any of them. I finally wrote what I thought would be a foolproof note: *Dear Madam: Will you please let this nigger boy*—I used the word *nigger* to make the librarian feel that I could not possibly be the author of the note—*have some books by H. L. Mencken?* I forged the white man's name.

40 I entered the library as I had always done when on errands for whites, but I felt that I would somehow slip up and betray myself. I doffed my hat, stood a respectful distance from the desk, looked as unbookish as possible, and waited for the white patrons to be taken care of. When the desk was clear of people, I still waited. The white librarian looked at me.

41 "What do you want, boy?"

42 As though I did not possess the power of speech, I stepped forward and simply handed her the forged note, not parting my lips.

43 "What books by Mencken does he want?" she asked.

44 "I don't know, ma'am," I said, avoiding her eyes.

45 "Who gave you this card?"

46 "Mr. Falk," I said.

47 "Where is he?"

48. "He's at work, at the M—Optical Company," I said. "I've been in here for him before."

49 "I remember," the woman said. "But he never wrote notes like this."

50 Oh, God, she's suspicious. Perhaps she would not let me have the books? If she had turned her back at that moment, I would have ducked out the door and never gone back. Then I thought of a bold idea.

51 "You can call him up, ma'am," I said, my heart pounding.

52 "You're not using these books, are you?" she asked pointedly.

53 "Oh, no, ma'am. I can't read."

54 "I don't know what he wants by Mencken," she said under her breath.

55 I knew now that I had won; she was thinking of other things and the race question had gone out of her mind. She went to the shelves. Once or twice she looked over her shoulder at me, as though she was still doubtful. Finally she came forward with two books in her hand.

56 "I'm sending him two books," she said. "But tell Mr. Falk to come in next time, or send me the names of the books he wants. I don't know what he wants to read."

57 I said nothing. She stamped the card and handed me the books. Not daring to glance at them, I went out of the library, fearing that the woman would call me back for further questioning. A block away from the library I opened one of the books and read a title: *A Book of Prefaces*. I was nearing my nineteenth birthday and I did not know how to pronounce the word "preface." I thumbed the pages and saw strange words and strange names. I shook my head, disappointed. I looked at the other book; it was called *Prejudices*. I knew what that word meant; I had heard it all my life. And right off I was on guard against Mencken's books. Why would a man want to call a book *Prejudices*? The word was so stained with all my memories of racial hate that I could not conceive of anybody using it for a title. Perhaps I had made a mistake about Mencken? A man who had prejudices must be wrong.

58 When I showed the books to Mr. Falk, he looked at me and frowned.

59 "That librarian might telephone you," I warned him.

60 "That's all right," he said. "But when you're through reading those books, I want you to tell me what you get out of them."

61 That night in my rented room, while letting the hot water run over my can of pork and beans in the sink, I opened *A Book of Prefaces* and began to read. I was jarred and shocked by the style, the clear, clean, sweeping sentences. Why did he write like that? And how did one write like that? I pictured the man as a raging demon, slashing with his pen, consumed with hate, denouncing everything American, extolling everything European or German,

laughing at the weaknesses of people, mocking God, authority. What was this? I stood up, trying to realize what reality lay behind the meaning of the words. . . Yes, this man was fighting, fighting with words. He was using words as a weapon, using them as one would use a club. Could words be weapons? No. It frightened me. I read on and what amazed me was not what he said, but how on earth anybody had the courage to say it.

62 Occasionally I glanced up to reassure myself that I was alone in the room. Who were these men about whom Mencken was talking so passionately? Who was Anatole France? Joseph Conrad? Sinclair Lewis, Sherwood Anderson, Dostoevski, George Moore, Gustave Flaubert, Maupassant, Tolstoy, Frank Harris, Mark Twain, Thomas Hardy, Arnold Bennet, Stephen Crane, Zola, Norris, Gorky, Bergson, Ibsen, Balzac, Bernard Shaw, Dumas, Poe, Thomas Mann, O. Henry, Dreiser, H. G. Wells, Gogol, T. S. Eliot, Gide, Baudelaire, Edgar Lee Masters, Stendhal, Turgenev, Huneker, Nietzche, and scores of others? Were these men real? Did they exist or had they existed? And how did one pronounce their names?

63 I ran across many words whose meanings I did not know, and I either looked them up in a dictionary or, before I had a chance to do that, encountered the word in a context that made its meaning clear. But what strange world was this? I concluded the book with the conviction that I had somehow overlooked something terribly important in life. I had once tried to write, had once reveled in feeling, had let my crude imagination roam, but the impulse to dream had been slowly beaten out of me by experience. Now it surged up again and I hungered for books, new ways of looking and seeing. It was not a matter of believing or disbelieving what I read, but of feeling something new, of being affected by something that made the look of the world different.

64 As dawn broke I ate my pork and beans, feeling dopey, sleepy. I went to work, but the mood of the book would not die; it lingered, coloring everything I saw, heard, did. I now felt that I knew what the white men were feeling. Merely because I had read a book that had spoken of how they lived and thought, I identified myself with that book. I felt vaguely guilty. Would I, filled with bookish notions, act in a manner that would make the whites dislike me?

65 I forged more notes and my trips to the library became frequent. Reading grew into a passion. My first serious novel was Sinclair Lewis's *Main Street*. It made me see my boss, Mr. Gerald, and identify him as an American type. I would smile when I saw him lugging his golf bags into the office. I had always felt a vast distance separating me from the boss, and now I felt closer to him, though still distant. I felt now that I knew him, that I could feel the very limits of his narrow life. And this had happened because I had read a novel about a mythical man called George F. Babbitt.

66 The plots and stories in the novels did not interest me so much as the point of view revealed. I gave myself over to each novel without reserve, without trying to criticize it; it was enough for me to see and feel something different. And for me, everything was something different. Reading was like a

drug, a dope. The novels created moods in which I lived for days. But I could not conquer my sense of guilt, my feeling that the white men around me knew that I was changing, that I had begun to regard them differently.

67 Whenever I brought a book to the job, I wrapped it in newspaper—a habit that was to persist for years in other cities and under other circumstances. But some of the white men pried into my packages when I was absent and they questioned me.

68 "Boy, what are you reading those books for?"

69 "Oh, I don't know, sir."

70 "That's deep stuff you're reading, boy."

71 "I'm just killing time, sir."

72 "You'll addle your brains if you don't watch out."

73 I read Dreiser's *Jennie Gerhardt* and *Sister Carrie* and they revived in me a vivid sense of my mother's suffering; I was overwhelmed. I grew silent, wondering about the life around me. It would have been impossible for me to have told anyone what I derived from these novels, for it was nothing less than a sense of life itself. All my life had shaped me for the realism, the naturalism of the modern novel, and I could not read enough of them.

74 Steeped in new moods and ideas, I bought a ream of paper and tried to write; but nothing would come, or what did come was flat beyond telling. I discovered that more than desire and feeling were necessary to write and I dropped the idea. Yet I still wondered how it was possible to know people sufficiently to write about them? Could I ever learn about life and people? To me, with my vast ignorance, my Jim Crow[3] station in life, it seemed a task impossible of achievement. I now knew what being a Negro meant. I could endure the hunger. I had learned to live with hate. But to feel that there were feelings denied me, that the very breath of life itself was beyond my reach, that more than anything else hurt, wounded me. I had a new hunger.

75 In buoying me up, reading also cast me down, made me see what was possible, what I had missed. My tension returned, new, terrible, bitter, surging, almost too great to be contained. I no longer *felt* that the world about me was hostile, killing; I *knew* it. A million times I asked myself what I could do to save myself, and there were no answers. I seemed forever condemned, ringed by walls.

76 I did not discuss my reading with Mr. Falk, who had lent me his library card; it would have meant talking about myself and that would have been too painful. I smiled each day, fighting desperately to maintain my old behavior, to keep my disposition seemingly sunny. But some of the white men discerned that I had begun to brood.

77 "Wake up there, boy!" Mr. Olin said one day.

---

3. **Jim Crow** Another term for segregation, meaning separate facilities, services, and policies for blacks and whites. When Wright refers to his "Jim Crow station in life," he means the discrimination he encountered on a daily basis as a black living in a world where whites had all the privileges.

78 "Sir!" I answered for the lack of a better word.

79 "You act like you've stolen something," he said.

80 I laughed in the way I knew he expected me to laugh, but I resolved to be more conscious of myself, to watch my every act, to guard and hide the new knowledge that was dawning within me.

81 If I went north, would it be possible for me to build a new life then? But how could a man build a life upon vague, unformed yearnings? I wanted to write and I did not even know the English language. I bought English grammars and found them dull. I felt that I was getting a better sense of the language from novels than from grammars. I read hard, discarding a writer as soon as I felt that I had grasped his point of view. At night the printed page stood before my eyes in sleep.

82 Mrs. Moss, my landlady, asked me one Sunday morning: "Son, what is this you keep on reading?"

83 "Oh, nothing. Just novels."

84 "What you get out of 'em?"

85 "I'm just killing time," I said.

86 "I hope you know your own mind," she said in a tone which implied that she doubted if I had a mind.

87 I knew of no Negroes who read the books I liked and I wondered if any Negroes ever thought of them. I knew that there were Negro doctors, lawyers, newspapermen, but I never saw any of them. When I read a Negro newspaper I never caught the faintest echo of my preoccupation in its pages. I felt trapped and occasionally, for a few days, I would stop reading. But a vague hunger would come over me for books, books that opened up new avenues of feeling and seeing, and again I would forge another note to the white librarian. Again I would read and wonder as only the naive and unlettered can read and wonder, feeling that I carried a secret, criminal burden about with me each day.

88 That winter my mother and brother came and we set up housekeeping, buying furniture on the installment plan, being cheated and yet knowing no way to avoid it. I began to eat warm food and to my surprise found that regular meals enabled me to read faster. I may have lived through many illnesses and survived them, never suspecting that I was ill. My brother obtained a job and we began to save toward the trip north, plotting our time, setting tentative dates for departure. I told none of the white men on the job that I was planning to go north; I knew that the moment they felt I was thinking of the North they would change toward me. It would have made them feel that I did not like the life I was living, and because my life was completely conditioned by what they said or did, it would have been tantamount to challenging them.

89 I could calculate my chances for life in the South as a Negro fairly clearly now.

90 I could fight the southern whites by organizing with other Negroes, as my grandfather had done. But I knew that I could never win that way; there were many whites and there were but few blacks. They were strong and we

were weak. Outright black rebellion could never win. If I fought openly I would die and I did not want to die. News of lynchings were frequent.

91   I could submit and live the life of a genial slave, but that was impossible. All of my life had shaped me to live by my own feelings and thoughts. I could make up to Bess and marry her and inherit the house. But that, too, would be the life of a slave; if I did that, I would crush to death something within me, and I would hate myself as much as I knew the whites already hated those who had submitted. Neither could I ever willingly present myself to be kicked, as Shorty had done. I would rather have died than do that.

92   I could drain off my restlessness by fighting with Shorty and Harrison. I had seen many Negroes solve the problem of being black by transferring their hatred of themselves to others with a black skin and fighting them. I would have to be cold to do that, and I was not cold and I could never be.

93   I could, of course, forget what I had read, thrust the whites out of my mind, forget them, and find release from anxiety and longing in sex and alcohol. But the memory of how my father had conducted himself made that course repugnant. If I did not want others to violate my life, how could I voluntarily violate it myself?

94   I had no hope whatever of being a professional man. Not only had I been so conditioned that I did not desire it, but the fulfillment of such an ambition was beyond my capabilities. Well-to-do Negroes lived in a world that was almost as alien to me as the world inhabited by whites.

95   What, then, was there? I held my life in my mind, in my consciousness each day, feeling at times that I would stumble and drop it, spill it forever. My reading had created a vast sense of distance between me and the world in which I lived and tried to make a living, and that sense of distance was increasing each day. My days and nights were one long, quiet, continuously contained dream of terror, tension, and anxiety. I wondered how long I could bear it.

Number of words: 3,883
Reading Times
1st reading _____ minutes
3rd reading _____ minutes

Reading Speed
15 minutes = 259 wpm
13 minutes = 299 wpm
11 minutes = 353 wpm
10 minutes = 388 wpm
9 minutes = 431 wpm

2.2
Second Reading

Go back and read the passage again. Take as much time as you need. Look up some of the unfamiliar words in the glossary at the end of the book or in your dictionary if you wish.

2.3
Third Reading

Read the passage quickly a third time. Concentrate on understanding the main ideas of the passage and the meanings of new vocabulary words in the contexts in which they appear.

2.4
Reader Response

In order to explore your response to this reading, write for 15 minutes about anything that interested you in this excerpt. You may wish to write about your reactions to some of the ideas presented here. Try to explore *your own thoughts and feelings* as much as possible. Do *not* merely summarize or restate the ideas in this passage.

2.5
Response Sharing

Read your response to two or three other people in your class. Listen carefully to what the others have written. After you have discussed each other's responses, talk about other points of interest in the passage.

2.6
Understanding Point of View

Every person looks at the world in a unique way based on individual experience and a combination of hopes, dreams, and expectations; this point of view is important in literature as well as in life. In this excerpt from *Black Boy*, we see that the library card symbolizes different things to each of the characters because of each character's point of view.

Example:

Richard Wright, the narrator:

To Richard Wright, the library card symbolizes many powerful and conflicting ideas. For example, on one level it represents freedom. The library card gives him access through the imagination to a world he has never lived in; at the same time, it cuts him off from the grim world he does live in. The card lets him see how other people, mainly white people, live and think. He begins to understand why they act as they do; after reading Sinclair Lewis's *Main Street*, he sees why his boss acts the way he does. At the same time, the library card symbolizes danger. Wright knows that if he is discovered using the library card for his own purposes, the consequences will be severe. People will believe that he is challenging the social and legal code of the society he lives in. There could be harsh retributions if he is found out; he could lose his job and what little standing he currently has in society. The library card enables him not only to think in new ways but also to learn a vastly richer language. The library card represents guilt; he knows he is breaking the laws of the society he lives in by using the library card, and he is afraid of what will happen to him if he is discovered. Yet he is powerless to stop reading. The card also represents frustration. By opening up his mind, it makes him recognize and reject the dead-end possibilities of his current life; yet it does not show him the way out—how he can escape his limited life and become part of this other richer world of unrestricted opportunity.

Using this example as a guide, work with the same small group. Choose one of the other characters and explain what the library card symbolizes to that person (e.g., Mr. Falk, Wright's Catholic coworker who lends his library card; the white librarian; one of Wright's white coworkers; or Mrs. Moss, his landlady.) Begin by putting yourself in that person's shoes; try seeing the world through his or her eyes. What does the library card represent to that person? How would that person feel about the narrator using the library card if he or she found out? Would the person approve? Why or why not? Explain and give specific examples and details.

2.7
Analyzing the Text

Work with your group members on this exercise. Discuss the answers carefully, particularly if there are disagreements among members of your group. In some cases there may be more than one possible interpretation.

1. The title of Richard Wright's autobiography is *Black Boy*. Yet in this excerpt Wright is not a boy. He is a young working man almost 19 years old with adult responsibilities. Why, then, did Wright choose to call his book *Black Boy* rather than *Black Man*? Explain the point Wright was trying to make. How does this title fit in with Wright's theme of racism and its devastating impact on human lives?

2. Define racism and give three examples of racism from this excerpt.

3. Read each statement carefully, decide if it is true or false according to the reading, and then write *T* (true) or *F* (false) on the line in front of the statement.

a. _____ H. L. Mencken was hated by many white southerners because of his race.

b. _____ Wright was curious about what Mencken had written that made some white people so angry.

c. _____ Reading opened up the world for Wright and made him more satisfied with his life and aware of its possibilites.

d. _____ Reading opened up the world for Wright and made him frustrated because he was now more aware of the limitations of his life.

e. _____ At the end of the passage, it was not clear where Wright's reading would lead him.

4. Write the word *racism* on a piece of paper. Then write down as many words and phrases as you can think of that are associated with this word in your mind. After you finish, compare your list of words with the lists of others in your group. What are the similarities and differences in your lists? What words would you like to add to your list now?

5. What is the main problem or issue in this reading that causes the writer to feel a conflict? Do you believe the writer will be able to resolve the conflict? Why or why not? Be as specific as possible in your answer.

2.8
Vocabulary Study

Study the italicized words and phrases in their contexts and guess at their meanings. Write your guess in the first blank. Then look up the word or phrase in your dictionary and write the definition in the second blank.

1 and 2. (paragraph 1) I came finally to the editorial page and saw an article dealing with one H. L. Mencken. I knew by *hearsay* that he was the editor of the *American Mercury*, but aside from that I knew nothing about him. The article was a furious *denunciation* of Mencken, concluding with one, hot, short sentence: Mencken is a fool.

hearsay

a. (guess) _____

b. (dictionary) _____

denunciation

a. (guess) _____

b. (dictionary) _____

3 and **4.** (paragraph 2) Then what ideas did Mencken hold that made a newspaper like the *Commercial Appeal castigate* him publicly? Undoubtedly he must be *advocating* ideas that the South did not like.

castigate

a. (guess) _____

b. (dictionary) _____

advocating

a. (guess) _____

b. (dictionary) _____

5. (paragraph 3) There was a huge library near the riverfront, but I knew that Negroes were not allowed to *patronize* its shelves any more than they were the parks and playgrounds of the city.

a. (guess) _____

b. (dictionary) _____

6. (paragraph 27) I turned from him and he called me back. He stared at me *quizzically.*

a. (guess) _____

b. (dictionary) _____

7. (paragraph 61) I pictured the man as a raging demon, slashing with his pen, consumed with hate, denouncing everything American, *extolling* everything European or German, laughing at the weaknesses of people, mocking God, authority.

a. (guess) _____

b. (dictionary) _____

8. (paragraph 65) I had always felt a vast distance separating me from the boss, and now I felt closer to him, though still distant. I felt now that I knew him, that I could feel the very limits of his narrow life. And this had happened because I had read a novel about a *mythical* man called George F. Babbitt.

a. (guess) _____

b. (dictionary) _____

9. (paragraph 74) I now knew what being a Negro meant. I could endure the hunger. I had learned to live with hate. But to feel that there were feelings *denied* me, that the very breath of life itself was beyond my reach, that more than anything else hurt, wounded me. I had a new hunger.

a. (guess) _____

b. (dictionary) _____

10. (paragraph 75) In *buoying* me up, reading also cast me down, made me see what was possible, what I had missed.

a. (guess) _____

b. (dictionary) _____

2.9

Paragraph Organization and Development

It is important to understand how information is presented in a well-organized and developed paragraph. Study the example below. How do you know what order the sentences follow? Consider both syntactic (structure) and semantic (meaning) clues.

Example:

a. ___1___ One morning I paused before the Catholic fellow's desk.

b. ___5___ He looked at me suspiciously. "My card is full most of the time."

c. ___2___ "What is it?"

d. ___3___ "I want to ask you a favor," I whispered to him.

e. ___4___ "I want to read. I can't get books from the library. I wonder if you'd let me use your card?"

Look at the sentences below and determine their order. Take a pencil and lightly mark every word or punctuation mark that gave you a clue.

a. _____ One morning I arrived early at work and went into the bank lobby where the Negro porter was mopping.

b. _____ The article was a furious denunciation of Mencken, concluding with one, hot, short sentence:

c. _____ I came finally to the editorial page and saw an article dealing with one H. L. Mencken.

d. _____ Mencken is a fool.

e. _____ I stood at a counter and picked up the Memphis *Commercial Appeal* and began my free reading of the press.

f. _____ I knew by hearsay that he was the editor of the *American Mercury*, but aside from that I knew nothing about him.

2.10
Application, Critical Evaluation, and Synthesis

Choose one or more topics to discuss with your small group or to write about.

1. The passage you have just read from *Black Boy* begins with a seemingly ordinary event: Wright (the narrator) happens to read an editorial in a white newspaper in which one white person furiously denounces and condemns another white, H. L. Mencken, and calls him a fool because of something Mencken has written that criticizes the South. This seemingly ordinary event, however, becomes a critical event in Wright's life, meaning that it becomes the first step in his transformation. Explain how and why this event changed Wright's life. First, discuss his life before the transforming experience. Then discuss how the experience led him to secretly scheme to get access to a library card. Explain the consequences of his getting the card and how his life began to unfold in a new direction. Comment on how his reading changed him mentally and emotionally. Finally, speculate on how Wright's life must have developed after this passage ends. Conclude with a paragraph about the power of reading to transform lives. Throughout your essay, try to give specific examples and details to explain your points and to make your meaning clear.

2. We have all had critical events in our lives that have affected and changed us greatly. Describe a critical event in your life. Discuss this event fully and explain its significance to you. Go on to show how your life changed and how you started to become a different person. Be sure to give specific examples and details of the change to make your meaning clear to your reader.

3. *Black Boy* is not only about growing up and the passage from childhood to adulthood; it is also about growing up in a segregated society where the separation between races meant that African Americans (or Negroes as Wright calls them) were denied equal opportunity. Look up *segregation* in an encyclopedia (see Expansion section, 4.7.2, p. 244). Summarize the information and then write about some of the examples and consequences of segregation that you notice in this excerpt. Be sure to note when segregation legally ended in the United States.

4. Time and place strongly affect what happens in both fiction and nonfiction. Explain the importance of time and place in "The Library Card." Why does the reader need to know something about American history to understand this passage? If you were explaining the meaning of this passage to someone from another culture, what would you say? What background would the person need to fully appreciate the meaning of the passage?

5. Discrimination is unfortunately a part of daily life for many people. Most of us have faced discrimination for race, ethnic background, religion, social class, or gender reasons at some point in our lives. Tell about a time when you were a victim of discrimination. Describe the situation in detail. What happened? Where, when, how, and why did the situation occur? How did you feel? What did you do about the situation? What, if anything, did you learn from the experience?

CHAPTER THREE

The Art of Reading

L in Yu-T'ang (1895–1976) was born in China. However, he attended Harvard University and the University of Leipzig in the West. He has written both nonfiction and novels explaining modern China to readers from other cultural backgrounds. A highly respected educator and writer, he taught at Peking National University for many years and was chancellor of Nanyang University in Singapore, as well as the head of the Arts division of UNESCO in 1948 and 1949. His best known books are *My Country and My People* and *The Importance of Understanding,* from which the following selection was taken. Reprinted with permission of Ayer Company Publishers, Inc.

3.1

First Reading

Read this selection quickly for the main ideas. Do *not* stop to look up words in your dictionary.

1 Reading or the enjoyment of books has always been regarded among the charms of a cultured life and is respected and envied by those who rarely give themselves that privilege. This is easy to understand when we compare the difference between the life of a man who does no reading and that of a man who does.[1] The man who has not the habit of reading is imprisoned in his immediate world, in respect to time and space. His life falls into a set routine; he is limited to contact and conversation with a few friends and acquaintances, and he sees only what happens in his immediate neighborhood. From this prison there is no escape. But the moment he takes up a book, he immediately enters a different world, and if it is a good book, he is immediately put in touch with one of the best talkers of the world. This talker leads him on and carries him into a different country or a different age, or unburdens to him some of his personal regrets, or discusses with him some special line or aspect of life that the reader knows nothing about. An ancient author puts him in communion with a dead spirit of long ago, and as he reads along, he begins to imagine what that ancient author

---

1. Before the mid-1970s, writers used "man" to refer to both men and women and masculine pronouns to refer to both genders. Lin Yu-T'ang is referring to both men and women in the masculine in this passage as was customary at the time this piece was written. As consciousness about women's equality increased in the 1970s, writers began to avoid the masculine to represent both genders either by using "people" and plural pronouns (e.g., they, their, them) or, in the singular, using "person" and both masculine and feminine pronouns (e.g., he and she, his and her, him and her).

219

looked like and what type of person he was. Both Mencius and Ssema Ch'ien, China's greatest historian, have expressed the same idea. Now to be able to live two hours out of twelve in a different world and take one's thoughts off the claims of the immediate present is, of course, a privilege to be envied by people shut up in their bodily prison. Such a change of environment is really similar to travel in its psychological effect.

2   But there is more to it than this. The reader is always carried away into a world of thought and reflection. Even if it is a book about physical events, there is a difference between seeing such events in person or living through them, and reading about them in books, for then the events always assume the quality of the spectacle and the reader becomes a detached spectator. The best reading is therefore that which leads us into this contemplative mood, and not that which is merely occupied with the report of events. The tremendous amount of time spent on newspapers I regard as not reading at all, for the average readers of papers are mainly concerned with getting reports about events and happenings without contemplative value.

3   The best formula for the object of reading, in my opinion, was stated by Huang Shanku, a Sung poet and friend of Su Tungp'o. He said, "A scholar who hasn't read anything for three days feels that his tal*k has no flavor* (becomes insipid), *and his own face becomes hateful to look at* (in the mirror)." What he means, of course, is that reading gives a man a certain charm and flavor, which is the entire object of reading, and only reading with this object can be called an art. One doesn't read to "improve one's mind," because when one begins to think of improving his mind, all the pleasure of reading is gone. He is the type of person who says to himself: "I must read Shakespeare, and I must read Sophocles, and I must read the entire Five-foot Shelf of Dr. Eliot, so I can become an educated man." I'm sure that man will never become educated. He will force himself one evening to read Shakespeare's Hamlet and come away, as if from a bad dream, with no greater benefit than that he is able to say that he had "read" Hamlet. Anyone who reads a book with a sense of obligation does not understand the art of reading. This type of reading with a business purpose is in no way different from a senator's reading up on files and reports before he makes a speech. It is asking for business advice and information, and not reading at all.

4   Reading for the cultivation of personal charm of appearance and flavor in speech is then, according to Huang, the only admissible kind of reading. This charm of appearance must evidently be interpreted as something other than physical beauty. What Huang means by "hateful to look at" is not physical ugliness. There are ugly faces that have a fascinating charm and beautiful faces that are insipid to look at. I have among my Chinese friends one whose head is shaped like a bomb and yet who is nevertheless always a pleasure to see. The most beautiful face among Western authors, so far as I have seen them in pictures, was that of G. K. Chesterton. There was such a diabolical conglomeration of mustache, glasses, fairly bushy eyebrows and knitted lines where the eyebrows met. One felt there were a vast number of ideas playing about inside that forehead, ready at any time to burst out

from those quizzically penetrating eyes. That is what Huang would call a beautiful face, a face not made up by powder and rouge, but by the sheer force of thinking. As for flavor of speech, it all depends on one's way of reading. Whether one has "flavor" or not in his talk, depends on his method of reading. If a reader gets the flavor of books, he will show that flavor in his conversations, and if he has flavor in his conversations, he cannot help also having a flavor in his writing.

5 Hence I consider flavor or taste as the key to all reading. It necessarily follows that taste is selective and individual, like the taste for food. The most hygienic way of eating is, after all, eating what one likes, for then one is sure of his digestion. In reading as in eating, what is one man's meat may be another's poison. A teacher cannot force his pupils to like what he likes in reading, and a parent cannot expect his children to have the same tastes as himself. And if the reader has no taste for what he reads, all the time is wasted. As Yuan Chunglang says, "You can leave the books that you don't like alone, *and let other people read them.*"

6 There can be, therefore, no books that one absolutely must read. For our intellectual interests grow like a tree or flow like a river. So long as there is proper sap, the tree will grow anyhow, and so long as there is fresh current from the spring, the water will flow. When water strikes a granite cliff, it just goes around it; when it finds itself in a pleasant low valley, it stops and meanders there a while; when it finds itself in a deep mountain pond, it is content to stay there; when it finds itself traveling over rapids, it hurries forward. Thus, without any effort or determined aim, it is sure of reaching the sea some day. There are no books in this world that everybody must read, but only books that a person must read at a certain time in a given place under given circumstances and at a given period of his life. I rather think that reading, like matrimony, is determined by fate or *yinyuan*. Even if there is a certain book that everyone must read, like the Bible, there is a time for it. When one's thoughts and experience have not reached a certain point for reading a masterpiece, the masterpiece will leave only a bad flavor on his palate. Confucius said, "When one is fifty, one may read the *Book of Changes*," which means that one should not read it at forty-five. The extremely mild flavor of Confucius' own sayings in the *Analects* and his mature wisdom cannot be appreciated until one becomes mature himself.

7 I regard the discovery of one's favorite author as the most critical event in one's intellectual development. There is such a thing as the affinity of spirits, and among the authors of ancient and modern times, one must try to find an author whose spirit is akin with his own. Only in this way can one get any real good out of reading. One has to be independent and search out his masters. Who is one's favorite author, no one can tell, probably not even the man himself. It is like love at first sight. The reader cannot be told to love this one or that one, but when he has found the author he loves, he knows it himself by a kind of instinct. We have such famous cases of discoveries of authors. Scholars seem to have lived in different ages, separated by centuries, and yet their modes of thinking and feeling were so akin that

their coming together across the pages of a book was like a person finding his own image. In Chinese phraseology, we speak of these kindred spirits as reincarnations of the same soul, as Su Tungp'o was said to be a reincarnation of Chuangtse or T'ao Yuanming, and Yuan Chunglang was said to be the reincarnation of Su Tungp'o. Su Tungp'o said that when he first read Chuangtse, he felt as if all the time since his childhood he had been thinking the same things and taking the same views himself. When Yuan Chunglang discovered one night Hsu Wench'ang, a contemporary unknown to him, in a small book of poems, he jumped out of bed and shouted to his friend, and his friend began to read it and shout in turn, and then they both read and shouted again until their servant was completely puzzled. George Eliot described her first reading of Rousseau as an electric shock. Nietzsche felt the same thing about Schopenhauer, but Schopenhauer was a peevish master and Nietzsche was a violent-tempered pupil, and it was natural that the pupil later rebelled against the teacher.

8   It is only this kind of reading, this discovery of one's favorite author, that will do one any good at all. Like a man falling in love with his sweetheart at first sight, everything is right. She is of the right height, has the right face, the right color of hair, the right quality of voice and the right way of speaking and smiling. This author is just right for him; his style, his taste, his point of view, his mode of thinking, are all right. And then the reader proceeds to devour every word and every line that the author writes, and because there is a spiritual affinity, he absorbs and readily digests everything. The author has cast a spell over him, and he is glad to be under the spell, and in time his own voice and manner and way of smiling and way of talking become like the author's own. Thus he truly steeps himself in his literary lover and derives from these books sustenance for his soul. After a few years, the spell is over and he grows a little tired of this lover and seeks for new literary lovers, and after he has had three or four lovers and completely eaten them up, he emerges as an author himself. There are many readers who never fall in love, like many young men and women who flirt around and are incapable of forming a deep attachment to a particular person. They can read any and all authors, and they never amount to anything.

9   Such a conception of the art of reading completely precludes the idea of reading as a duty or as an obligation. In China, one often encourages students to "study bitterly." There was a famous scholar who studied bitterly and who stuck an awl[2] in his calf when he fell asleep while studying at night. There was another scholar who had a maid stand by his side as he was studying at night, to wake him up every time he fell asleep. This was nonsensical. If one has a book lying before him and falls asleep while some wise ancient author is talking to him, he should just go to bed. No amount of sticking an awl in his calf or of shaking him up by a maid will do him any good. Such a man has lost all sense of pleasure of reading. Scholars who

---

2. An **awl** is a small, sharply pointed tool used to make holes in leather.

are worth anything at all never know what is called "a hard grind" or what "bitter study" means. They merely love books and read on because they cannot help themselves.

10 What, then is the true art of reading? The simple answer is to just take up a book and read when the mood comes. To be thoroughly enjoyed, reading must be entirely spontaneous.

Number of words: 2,259

Reading Times		Reading Speed
1st reading _____ minutes		10 minutes = 226 wpm
3rd reading _____ minutes		9 minutes = 251 wpm
		8 minutes = 282 wpm
		7 minutes = 323 wpm
		6 minutes = 377 wpm

3.2
Second Reading

Go back and read the passage again. Take as much time as you need. Look up some of the unfamiliar words in the glossary at the end of the book or in your dictionary if you wish.

3.3
Third Reading

Read the passage quickly a third time. Concentrate on understanding the main ideas of the passage and the meanings of new vocabulary words in the contexts in which they appear.

3.4
Reader Response

In order to explore your response to this reading, write for 15 minutes about anything that interested you in this passage. You may wish to write about your reactions to some of the themes and ideas presented here—or you may wish to disagree with something in the passage. Try to explore your *own thoughts and feelings* as much as possible. Do *not* merely summarize or restate the ideas in this passage.

3.5
Response Sharing

Read your response to two or three other people in your class. Listen carefully to what the others have written. After you have discussed each other's responses, talk about other points of interest in the passage.

3.6
Identifying Main Ideas

Working with the same small group, make a list of the main ideas in this passage. Be sure to state the main ideas in your own words. Don't just copy sentences directly from the text. Think carefully about what the writer is trying to tell you.

3.7
Analyzing the Text

Work with your group members on this exercise. Discuss the answers carefully, particularly if there are disagreements among members of your group. In some cases there may be more than one possible interpretation.

1. How does the title relate to the passage? What point is the author making with this title?

2. Lin Yu-T'ang makes the point that seeing or living through an event is different from reading about the event. What is the difference as he sees it? What do you think he means by the "contemplative mood"? What is the role of the contemplative mood in reading?

3. Read each statement carefully, decide if it is true or false according to this article, and then write *T* (true) or *F* (false) on the line in front of the statement.

   a. _____ According to this passage, the main reason to read is to acquire information and to learn about events in the world.

   b. _____ The world is a prison for the person who does not read, according to this writer.

   c. _____ There are certain books everyone should read, according to this passage.

   d. _____ What one reads should depend upon one's tastes.

   e. _____ Reading should not be considered a duty or obligation, according to this passage.

4. Read the following sentences and explain what they mean:

   a. "The man who has not the habit of reading is imprisoned in his immediate world in regard to time and space. . . . From this prison there is no escape."

   b. "One doesn't read to 'improve one's mind,' because when one begins to think of improving his mind, all the pleasure of reading is gone."

   c. "Hence I consider flavor or taste as the key to all reading."

   d. "I regard the discovery of one's favorite author as the most critical event in one's intellectual development."

   e. "To be thoroughly enjoyed, reading must be entirely spontaneous."

5. Rewrite the following passage to avoid using the masculine to refer to both men and women. Consider different options and think about the advantages and disadvantages of each option.

The man who has not the habit of reading is imprioned in his immediate world, in respect to time and space. His life falls into a set routine; he is limited to contact and conversation with a few friends and acquaintances, and he sees only what happens in his immediate neighborhood.

3.8
Vocabulary Study

Study the italicized words and phrases in their contexts and guess at their meanings. Write your guess in the first blank. Then look up the word or phrase in your dictionary and write the definition in the second blank.

1 and 2. (paragraph 1) This talker leads him on and carries him into a different country or a different age, or *unburdens* to him some of his personal regrets, or discusses with him some special line or *aspect* of life that the reader knows nothing about.

unburdens

a. (guess) _____

b. (dictionary) _____

aspect

a. (guess) _____

b. (dictionary) _____

3 and 4. (paragraph 1) An *ancient* author puts him in *communion* with a dead spirit of long ago, and as he reads along, he begins to imagine what that ancient author looked like and what type of person he was.

ancient

a. (guess) _____

b. (dictionary) _____

communion

a. (guess) _____

b. (dictionary) _____

5, 6, and **7.** (paragraph 2) The reader is always carried away into a world of thought and *reflection*. Even if it is a book about physical events, there is a difference between seeing such events in person or living through them, and reading about them in books, for then the events always *assume* the quality of the spectacle and the reader becomes a *detached* spectator.

reflection

a. (guess) _____

b. (dictionary) _____

assume

a. (guess) _____

b. (dictionary) _____

detached

a. (guess) _____

b. (dictionary) _____

8. (paragraph 3) Anyone who reads a book with a sense of *obligation* does not understand the art of reading.

a. (guess) _____

b. (dictionary) _____

9 and **10.** (paragraph 4) The most beautiful face among Western authors, so far as I have seen them in pictures, was that of G. K. Chesterton. There was such a *diabolical conglomeration* of mustache, glasses, fairly bushy eyebrows and knitted lines where the eyebrows met.

diabolical

a. (guess) _____

b. (dictionary) _____

conglomeration

a. (guess) _____

b. (dictionary) _____

3.9
Paragraph Organization and Development

It is important in both reading and writing to understand how information is presented in a well-organized and developed paragraph. Study the example below. How can you figure out what order the sentences follow? Consider both syntactic (structure) and semantic (meaning) clues.

Example:

a. __1__   Reading or the enjoyment of books has always been regarded among the charms of a cultured life and is respected and envied by those who rarely give themselves that privilege.

b. ___3___ The man who has not the habit of reading is imprisoned in his immediate world, in respect to time and space.

c. ___2___ This is easy to understand when we compare the difference between the life of a man who does no reading and that of a man who does.

d. ___4___ His life falls into a set routine; he is limited to contact and conversation with a few friends and acquaintances, and he sees only what happens in his immediate neighborhood.

Study the sentences below and determine their order. With a pencil, lightly mark every word or punctuation mark that gave you a clue.

a. _____ What he means, of course, is that reading gives a man a certain charm and flavor, which is the entire object of reading, and only reading with this object can be called an art.

b. _____ He said, "A scholar who hasn't read anything for three days feels that his talk has no flavor (becomes insipid), *and his own face becomes hateful to look at* (in the mirror)."

c. _____ One doesn't read to "improve one's mind," because when one begins to think of improving his mind, all the pleasure of reading is gone.

d. _____ The best formula for the object of reading, in my opinion, was stated by Huang Shanku, a Sung poet and friend of Su Tungp'o.

3.10
Application, Critical Evaluation, and Synthesis

Choose one or more topics to discuss with your small group or to write about.

1. Lin Yu-T'ang argues that reading is an art. He states, "Reading or the enjoyment of books has always been regarded among the charms of a cultured life and is respected and envied by those who rarely give themselves that privilege." Do you think reading is an art or a skill or, perhaps, both? Do you think it is possible to be cultured without being a reader? What does it mean to be cultured and what does that have to do with reading?

2. Lin Yu-T'ang claims that finding one's favorite author is critically important. He goes on to say, "It is only this kind of reading, this discovery of one's favorite author, that will do one any good at all. Like a man falling in love with his sweetheart at first sight, everything is right." Have you had the experience of falling in love with an author? If so, who was the author and what was the book that attracted you to this writer? What appealed to you? How long did your infatuation or love affair with this author continue?

3. Lin Yu-T'ang insists that no one should be required to read a particular book ("There can be, therefore, no books that one absolutely must read.") This is a controversial statement, and many educators, particularly literature teachers, would disagree. What do you think? Should reading be entirely spontaneous and up to the individual or should a person be required to read certain books? Explain your point of view clearly and give examples to support your main ideas.

4. This unit is entitled *Opening Up the Mind*. Helen Keller, Richard Wright, and Lin Yu-T'ang write about some of the same themes, and yet each has his or her own critically important slant. What are the similarities and differences among these writers? How would you compare and contrast their ideas? What are the main points each is making? Which writer has the most appeal for you? Why?

AT THE END OF EVERY UNIT, YOU ARE INVITED TO TURN TO THE EXPANSION SECTION BEGINNING ON PAGE 233. THIS SECTION CONCENTRATES ON THE FUNDAMENTALS OF LIBRARY RESEARCH AND REPORT WRITING.

Vocabulary Games

H ere is a chance to review some of the vocabulary you have encountered in this unit. After you finish the game quizzes on your own, discuss
your answers with your group members. You may use your dictionary to look up
items to resolve disagreements. Scoring: 5 points for each correct answer.

Synonyms

Read each passage carefully and then draw a circle around the word or phrase
that means the same thing (or almost the same thing) as the italicized word or
phrase. If a word or phrase has more than one meaning, choose the meaning
that fits the context in the passage.

Example: She paused momentarily as she *groped for* words to express her
surprise at his sudden outburst.

a. searched hesitantly for   b. softly touched   c. grabbed

Passage One

The children quickly saw the relationships between the *tangible* objects on the
table and the *concept* of number. The teacher *seized* the opportunity to encourage them to *persist* at the number games. They were enjoying themselves so
much that they were not at all *conscious* of the difficulty of the task.

1. *tangible*

　　a. material   b. handmade   c. soft feeling

2. *concept*

　　a. beginning   b. abstract idea   c. picture

3. *seized*

　　a. grabbed   b. stopped   c. took advantage of

4. *persist*

　　a. continue   b. play   c. work

5. *conscious*

　　a. alert   b. awake   c. aware

Passage Two

At first Helen Keller was *puzzled* and *frustrated* by her teacher's lessons, but gradually she reported that the *dense* fog in her mind began to lift, and she began to *apprehend* the remarkable idea that everything has a name. There were still enormous obstacles before her, but from this moment on, she began to *acquire* a new level of language.

6. *puzzled*

a. offended   b. confused   c. pleased

7. *frustrated*

a. challenged (by something)   b. curious (about something)
c. irritated at being unable to succeed (at something)

8. *dense*

a. dark   b. moist   c. thick

9. *apprehend*

a. understand   b. catch   c. take

10. *acquire*

a. buy   b. ask about (something)   c. attain

Antonyms

Antonyms are words that have opposite meanings, e.g., cold-hot; tall-short; dark-light. Read each passage carefully and then draw a circle around the word or phrase that means the opposite (or almost the opposite) of the italicized word or phrase. If a word or phrase has more than one meaning, choose the meaning that fits the context in the passage.

Example: He was full of *despair* over the terrible news.

a. anguish   b. anger   (c. pleasure)

[*Pleasure* is the antonym of *despair*.]

Passage Three

Is language *innate* in humans or is it developed entirely through life experience? It is true that small children *imitate* the speech of others, but they also *create* their own speech. They quickly develop a sense of what is *appropriate* or inappropriate in a particular situation. Language is certainly very *complex*; yet children are born knowing how to learn it.

11. *innate*

a. inborn   b. developed through the environment   c. original

12. *imitate*

    a. create   b. comprehend   c. mimic

13. *create*

    a. make   b. destroy   c. invent

14. *appropriate*

    a. correct   b. wrong   c. right

15. *complex*

    a. hard to learn   b. complicated   c. simple

Logical Relationships

Look at the first pair of words, determine the relationship between them (are they synonyms or antonyms?). Then circle the word or phrase that fills in the blank to logically make a similar type of relationship.

    Example: happy : sad = joy : _____

            (a. sorrow)   b. laughter   c. tears

            [*Happy* is related to *sad* in the same way *joy* is related to *sorrow*.]

16. apprehend : understand = perceive : _____

    a. decide   b. remember   c. recognize

[*Apprehend* is related to *understand* in the same way as *perceive* is related to _____.]

17. augment : add = demonstrate : _____

    a. understand   b. show   c. plan

18. inadequate : sufficient: gentle : _____

    a. rough   b. kind   c. patient

[*Hint: Inadequate* and *sufficient* are antonyms.]

19. engrave : write = puzzle : _____

    a. enlighten   b. clarify   c. mystify

20. consciousness : awareness = barriers : _____

    a. openings   b. obstacles   c. gates

SCORE: Number of correct answers _____ × **5** = _____

Developing Research
and Writing Skills

When you finish each unit, you should turn to this section if you want to work more on writing and learn how to do basic library research for a research paper. We suggest that you read through this entire section first to give yourself an overview. After that, you should refer to various topics as needed. For example, you will probably need to review the Getting Started section and the Library Research topic several times before you understand all of the points mentioned. You may need several study sessions to learn the uses of direct quotation and paraphrasing and the differences between them. Finally, use this section as a resource manual; refer to various parts of it from time to time to help you learn how to do process writing, basic library research, and write research papers.

Contents

4.1
Choosing a Writing Topic

At the end of every chapter we give you ideas for topics you could write about. These are only suggestions, and you may wish to make up your own writing topics from time to time. Your teacher and/or your group members may help you select a topic sometimes. We suggest that you try if possible to choose or make up a topic that is interesting to you because it will be easier for you to write about something you are interested in.

4.2
Getting Started

Once you have chosen a topic, you obviously have to get started writing. Getting started is the hardest part of writing for most people. However, there are ways of making this task easier, and we would like to introduce you to some of these techniques.

We suggest that you try all of the techniques a few times until you find the one or ones that help you the most. All of these techniques are useful, but you may find one of them works better than another for helping you develop ideas on a certain topic.

1. Brainstorming

Brainstorming helps you get ideas for your writing project. Here is how you do it. First, you take a pen or pencil and a piece of paper (scrap paper is fine for this task) and write your topic on your paper. Read your topic over a few times to yourself. Then let your mind wander. Write down any words or phrases that come to your mind in connection with your topic. Here's an example. Let's suppose your general topic is nutrition. First, write your topic on your paper as we suggested. And then jot down (write down quickly) any ideas that come to mind related to your topic.

nutrition	*fat*	*bulimia*
eating well	*sugars*	*pressure to be thin*
vitamins	*fruits*	*anxiety*
minerals	*vegetables*	*social pressures*
whole grains	*eating disorders*	
carbohydrates	*anorexia*	

Brainstorming with other people: This is an excellent group activity if you are working with others on developing a writing or discussion project. How do you brainstorm with a group? First, choose one person to be the group recorder. This person will be in charge of writing down any words or phrases group members suggest. This can be done on paper, on a blackboard, or on a flip-chart.

Making connections: After you brainstorm, the next step is to make connections between your ideas. Look at your list. Ask yourself (or the group members, if you are working with a group) these questions:

   a. Is anything on this list related to anything else on this list? If yes, draw a line between those ideas to connect them.

nutrition	fat	bulimia
eating well	sugars	pressure to be thin
vitamins	fruits	anxiety
minerals	vegetables	social pressures
whole grains	eating disorders	
carbohydrates	anorexia	

   b. As you make connections, do you suddenly think of something new, something that you didn't have on your list? Good! Write it in now anywhere on the list. Read over the items on your list several times and see if there are any more additions you want to make.

   c. Is there anything you want to leave out? Is there something on your list that you now think is not really closely related to your topic? What do you do? Cross it out. Read over your list again and cross out any other items that are not interesting to you or are not closely related to your topic.

   d. Can you put your ideas in an order? Write "1" by the idea you want to write about first, "2" by the idea you want to write about second, etc.

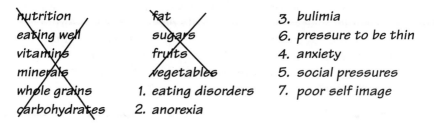

~~nutrition~~	~~fat~~	3. bulimia
~~eating well~~	~~sugars~~	6. pressure to be thin
~~vitamins~~	~~fruits~~	4. anxiety
~~minerals~~	~~vegetables~~	5. social pressures
~~whole grains~~	1. eating disorders	7. poor self image
~~carbohydrates~~	2. anorexia	

Making a list

We have mentioned making a list above, but in fact, there are several ways to make a list as you are brainstorming. One technique is not necessarily better than another, but one may prove more useful to you under certain circumstances. Again, we suggest you experiment with different techniques.

Here are examples of the most common listing techniques. The writer is listing the advantages and disadvantages of having a national school curriculum.

A National School Curriculum	
Advantages	*Disadvantages*
• common standards	• discourages creativity
• clear goals	• discourages innovation
• society understands standards	• may discriminate against certain groups
• makes changing schools easier	• makes it difficult to change the curriculum as needed to keep up with society
• employers understand diploma	• standards don't guarantee value
• promotes clarity of vision	• promotes "gray" vision

A list of this kind is especially useful for exploring issues when you are trying to look at two sides of a subject—for example, the advantages and disadvantages of something, reasons for doing and not doing something.

Mapping and clustering

Another useful listing technique is mapping or clustering. Instead of making a linear list, as illustrated above, you start by writing your topic in the center of your page in a box. Then, as you brainstorm for ideas, you write your ideas around the topic. As you write one idea down, you may think of another idea related to it, so you could write this second idea close to the first idea in a cluster (a group of ideas).

Here is an example of a map with some clusters. The topic is conformity, and it is written in the box in the middle of the page.

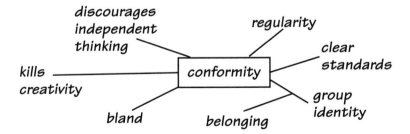

Mapping and clustering can be useful for helping you see relationships between ideas.

Mapping can be very useful for showing important events or ideas in relation to each other. In the example below, a student has drawn a map of her life. We can easily see both the high points and low points of her life from this map; we can also see which events stand out in some way for her.

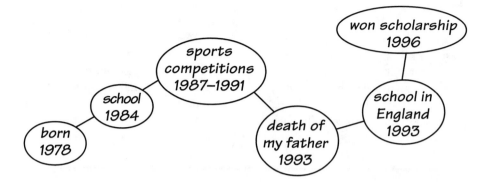

If you are telling a story or recounting an experience, mapping can help you organize the experience in order. Additionally, it will help you see which events are the most important and thus need to be emphasized in the telling or writing.

It doesn't matter what form your brainstorming takes—linear lists, mapping, clustering— and it doesn't matter what you make your notes on—a clean piece of paper, the back of an old envelope, a paper napkin, any kind of scrap paper. This is just an activity for your eyes only—to help you explore your own thoughts and feelings relating to the topic as the first step in writing about the topic.

2. *Freewriting*

Another way to get started and explore your ideas on a topic is to do some freewriting at the beginning. You can do freewriting after or in place of brainstorming.

How do you freewrite? You write for 10–15 minutes about your topic. *You should write anything that comes into your mind. If nothing comes into your mind, just write "I can't think of anything," but keep on writing. Don't stop writing. Keep your pen or pencil moving across your paper for the entire time.*

When you are freewriting, don't think about grammar, spelling, or punctuation. Just write! And don't stop writing until your time is up.

After you finish, read over what you have written. Draw a line under anything that seems interesting to you—a sentence or two, maybe just a phrase. You can freewrite again beginning with this *kernel* (the part you underlined). You can continue to freewrite several times. Each time you freewrite, you bring your ideas on your topic more and more into focus.

Here is an example of freewriting. The writer (Isha) is freewriting on the topic of immigration. After she finished, she underlined the part she thought was the most important and interesting to her (the kernel). (Note: Grammar and spelling have not been corrected.)

> *Immigration. Immigrants often seek new opportunities in their new country, for example, better jobs and educational opportunities. Often they support themselves and send money back to their relatives at home.*

It's not all a bed of roses though. I mean they face problems as well. The customs and traditions in the new country are different from theirs. They may feel lonely and strange and different from everyone else. Everything is different and unusual for them, the language, the customs. It is hard to learn a new language, especialy if your an adult. Children can learn languages more easy because they go to school and play with other kids. <u>*Sometimes the childern get a little mixed up and grow apart from their parents. What I mean is children of immigrants try to be like the other children in school. They may forget their own traditions while they try to be like all the other kids. This may cause a problem in their family, a problem with their parents. They—the parents and the children—may grow apart. They may have problems communicating with each other. The children can lose their roots and not know about their traditions. They become like weeds growing in their shallow new soil and they can lose some of the beauty of their past.*</u>

Isha decided to do another freewriting, so she began by writing her kernel sentence on her paper. She freewrote for 10 minutes with this new beginning. As you can see, her second freewriting is more focused and directed than her first freewriting because she is beginning to discover what is interesting and important for her in this topic.

<u>*Sometimes the childern get a little mixed up and grow apart from their parents. What I mean is children of immigrants try to be like the other children in school. They may forget their own traditions while they try to be like all the other kids. This may cause a problem in their family, a problem with their parents. They—the parents and the children—may grow apart. They may have problems communicating with each other. The children can lose their roots and not know about their traditions.*</u> *In my high school, there were many children of immigrants, especially from Pakistan and India. Most of them kept the old traditions of their families while learning some of the new ones in their new country. They celebrated their Hindu or Muslim holidays, for example, and spoke their native language at home with their parents. Sometimes they wore saris and salwar kameez for special occasions, and sometimes they wore jeans and sweatshirts, like other American kids. They could fit into bothe worlds. Some of the immigrant children, however, did not want to keep the old traditions. They wanted to be "real" Americans (as they thought) and so they tried to deny their roots. They did not want to celebrate the holidays of their native country or to speak their native language. Some of them began to run around with a bad crowd and to smoke and drink and even use illegal drugs, all strongly forbidden by our religions. I knew a boy named Rashid, for example. He changed his name to Richy when we were about 14 and during the years we were in high school, I saw*

him become a lost person, a drifter, a person without a past and, I am
afraid, without a future. He was a lost soul, and I felt very sorry for him.
Richy was like a weed growing in shallow, poor soil.

Isha ended up writing a paper on the psychological importance of
biculturalism, a subject she had not thought much about before she did her two
freewritings. As you can see, the freewriting helped her to explore her ideas and
to focus them in an area of interest to her.

Finally, brainstorming and freewriting are techniques that help you get started.
And, remember, getting started is the tough part. Once you have started, the
writing process becomes much easier because you have some ideas to work with.

4.3
Choosing a Topic for Library Research

We suggest that you choose a topic related to a unit theme if you want to do a
library research project. This will allow you to use some of the ideas, information,
and vocabulary from the unit and thus build on knowledge you already have. The
following are suggestions for topics. However, feel free to come up with your own
topic related to the unit theme.

Unit 1: Leaving Home
Contributions immigrants make to society in _____
(a country or city)

Discrimination against immigrants

Living in two cultures

Brain drain through emigration

Disappointments immigrants face in _____ (a country)

_____ (your suggestion)

Unit 2: You Are What You Eat
Good nutrition in _____ (a country or region of a country)

World food production

New technologies in food production

Holiday foods in _____ (a country or region of a
country)

_____ (your suggestion)

Unit 3: Why Do People Behave the Way They Do?
The benefits of conformity
The drawbacks of conformity
Social behavior in _____ (a country or region of
a country)

How people learn to be good citizens in _____
(a country)
_____ (your suggestion)

Unit 4: The Brain and How It Works
Alzheimer's disease
How to remember names or numbers
How a stroke damages the brain
The speech center of the brain
Instinct and the brain
_____ (your suggestion)

Unit 5: Opening Up the Mind
A book that changed history
My favorite poem
A book (or movie) that changed my ideas about _____ (e.g., another culture, a particular event, a person or a group of people)
Education and democracy
The importance of free public education for all
_____ (your suggestion)

4.4
Exploring the Topic

Go back to the "Getting Started" section, **4.2**. Start off by brainstorming about your topic and then follow up by freewriting to get ideas for your writing project. Freewrite a couple of times, if possible, to bring your ideas into focus.

When you have finished your freewriting, be sure to pick out the most interesting part or parts. Underline these parts to use later. If possible, do a second freewrite to bring your ideas into focus more clearly. Start off with your kernel.

4.5
Narrowing the Topic

Now, think of some specific questions that you want to ask about your topic.

Example: Discrimination against immigrants

1. What are some reasons for discrimination against immigrants?
2. Who discriminates against immigrants? Why?
3. What are some examples of discrimination against immigrants?
4. Is discrimination related to the current economic and/or political situation?
5. Do all immigrants face discrimination or is it likely to be aimed at certain groups of immigrants? If so, which groups?

Example: Teenagers and Junk Food

1. What is junk food and why is it called junk food?

2. Why do teenagers in particular eat junk food even when they know it is not nutritious?

3. What are some examples of junk food that are popular around the world?

4. How does advertising promote junk food?

5. Do you think parents should not allow their children to eat junk food? Explain.

6. Does junk food have absolutely no nutrition?

7. Could a person sustain life on junk food only?

8. How is junk food related to culture?

You should try to think of at least six or seven questions, more if possible. You may not use all of your questions, but they can help you focus your ideas and provide a direction for your research.

One reason it is a good idea to have as many questions as possible is that you may not be able to find information on some of your questions when you are doing your research.

4.6
Developing the Topic

Look at your questions in **4.5** above. Which of your questions seem most interesting to you? Which most important?

1. Pick out three or four of your best questions. *Note:* You can change your questions at any time if you want to add new ones, combine old ones, restate them in a different way, etc. For example, you may suddenly realize that you have left a very important question out. You can just add it to your list at any time.

2. Now, think about where you could get information to answer each question.

Example: Contributions immigrants have made to society

What are some of the contributions immigrants have made to society in _____ (a country)?

Sources of information: Here are some of the places you could find information to answer this question.

- Library (books, magazines, newspapers)
- Other media (television, radio, movies)
- Personal observations and experiences
- Interviews

4.7
Doing Library Research

You will probably need to look up information in a library. If you have never done research in a library before, ask one of the librarians to help you. The librarian can tell you where to find information on your topic. Here are some of the library resources the librarian may suggest.

1. The card catalog

This is the place to look up books on your subject. If you look up your general subject area—for example, *family*—you can see whether there are books on your subject. *Note:* You may need to think of related words and look in several places in the card catalog to find your subject (e.g., *family, marriage, living arrangements, divorce, children, parents, parenting*).

Here are examples of cards from a card catalog. Cards are filed alphabetically according to author, book title, and general subject area. The first card is filed according to subject (in this case, *family*).

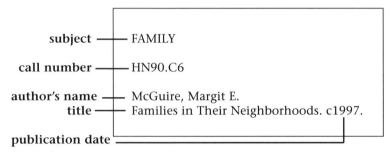

The next card is filed according to author. If you know the name of a particular author, you could look up books by that author by looking through the card catalog for the author's last name.

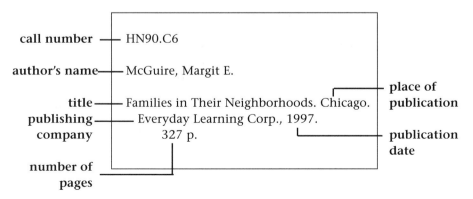

The next card is filed according to title.

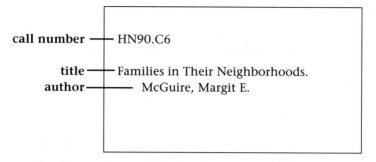

call number —— HN90.C6

title —— Families in Their Neighborhoods.
author —— McGuire, Margit E.

The *call number* tells you where to find the book in the library. Most libraries post a chart showing the location of books by call number areas. However, you can always ask the librarian to tell you where to find a book.

Note: In many libraries, card catalogs have now been put on computer. You can look things up in exactly the same way in a computerized catalog—alphabetically by author, book title, or general subject area. Ask a librarian to show you how to use the computer.

2. Encyclopedias

For certain types of subjects, you may be able to find general background information in an encyclopedia. For example, if you wanted a general historical overview of the family, you might look up *family* and *childrearing* in an encyclopedia. There are many specialized encyclopedias: art, music, sports, etc. You can usually get more detailed information in these specialized encyclopedias. *Note:* Encyclopedias provide a good starting point for research—but don't stop there. You need to get more specific information from other sources. Many encyclopedias include a bibliography (a list of related books) at the end of an article.

3. Readers' Guide to Periodical Literature

You can look up magazine articles on your subject here. *RGPL* is an alphabetical index by author and subject of periodicals (magazines) of general interest published in the United States, and it is arranged by year. For example, if you wanted to see what articles appeared in U.S. magazines in 1996 relating to *family,* you would look in the 1996 volume under "family." On p. 245 is a partial listing of what you would find.

The next step is to write down the articles that seem to be related to your subject. Be sure to write the name of the magazine and its date of publication:

article ＿＿ "Secrets of happy families"

author ＿＿ M. Scarf. *Ladies' Home Journal.* ＿＿＿＿＿ **magazine.**

issue and pages ＿＿ v112 p104+   S'95 ＿＿＿＿＿＿＿ **date**

FAMILY

See also

Aged—Family relationships
AIDS patients—Family relationships
Air pilots' families
Alzheimer's disease patients—Family relationships
Athletes' families
Aunts
Authors' families
Birth order
Black family
Cancer patients—Family relationships
Cardiacs—Family relationships
Celebrities' families
Childlessness
Children
Church work with families
Contract with the American Family
Cousins
Dictators' families
Divorce
Extended family
Family policy councils
Family values
Fathers
Fathers-in-law
Focus on the Family (Organization)
Foster home care
Golfers' families
Grandparents
Handicapped—Family relationships
Home
Home schooling
Households
Husbands
Kinship
Marriage
Married couples
Mentally handicapped—Family relationships
Mentally ill—Family relationships
Mothers
Mothers-in-law
Pan American Flight 103 disaster, 1988—Families of victims
Parent-child relationship
Parents
Patriarchy
Physicians' families
Presidents—Families
Public officers' families
Servicemen's families
Siblings
Sick—Family relationships
Single parent families
Stepparents and stepchildren
Stroke patients—Family relationships
TWA Flight 800 disaster, 1996—Families of victims
Uncles
Victims of crime—Families
Wives
Work and family

6 ways to strengthen your family. M. B. Pipher. il *Good Housekeeping* v222 p110-12 My '96
10 steps to a better-balanced life. N. Samalin. il *Working Mother* v19 p34-8 S '96
Anger and resentment can trigger discord [family relationships; views of Ethel Glenn] il *USA Today (Periodical)* v124 p3 Ap '96
BH&G kids. B. H. Palar. See issues of Better Homes and Gardens beginning May 1994
Biology and family, partners in crime [research by Adrian Raine] *Science News* v150 p11 Jl 6 '96
Can government save the family? [symposium] il *Policy Review* no79 p43-7 S/O '96
Candidates court family values vote [presidential race] J. W. Kennedy. il pors *Christianity Today* v40 p76-81 O 7 '96
The children of Beatrice Webb [H. R. Clinton's book It takes a village] A. Cockburn. *The Nation* v262 p9-10 F 12 '96
Disintegration of the family is the real root cause of violent crime. P. Fagan. il *USA Today (Periodical)* v124 p36-8 My '96
Family [celebrating the holidays] C. Tevis. il *Successful Farming* v93 p41 D '95
Family network. See issues of Better Homes and Gardens beginning May 1986

They look at the list of other subject categories ("See also"). You may find additional information in one of these subject categories.

Ask the librarian if the magazines you want are available in your library and, if so, how you may locate the ones you need. Remember, the *Readers' Guide to Periodical Literature* is a good place to look for current information on your topic.

Note: If you are doing research outside of the United States, ask the librarian if the library has some sort of guide to periodical literature.

4. *The New York Times Index*

This is a good place to look for newspaper articles on your topic. *Note:* If your library does not have this particular index, ask the librarian if they have another index of newspaper articles. Many major newspapers have such an index.

This is a sample partial entry under the category "Families and Family Life" of articles that appeared in *The New York Times* in the year 1995. (Some of these

---

FAMILIES AND FAMILY LIFE. See also
Adoptions
Africa, Ja 14
Births
Child Abuse
Child Custody and Support
Children and Youth
Christmas, D 21,24
Computers and Information Systems, D 25
Crime and Criminals, My 31
Domestic Violence
Drug Abuse and Traffic, My 7
Executives and Management, My 7, Je 18, Jl 23, S 24
Football, Je 18
Gambling, O 18
Immigration and Refugees, Je 5
Labor, Je 18
Magazines, O 1
Marriages
Medicine and Health, Mr 12
Murders and Attempted Murders, D 1
Presidential Election of 1996, Ap 20
Taxation, O 16
   About Men article by Steven Lewis on raising family of seven children notes profound differences between large and small families; drawing (M), Mr 12,VI,36:3
   Andrew J Cherlin Op-Ed article says stepmothers in America still labor under malevolent image, despite sociological changes, and that Mother's Day offers perfect moment to try to coin new term in English that replaces largely outdated stigma, My 14,IV,15:2
   Report by Population Council finds structure of family life, in rich and poor countries alike, is undergoing profound changes; says idea that family is stable and cohesive unit in which father serves as economic provider and mother as emotional care giver is myth; findings highlighted; graphs (M), My 30,A,5:1
   Interview with Dr James Dobson, founder of not-for-profit Focus on the Family organization that producrs syndicated radio program of same name heard on more than 2,000 radio stations nationwide; photos (M), My 30,A,12:1
   Sean Elder article on being a full-time father, whose wife works full time, and the perspective this gives him on part-time dads who have read all the books on fathering; says these 'Gentlemen Fathers' can be especially annoying when they deny that any father could possibly experience frustration or anything less than fun and fulfillment in raising a child; drawing (M), Je 11,VI,30:1

---

articles might be relevant if you were researching the subject, "the changing family.")

Again, ask the librarian where the articles you are interested in are located.

4.8
Taking Notes

As you look through encyclopedias, newspapers, books, and other sources, you will need to take notes. In every case, you will want to

- keep related information together. You should develop a way to keep your notes on each subject separate from notes on all other subjects.
- be able to organize and reorganize your information in different ways easily. Your notes, when they are all put together, should function as a very rough draft of your report.

There are several ways of taking notes. Two common ways are
- *For a short report or composition (two or three pages):*

  On separate pieces of paper, write topic headings, one topic per page (e.g., nutrition, causes of malnutrition, sources of calcium, the importance of iron in the diet).

  As you find information relating to a topic, make notes on the page that deals with that topic. Do not mix topics on one page. If you find that a topic becomes longer or more complex than you expected, divide it onto separate pages, one page for each new subtopic. For each note that you write down, remember to include the source where you got the information (the book/magazine title, author, date of publication, page number).

  When you are finished taking notes, number the points on each page in the order in which you want to use them in your report. You can then organize these pages into the general format of your report. The information on sources will be useful for quotations, footnotes, and references.

- *For longer reports and general note taking:*

  The most common way to take notes is on 3-by-5-inch index cards. Generally, you use one card per item of information. At the top of each card, write the topic and the source, then use the card to write out the information you want. (Rather than repeating the full information about the source on each card, you may want to keep a separate list with this information—title, author, date of publication—and just write the title and page number on each index card.)

  When you are finished with your research, you may have up to several hundred cards for a long report. You can then organize and reorganize these cards into the format for your report.

4.9
Quoting and Paraphrasing

When you are using information from books and articles, it is important to know how to quote and how to paraphrase.

1. Quoting

When you are using the *exact words* from a book or article, you must use quotation marks around the words to show that you are borrowing someone else's words.

Example:

"Principles are guidelines for human conduct that are proven to have enduring, permanent value."

Note: The quotation marks (") go at the beginning of the quoted passage and at the end of the quoted passage (". . ."). The final quotation mark goes after the period or other punctuation.

Goethe once said, "Things which matter most must never be at the mercy of things which matter least."

Directly quoting (using the exact words of someone else) can be quite effective if

- the information is very important
- the ideas are well-expressed
- the statement is made by an important person, for example, a recognized expert in the field or a highly placed official.

Example:

"A team of international scientists has recently discovered a jaw estimated to be 2.33 million years old in northern Ethiopia."

On the other hand, *do not quote:*

- *too much.* A very long quote (a page or more) is not effective. Just pick out the most important information to quote.
- *everyday, commonplace information.*
  "The weather in Belgium is often rainy. However, there were several sunny days in July."

- *too often.* Quotations become ineffective and meaningless if you have too many of them. Save them for special and important information.

2. Paraphrasing

When you restate an idea in your own words, you are paraphrasing. Notice the difference between quoting and paraphrasing in the following examples:

Quoting: John Chiu, president of Internet Productions, says, "We are teetering on the brink of a major technological shift, one that has the power to radically change the course of history."

Paraphrasing: According to John Chiu, president of Internet Productions, human beings are teetering on the brink of a major technological shift, one which has the power to radically change the course of history.

Quoting: Dr. Mejia said, "Sandra, you should take this medicine two times a day."

Paraphrasing: Dr. Mejia told Sandra to take the medicine two times a day.

Quoting should be saved for the special situations discussed in Section 1 above. In other situations, it is preferable to paraphrase—to restate an idea in your own words.

Here is another example of the difference between quoting and paraphrasing. You decide which is a quotation and which is a paraphrase.

Boutros Boutros-Ghali, secretary general of the United Nations, said in a recent speech, "Poverty is the main enemy of people around the world today."

Boutros Boutros-Ghali, secretary general of the United Nations, said in a recent speech that poverty is the main enemy of people around the world today.

4.10
Footnotes and Bibliography

You show the sources for your information in the footnotes and the bibliography.

1. Footnotes

Your reader often wants to know where you got your information or you may need to prove where your information came from, particularly if you are dealing with an unusual or surprising bit of information. You should always footnote important information and direct quotes. There are several ways to footnote. After the statement to be footnoted in your report, you write a number. The first footnote would be "1", the second one "2", etc. The number should be written slightly above the line.

Example:
The stock market went up more than 400 points between July and November.[1]

At the bottom of the page—or at the end of the paper on a special page—you cite the reference from which you got this information. In other words, you tell your reader where you got your information.

It is becoming common to cite references right in the text in parentheses,

Example:
R. Murray (1996, p. 18) argues that the hidden curriculum often has more power than the overt curriculum.

The advantage of this form of citation is that the reader has immediate and easy access to the source of the information without looking at the bottom of the page or at the end of the chapter or paper for a footnote. The complete reference information will appear in the bibliography or reference section.

Ask your teacher where you should put your notes (at the bottom of the page, at the end of the paper, or in parentheses in the text itself) and the note form you should use. Your teacher may refer you to a style sheet such as the *MLA [Modern Language Association] Style Sheet,* which will explain and illustrate how to write notes.

2. Bibliography

A bibliography is a complete list of all sources of information you have used in the report: books, articles, interviews. The bibliography (sometimes called *References*) goes at the end of your paper. At the top of the page, write the word BIBLIOGRAPHY (or REFERENCES). Then you should list all of your sources alphabetically by the author's last name.

Ask your teacher what bibliographic form you should use. Here is a sample of a partial bibliography.

Castillo, Camilla, and Juan Gonzales-Rios. "Latino or Hispanic? Political and Social Implications." *Language and Culture*, 19:26-31. March 1997.

Godard, Marc. *Patterns of Immigration in the 1990s.* London: The Blackstone Arms Press, 1997.

Prataps, Sangeeta. Personal interview. New Delhi, India, May 12, 1998.

4.11
Interviewing

In addition to doing library research on your topic, you can get information about your topic by interviewing people. Here are some important points to keep in mind when you are setting up and conducting an interview.

1. Deciding on interview information areas

Think about what kind of information you want to get in an interview. Suppose your topic is "single parent families." You could interview some single parents to get information about their experiences.

If your topic were "divorce", you could interview someone who had had direct experience with divorce, someone who has been divorced or whose parents are divorced, for example.

2. Making up interview questions

After you have decided on what kind of information you want to get in an interview, you should make up a general list of interview questions. Try to think of questions that might elicit interesting answers that are related to your topic.

- You should have some yes–no questions.

  Were you very much affected by your parents' divorce?

- You should also have some open-ended information-gathering questions (you complete the sentences).

  How were you affected by your parents' divorce? What do you think about. . . ?   How would you advise. . . ? What are some of the reasons for. . . ? Did you   ever wonder about. . . ?)

Show your list of questions to two or three other people, if possible, and ask for their suggestions.

3. Selecting people to interview

Now you should choose some people to interview. Generally, two or three interviews are enough unless you are doing a long, in-depth study. Then you will need more. Ideally, the people you interview should have

- some direct experience related to the topic (e.g., some type of experience with divorce if you were researching divorce)

OR

- some important information or knowledge related to the topic. In other words, the person could be an expert in the area or an official who would have access to such information.

4. Conducting the interview

Always try to arrange your interviews at a time of convenience to the interviewee. You will get better results if you do. Try to be as relaxed and cordial as possible when you conduct your interviews to make your interviewee feel at ease. Listen carefully and be sure to ask additional questions if something interesting but unexpected comes up. Make brief notes to help you remember important responses. Jot down just enough information to help you reconstruct the essential information later, but don't try to write down everything.

Example:

What are some of the problems you have faced as a result of being divorced?

loneliness, isolation, not enough money

Be sure to thank your interviewee for taking the time for the interview and ask if you may check back with him or her later for additional information. You may find that you would like to ask another question or two later as you are looking over your notes.

Try to write up your interviews in some form as quickly as possible so that you don't forget essential information.

5. Using interview information

When you are writing your paper, in the body of the paper you can include information from your interviews.

- *Explain who you interviewed*
  Demi Arroyo is a divorced mother with two small children in Los Angeles. In a recent interview, Ms. Arroyo stated that arranging dependable and affordable childcare was the biggest challenge she faced.[2]

---

2. Arroyo, Demi. Personal interview. Los Angeles, CA. Sept. 9, 1998.

You should footnote this information so that your reader will know when the interview was conducted.

- *Quote sparingly and paraphrase extensively*

Write up most of the interview in third person, narrative form. In other words, paraphrase most of the interview. If your interviewee made a statement that was particularly important or well-expressed, then directly quote that statement. But, remember, don't quote too much! (You may wish to review the guidelines for quoting and paraphrasing in Sections 1 and 2 on page 248).

5.1
Making an Outline

After you have gathered information from a variety of sources, you can then begin to write your paper. Some people find it useful to make a general outline of how they want to organize their paper. Here is an example of an outline.

Devastating Effects of 1995 Hurricanes on the Gulf of Mexico

I. Introduction—General overview of the subject
   - A. General description of geographical area (setting the context)
   - B. Background historical information on hurricanes in area
   - C. General remarks about the 1995 hurricane season in area
   - D. General remarks about damage in area and effects

II. Body
   - A. Description of the major 1995 hurricanes
     1. How strong the winds were and how long they lasted
     2. When they occurred
     3. The extent to which people were prepared (or not prepared)
     4. The immediate aftermath of the major hurricanes
   - B. How people and businesses were affected
     1. Statistics on injuries and deaths
     2. People who were most affected and why (specific case studies, if possible)
     3. Damage to property
     4. Description of property damage
        - a. Types of damage
        - b. Examples
        - c. Effects on local people
        - d. Effects on local industries (e.g., tourism)
        - e. Statistics about damage
        - f. Location of damaged property

    C. Rescue and relief efforts

    D. National and international involvement

    E. Problems in rescue and relief efforts

        1. Destruction of hospitals, first aid centers, etc.

        2. Lack of medical and other supplies

        3. Transportation/sanitation problems

    F. Lessons to be learned from the 1995 hurricane season

        1. Importance of early warning

        2. Importance of preparation for disaster

        3. Precautions people can take

        4. Importance of people being trained to respond to hurricane disasters

III. Conclusion

    A. Summary

    B. Suggestions and recommendations for the future

Note: Many people find it useful to make a general outline before they begin writing. They believe the process of making an outline helps them plan and organize their ideas. When they are writing their paper or report, they can refer to their outline to make sure that they have not forgotten any parts. On the other hand, other people believe that they can organize and express their ideas more clearly if they do NOT make an outline before they begin.

Make an outline of your topic now, but DON'T be afraid to change it as necessary once you begin actually writing. DON'T be locked in by your outline. Use the outline as a way of thinking about the organization and content of your report and as a guide.

5.2
The Parts of a Composition

Most compositions and reports have four main parts, and each part has a specific function.

- **Title:** This is the name of your report or composition, and it should give the reader some idea of what the report or composition will cover.
  Example:
  The American School Year: Time for a Change?
- **Introduction:** Here is where you give the background of your subject and a general overview of what the paper or report will be about. It should give the reader a basic idea of what you will cover in general terms. Your thesis (main idea of the composition) should be clearly stated in the introduction.

Example of a thesis statement:

The American school year must be extended if American students are going to keep up with students from other industrialized countries.

- **Body:** Here is where you give reasons and examples to support your thesis statement. Generally, you state a reason, explain it if necessary, and then give specific examples to illustrate this reason. It is a good idea to include as many facts and relevant figures as possible here.

Examples of body paragraphs:

The American 180-day school year is based on a rural tradition that no longer fits the needs of a heavily industrialized, urban society. In the past, most American families lived on farms, and they needed their children to help them with the farm work in the summers, especially during harvest. Consequently, the school year was designed to give students a three-month vacation in the summer so they could work on the family farm. However, fewer than three percent of Americans live on farms now, so there is no longer a need for such a long summer vacation to supply farm labor.

In a major address in 1994, Ernest L. Boyer, president of the Carnegie Foundation for the Advancement of Teaching, said, "The time has come for radical change in the American school year if American students are to keep pace with students from the top industrial countries around the world."[1] Boyer proposed a longer school year so that American students could cover more material, particularly in math and science.

Note: If a quotation is five lines or shorter, it does not have to be indented and presented as a separate paragraph (see the Boyer quotation above). It simply continues as part of the text and quotation marks are used around it. If the quotation is longer than five lines, however, it should be indented and presented as a separate paragraph. Quotation marks should NOT be used.

Example of a longer quotation:

Ernest L. Boyer, president of the Carnegie Foundation for the Advancement of Teaching, said:

> *The time has come for radical change in the American school year if American students are to keep pace with students from the top industrial countries around the world. Japanese students go to school 243 days a year, while American students go just 180 days. American students simply cannot keep up.[3]*

The body is the longest part of a composition. It contains the specific information, concrete examples, and statistics (see example above). The length of the body varies according to the length of your report or composition. In a short composition, the body might be two or three paragraphs. In a long report, the body would be many pages.

- **Conclusion:** You restate the thesis in slightly different words, briefly review the major points of your report, and make a few general remarks about the thesis. Do NOT introduce any new information here. You may want to compare, contrast, or highlight some information that you thought was especially important in the body. Also, people frequently make recommendations for some sort of change or additional research in the conclusion based upon the findings in their report.

Remember: The conclusion is a kind of brief summary; keep it short. If the reader has not read the whole report or composition, the reader should be able to read the conclusion and get a general idea of the whole report or composition.

Example:

In conclusion, educational experts agree that it is time to extend the American school year. The 180-day year, with its long summer vacation, no longer fits the needs of our urban industrial society, and we cannot keep up with other industrialized countries, where students go to school up to 63 days more a year. It is time for a change, a radical change, as America prepares to face the challenges of the next century.

5.3
Writing and Getting Feedback on the First Draft

In this section we give you suggestions for how to write the first draft of your report and get feedback on it.

1. Writing the first draft

Beginning with any part of your report, write the first draft. *Note:* You do not have to write the introduction first. If you find it easier to begin with the body, start there. You may wish to write in pencil and double- or triple-space so you have room to make changes as you go along. As you are writing, read over what you have written from time to time. This can help you get ideas for continuing.

2. Getting feedback on the first draft

Show your draft to one or two other people. Ask them to tell you which parts they liked best and which parts are unclear or incomplete and need to be changed. Where do you need to have more information? more examples? Which points are unclear? Be sure to discuss problem areas thoroughly so that you can decide how to rewrite them. Concentrate primarily on ideas and making sure they are expressed clearly. Don't worry about form (grammar, punctuation, and spelling) yet. That will come later.

5.4
Writing and Getting Feedback on the Second Draft

In this section, we give you some suggestions on how to use feedback on your first draft to revise and then how to edit your report for form.

1. *Using feedback to revise content*

After you have discussed the changes suggested to you by the person giving you feedback on your first draft, you should write your composition again, trying to incorporate these changes. Usually this means that you have to add examples and perhaps explain how these examples are connected to your main points. Maybe your introduction was not as strong as it could have been. Whatever the problem areas are, now is the time to clear them up. At this point, your goals are to make your ideas as clear and as complete as possible. You should be trying to establish a closer connection with your reader and making it as easy as possible for your reader to understand your meaning.

As you are writing your second draft, read it over to yourself to see if you are making your ideas clear.

2. *Getting feedback on the second draft*

Show your second draft to the person or persons who read your first draft. Make sure your revisions are clear. If your ideas are still not clear or complete, write in the necessary changes.

3. *Editing for form*

When the meaning is clear, check over grammar, punctuation, and spelling with the person or persons reading your draft. *Note:* Don't worry about grammar, punctuation, and spelling until the meaning is clear.

Try to learn to recognize your problem areas in form. For example, do you sometimes make mistakes in verb endings, such as leaving off -*s* or -*ed*? Do you sometimes mix up *there*, *their*, and *they're*, or *its* and *it's*? Try to identify and correct these errors in form at this time. If you are using a computer, be sure to use spell-check to catch any spelling errors, but remember that a word can be spelled correctly and still be incorrect in a certain context, as in the examples just noted. The best spelling and meaning checker is still you.

5.5
Writing the Final Draft

Write or type your final draft. If you write your final draft by hand, be sure to use a pen. Write neatly and clearly on lined paper. It is usually advisable to skip lines because it will be easier for your reader to read. If you type or use a computer, double space. Hand in your final draft to your teacher.

If you write several drafts of a paper, the final product will be much better. Also, remember to concentrate on content (clear expression of ideas) first, and then work on form (grammar, punctuation, and spelling).

One final note: GOOD WRITING IS REWRITING. All good writers are really rewriters.

In this glossary, words are defined as they are used in the readings. Since many of these words may also have other meanings, you may want to look in your own dictionary for the full range of meanings of a word. Page numbers refer to the page on which a word appears in this book.

abstract   *adj.* General; theoretical. *Ex.* It is hard to define abstract ideas such as "love" or "truth." (p. 192)

accelerate   *v.* To go faster. *Ex.* The car accelerated as it entered the highway. (p. 147)

accord   *n.* An agreement; peace. *Ex.* The two countries came to an accord and signed a peace agreement. (p. 22)

accumulate   *v.* To gather; to collect. *Ex.* When Ms. Richie accumulates enough money, she will buy a car. (p. 54)

accuse   *v.* To say someone has done something wrong. *Ex.* She accused him of stealing the money. (p. 80)

acute   *adj.* Very sensitive or intense. *Ex.* Charlie suffered acute embarrassment when he spilled soup on his shirt at the dinner party. (p. 159)

adjacent   *adj.* Next to each other. *Ex.* The Petersons and the Lees live in adjacent houses. (p. 176)

advocate   *n.* A supporter. *Ex.* Advocates for clean air want the government to control air pollution (p. 67)

affectionate   *adj.* Showing love; caring. *Ex.* Mr. and Mrs. Sprogis are very affectionate with each other. (p. 151)

affinity   *n.* A strong natural attraction. *Ex.* Martin has an affinity for fast cars and loud music. (p. 221)

afraid   (**I'm afraid that**, phrase) I'm sorry to tell you; I regret that. *Ex.* I'm afraid that I won't be able to attend your party; I already have other plans for Saturday night. (p. 125)

aggression   *n.* Very forceful, harmful behavior; appearing ready to fight. *Ex.* The warring countries carried out acts of aggression against each other. (p. 146)

agitated   *adj.* Excited; very emotional. *Ex.* He became very agitated when he heard the bad news. (p. 176)

agonizing   *adj.* Feeling great mental or physical pain. *Ex.* I was in agonizing pain after I broke my arm.

aim   *n.* Goal. *Ex.* It is my aim to finish college. (p. 221)

akin   *adj.* Similar to; related to. *Ex.* "I can't believe you like to eat raw eggs," she said with a look akin to disgust. (p. 221)

alter   *v.* To change. *Ex.* Please don't alter your plans just for me. (p. 64)

amass   *v.* To accumulate; to gather. *Ex.* The art collector began amassing paintings when he was in college. (p. 165)

Amazon   *n.* In Greek mythology, the Amazons were a society of strong, independent women warriors who lived without men; the word is now used (sometimes impolitely) to describe a tall, strong woman. (p. 4)

ambiguous   *adj.* Unclear; vague. Ex: His answer was ambiguous, so it is difficult to understand what he means. (p. 109)

ambush   *v.* To attack after hiding and waiting. *Ex.* The cat ambushed the birds while they were drinking from a puddle. (p. 159)

ammunition   *n.* Information that supports your point of view. *Ex.* With these petitions and studies as ammunition, we can prove to the City Council that Main Street needs more traffic lights. (p. 163)

amnesty   *n.* Being forgiven for a crime (used mostly for political situations). *Ex.* The political prisoners received amnesty and returned home. (p. 33)

amputate   *v.* (amputation   *n.*) To cut off a part of the body. *Ex.* The doctor had to amputate Sergei's foot after it got caught in the machine. (p. 165)

apparent   *adj.* Seeming as if something is true (but not necessarily true). *Ex.* Pietro has an apparent advantage as a basketball player because he is tall. (p. 37)

arduous   *adj.* Very difficult. *Ex.* His journey through the mountains was long and arduous. (p. 127)

aspect   *n.* One part of of something. *Ex.* Spain has had a great influence on many aspects of Latin American life and culture. (p. 109)

assimilate   *v.* To become part of the community. *Ex.* The children of immigrants often find it easier to assimilate into the culture than their parents do. (p. 38)

audible   *adj.* Loud enough to be heard. *Ex.* The students made audible sounds of happiness or disappointment when they saw their test grades. (p. 127)

avail   (to no avail   *phrase*). Of no use. *Ex.* I tried to get tickets to the popular play but to no avail; they are sold out for months. (p. 176)

awkwardly   *adv.* In a clumsy or embarrassed way. *Ex.* Juris moved awkwardly as he learned the new dance. (p. 97)

barren   *adj.* Empty; unable to maintain life. *Ex.* The moon is a barren world of rocks and sand. (p. 20)

barrier   *n.* An obstacle that holds something back. *Ex.* Since Ms. Ortega arrived here as a poor refugee, she has overcome many obstacles to become a successful businessperson. (p. 110)

base   *n.* The bottom part. *Ex.* The off-on switch is at the base of the lamp. (p. 55)

betray   *v.* To be disloyal; to do something that hurts a person who trusts you. *Ex.* I would never betray my friends. (p. 204)

blend in   *v.* To combine completely with other things. *Ex.* Mauritz blends in so well to our group that it is hard to believe he just began working here last week. (p. 111)

blurred   *adj.* Become unclear. *Ex.* If you don't focus the camera well, your pictures will be blurred. (p. 54)

blushingly   *adv.* Becoming red in the face from embarrassment or modesty. *Ex.* "I painted that picture and it won an award," she said blushingly. (p. 18)

boisterous   *adj.* Noisy and lively. *Ex.* The college students had a boisterous party on Friday night. (p. 21)

bold   *adj.* Brave. *Ex.* Only a bold skier would ski down that mountain! (p. 206)

bonus   *adj.* Something extra. *Ex.* Everybody at my company gets a bonus paycheck on New Year's Day. (p. 55)

boost   *v.* To raise up. *Ex.* A strong economy always boosts car sales. (p. 32)

breakthrough   *n.* An important achievement that leads to further progress. *Ex.* There was a major breakthrough in the labor negotiations—both sides agreed on the vacation policy. (p. 64)

brood   *v.* To think sad thoughts without stopping. *Ex.* Kathy brooded over her mistakes and was never happy. (p. 208)

bundle   *n.* Several things tied together in one package. *Ex.* Reiko carried a bundle of dirty clothes to the laundromat. (p. 177)

burnished   *adj.* Made brighter and smoother (by polishing). *Ex.* The palace was filled with burnished objects of gold and silver. (p. 18)

by all means   *phrase.* Certainly; allowing someone to do something. *Ex.* If you like those peaches, by all means eat another one. (p. 55)

calculus   *n.* A type of mathematics. *Ex.* Engineering requires the study of calculus and physics. (p. 38)

calf   *n.* The large muscle in the back of your leg below your knee. *Ex.* The calf muscles on a football player must be very strong. (p. 222)

cast a spell over   *phrase.* To cause a magic effect. *Ex.* The wicked queen cast a spell over the princess and she slept for one hundred years. (p. 222)

cast-off   *adj.* Thrown away; no longer wanted. *Ex.* The poor children wore cast-off clothes and second-hand shoes. (p. 18)

catch (a catch)   *n.* Something that is hard to get. *Ex.* Getting that good job was quite a catch for Giovanni. (p. 17)

cautiously   *adv.* Being very careful in order to avoid danger or trouble. *Ex.* We walked through the tall grass cautiously, watching out for snakes. (p. 65)

cease   *v.* (**cessation**   *n.*) To stop. *Ex.* Cease that noise right now! (p. 195)

charm   *n.* Pleasing and attractive; appeal. *Ex.* I enjoy the charm of small fishing villages. (p. 219)

cheer   *v.* To shout your approval or encouragement. *Ex.* The crowd cheered loudly as the horse crossed the finish line. (p. 127)

cherished   *adj.* Beloved; greatly loved. *Ex.* They lost their cherished possessions in the fire. (p. 163)

chitchat   *n.* Informal conversation, often about unimportant things. *Ex.* The students enjoyed a little chitchat between classes. (p. 164)

chunk   *n.* A section. *Ex.* She cut a chunk of cheese and ate it with some bread. (p. 78)

churn out   *v.* To produce a lot of something very quickly. *Ex.* The song writer churned out hundreds of songs in her lifetime. (p. 164)

circuit   *n.* A path that goes around a specific area. *Ex.* The brain circuits go to every part of the body. (p. 146)

civic   *adj.* Related to the community you live in. *Ex.* The mayor took his civic responsibilities seriously. (p. 94)

claim   *n.* A demand; a request. *Ex.* My job has a big claim on my time. (p. 220)

clench   *v.* To close one's hand tightly; to hold tightly. *Ex.* Maria clenched the package in her arms as she walked through the crowded store. (p. 177)

clinical trials   *phrase.* Scientific tests to determine if a new medicine is safe. *Ex.* The clinical trials proved that the stomach ulcer medicine was effective. (p. 34)

clump   *n.* A small group of things that stay close together. *Ex.* A clump of trees stood in the middle of the field. (p. 160)

clumsy   *adj.* Without skill; not graceful. *Ex.* Petra handled the vase in such a clumsy way that she dropped it. (p. 204)

cohesive   *adj.* Fit together well; joined with similar interests. *Ex.* The Japanese people have developed a very cohesive society. (p. 111)

commitment   *n.* A strong belief or promise. *Ex.* At their marriage ceremony, Chris and Camille made a commitment to love and help each other. (p. 130)

compromise   *v.* To agree by having each person give up something that he or she wants. *Ex.* Sue wanted a large car but Pete wanted a small one, so they compromised and bought a mid-size car. (p. 65)

concept   *n.* A general idea. *Ex.* Do you have any concept of how much that car would cost? (p. 177)

conclude   *v.* To decide after you have thought about something carefully. *Ex.* What can you conclude after hearing the two sides of the story? (p. 203)

conjure   *v.* To create in your mind or in your dreams. *Ex.* What does the word "vacation" conjure for you? (p. 22)

consult *v.* To ask the advice of. *Ex.* If you have legal problems, you should consult a lawyer. (p. 6)

contaminated *adj.* Become polluted by chemicals or bacteria. *Ex.* The river became so contaminated with garbage that all the fish died. (p. 109)

contemplative *adj.* Thoughtful; focusing one's attention on. *Ex.* People with contemplative minds often become writers or musicians. (p. 220)

content *adj.* Happy; satisfied. *Ex.* I am content to sit here and look at the flowers. (p. 221)

controversy *n.* An argument; a debate. *Ex.* There is a great controversy in the United States over gun control. (p. 65)

conversely *adv.* The opposite way. *Ex.* You can do your homework first and then eat dinner; conversely, you could eat dinner first. (p. 33)

convey *v.* To communicate; to give someone a message. *Ex.* In his speech, he conveyed a strong message about gun control. (p. 79)

conviction *n.* A strong belief. *Ex.* I have a conviction that I will become rich someday! (p. 207)

correlate *v.* To have a connection; to be related. *Ex.* His strong legs correlate with his ability to run fast. (p. 162)

craving *n.* A strong desire. *Ex.* Sometimes I have a craving for salty foods. (p. 19)

crumble *v.* To fall apart into little pieces. *Ex.* The dry soil crumbled in her hands. (p. 35)

culminate *v.* To reach the end. *Ex.* The wedding celebration culminated in a big dinner and party. (p. 147)

cultivation *n.* Development. *Ex.* I studied music and painting for the cultivation of my mind. (p. 220)

daintily *adv.* In a delicate or neat way. *Ex.* At the president's reception, the guests sipped their tea daintily. (p. 99)

dangle *v.* To hang down and swing. *Ex.* Long earrings dangled from her ears and a gold bracelet dangled from her wrist.

data *n.* Information. *Ex.* Scientists have been collecting data on Jupiter's moons for many years. (p. 160)

date *n.* 1. A social engagement, especially with a girlfriend or boyfriend. *Ex.* On their third date, Bill told Carolyn that he loved her. (p. 79) **2. to date**, *phrase* So far; up to now. *Ex.* To date, I have lived in three countries and learned two languages. (p. 19)

deal *v.* To give out (often used for handing out cards in a card game). *Ex.* Life has dealt me many joys and many sorrows. (p. 166)

defer *v.* To do something later than originally planned. *Ex.* Ali deferred his vacation from June to September. (p. 130)

defiantly   *adv.* Refusing to obey; ignoring someone's disapproval. *Ex.* "I don't want to go to bed," the child said defiantly. (p. 99)

deliberately   *adv.* On purpose; planned. *Ex.* I deliberately chose the blue one because I thought you would like it. (p. 22)

delighted   *adj.* Very happy. *Ex.* Hello, I'm delighted to meet you. (p. 193)

demonstrate   *v.* To show how something is done. *Ex.* Let me demonstrate how this vacuum cleaner works. (p. 64)

denounce   *v.* To speak against something. *Ex.* The newspaper denounced the government's plan to raise taxes. (p. 206)

deny   *v.* To refuse; to deprive of. *Ex.* The prisoner was denied his freedom. (p. 20)

derive   *v.* To receive. *Ex.* I derive great pleaslure from playing my guitar. (p. 208)

deteriorating   *adj.* Slowly becoming worse and worse. *Ex.* Because of his deteriorating health, he could no longer walk. (p. 20)

deviant   *adj.* Different from normal (and unacceptable). *Ex.* The criminal had a deviant personality. (p. 110)

devise   *v.* To create; to invent. *Ex.* Louis Braille devised a method by which blind people can read. (p. 175)

devour   *v.* To eat completely and quickly. *Ex.* I'm so hungry I could devour that whole pot of stew. (p. 222)

diagnosis   *n.* A specialist's decision about what is wrong with something. *Ex.* The mechanic's diagnosis is that my car needs new brakes. (p. 127)

digestion   *n.* (**digest**, *v.*) The process of changing the food you eat into basic nutrients that your body can use. *Ex.* She digested her lunch quickly and was hungry for a snack. (p. 221)

discern   *v.* To recognize; to detect. *Ex.* She discerned their meaning even though she didn't understand all the words. (p. 208)

discipline   *n.* Firmness; control. *Ex.* To go on a diet, you need a lot of self-discipline. (p. 151)

disconcertingly   *adv.* In an uneasy or worried way. *Ex.* "Do I really have to walk over that shaky little bridge?" she asked disconcertingly. (p. 5)

dissuasion   *n.* Persuading someone not to do something. *Ex.* Won't all my dissuasions convince you to change your mind? (p. 5)

distaste   *n.* Not liking something; thinking something is unpleasant. *Ex.* The idea of sleeping in a tent filled her with distaste. (p. 79)

distinguish   *v.* To see or hear clearly. *Ex.* Can you distinguish the original painting from the copy? (p. 193)

distracted   *adj.* Drawing someone's attention to another topic. *Ex.* I was so distracted by the noise outside that I didn't understand what you were saying. (p. 163)

diverse *adj.* Varied; many different kinds. *Ex.* The voters have diverse opinions about the candidates. (p. 112)

doomed *adj.* Certain to have an unpleasant future (which you cannot prevent). *Ex.* Their vacation was doomed from the beginning—their car broke down the first day and it rained. (p. 20)

dosage *n.* The amount of medicine that you take at one time. *Ex.* The typical dosage of aspirin is two tablets. (p. 54)

drawback *n.* A disadvantage; an undesirable aspect of something. *Ex.* One drawback of this apartment building is that it doesn't have an elevator. (p. 131)

drench *v.* To get very wet. *Ex.* I got drenched in the sudden rain storm. (p. 159)

dumb *adj.* Unable to speak. *Ex.* Martine was struck dumb from fear. (p. 189)

dunce *n.* A stupid person; a fool. *Ex.* I am a real dunce at mathematics. (p. 4)

duty *n.* Job, responsibility. *Ex.* The accountant's duties include balancing the budget and writing checks. (p. 222)

ecstatic *adj.* Very happy. *Ex.* Carolina was ecstatic over her promotion to senior administrator. (p. 175)

elaborate *adj.* Very detailed or complicated. *Ex.* Sangeeta and Mritiunjoy made elaborate plans for their wedding. (p. 126)

emporia *n.* plural (**emporium**, singular) Old-fashioned word for a store that sells many kinds of things; a department store. (p. 19)

encounter *v.* To meet unexpectedly; to be faced with. *Ex.* I encountered many new words in this book. (p. 207)

entrepreneur *n.* A person who starts a business. *Ex.* Many entrepreneurs in China are opening small factories. (p. 32)

envied *adj.* Having something that other people also want. *Ex.* He was envied for his good health and happy family life. (p. 219)

errand *n.* A short trip to do a specific task. *Ex.* I do all my personal errands on Saturday morning. (p. 205)

essential *adj.* Necessary. *Ex.* If you want to drive, it is essential to have a driver's license. (p. 54)

eventful *adj.* Full of important or memorable events. *Ex.* My wedding was the most eventful day of my life. (p. 189)

eventually *adv.* At some future time. *Ex.* You will eventually need to buy a new coat, so why don't you start saving for it now? (p. 54)

evidence *n.* Indication; proof. *Ex.* The fingerprints on the window are evidence of the crime. (p. 32)

evidently *adv.* Seeming to be true. *Ex.* Evidently, the people didn't like Mayor Costanza because they voted him out of office. (p. 220)

evolve   *n.* To develop from. *Ex.* Lions and cats evolved from the same prehistoric ancestor. (p. 145)

exactly   *adv.* Precisely the same; just like (something). *Ex.* Do exactly as the swimming instructor says, and you'll swim faster. (p. 65)

excel   *v.* To do something very well or better than others. *Ex.* Jonathan excels at soccer while Michael excels at swimming. (p. 159)

excessive   *adj.* Too much; extreme. *Ex.* Excessive stress is bad for you. (p. 7)

exclusively   *adv.* Only; entirely. *Ex.* The musician devoted his time exclusively to playing his violin. (p. 162)

excruciating   *adj.* Very painful; terrible. *Ex.* I have an excruciating headache. (p. 177)

exert   *v.* To make a strong effort in order to get a certain result. *Ex.* The parents exerted pressure on the school to include more science in its curriculum. (p. 110)

expense   (**at their expense**, *phrase*). In a way that causes harm, loss, or embarrassment. *Ex.* The other children made jokes at Clara's expense, and she became angry. (p. 37)

expose   *v.* To put in contact with; to be without protection. *Ex.* It is dangerous to be exposed to high levels of X-rays. (p. 65)

fade   *v.* (**faded**, *adj.*) Having lost color or brightness. *Ex.* I wear faded, old clothing when I wash my car. (p. 94)

faint   *adj.* Indistinct; not clear. *Ex.* The writing on the old letter was so faint that I could hardly read it. (p. 194)

farfetched   *adj.* Very unlikely; almost impossible to believe. *Ex.* Martha gave some farfetched excuse that her dog ate her homework. (p. 165)

fetus   *n.* The developing human or animal before birth. *Ex.* A human fetus spends nine months in its mother's uterus before being born. (p. 164)

firmly   *adv.* Tightly. *Ex.* Suteera tied the suitcase firmly to the top of the car. (p. 96)

fit   *adj.* In good physical condition. *Ex.* Ana stays fit by swimming three times a week. (p. 55)

flaw   *n.* Something that is wrong; a defect. *Ex.* There is a flaw in that diamond, so the price is very low. (p. 80)

flexible   *adj.* Can be changed easily. *Ex.* I have a flexible schedule, so I can meet you anytime. (p. 147)

flicker   *n.* and *v.* To go on and off quickly. *Ex.* The lamp flickered for a few minutes and then went out. (p. 176)

foolproof   *n.* Without any errors or problems. *Ex.* Belinda has a foolproof method for remembering names. (p. 205)

foothold   *n.* A small, safe position from which you can move forward. *Ex.* Rolf's store gained a foothold in the electronics market and he quickly opened five more stores. (p. 33)

forged   *adj.* False; not a real one. *Ex.* The signature on that check is forged. (p. 18)

fraction   *n.* A small part of something. *Ex.* It takes only a fraction of a second for the calculator to multiply those numbers. (p. 37)

fro   (to and fro, *phrase*). Back and forth. *Ex.* The flowers swayed to and fro in the wind. (p. 189)

frustratingly   *adv.* Filled with dissatisfaction because you cannot do what you want. *Ex.* We smiled at each other frustratingly; he spoke only Russian, I spoke only English. (p. 159)

function   1. *n.* Purpose. *Ex.* What is the function of the "redial" button on the telephone? (p. 147) 2. *v.* To work well or properly. *Ex.* If your car isn't functioning right, take it to a mechanic. (p. 51)

furious   *adj.* Extremely angry. *Ex.* Mr. Kwan became furious when he found out his car had been stolen. (p. 147)

gasp   *v.* To breathe in quickly when you are surprised. *Ex.* The crowd gasped as the tightrope walker performed amazing tricks high above their heads. (p. 128)

gauge   *v.* To measure. *Ex.* Scientists are trying to gauge our use of the earth's water. (p. 22)

generate   *v.* To create. *Ex.* If a lizard loses its tail, it can generate a new one. (p. 176)

genetically-altered   *phrase.* "Genetically" refers to the genes that determine individual characteristics. "Altered" means "changed." *Ex.* The genetically-altered oranges were able to grow in cold weather. (p.63)

genial   *adj.* Pleasant to be with; friendly. *Ex.* Mr. Amado has a genial personality and everyone likes him. (p. 210)

glance   *v.* To look quickly. *Ex.* He glanced at the books on the table and picked up the one that looked most interesting. (p. 206)

glimpse   *v.* To get a quick look; to see briefly. *Ex.* We glimpsed the countryside through the train window. (p. 160)

gnaw   *v.* To bite on something again and again. *Ex.* The dog gnawed on the big bone. (p. 79)

gracious   *adj.* Being polite and kind. *Ex.* Hassan is a gracious host and treats his guests well. (p. 127)

grim   *adj.* Without pleasure; harsh. *Ex.* The firefighters went about the grim work of rescuing the victims of the fire. (p. 19)

harassed   *adj.* Feeling worried because you have too many problems. *Ex.* During the busy holiday season when the stores are crowded, the salespeople look harassed. (p. 78)

hardpressed   *adj.* Finding it difficult; having problems. *Ex.* We were hardpressed to find a pharmacy open at 2 a.m. (p. 36)

heartily   *adv.* With great enjoyment; with enthusiasm. *Ex.* Mr. Egan greeted his guests heartily. (p. 80)

herbalist   *n.* A medical specialist who uses herbs and plants as medicines. *Ex.* The herblist suggested mint tea to calm my upset stomach. (p. 6)

hesitate   *v.* To stop for a short time while you decide what to do or say. *Ex.* Don't hesitate to call me if you need some help. (p. 99)

hint   *n.* A clue; a suggestion made in an indirect way. *Ex.* Don't give Roger any hint that we're making a party for him; it's a surprise! (p. 162)

hostility   *n.* Opposition and anger. *Ex.* There was a great deal of hostility between the prisoners and the guards. (p. 204)

hum   *v.* To sing a song with your mouth closed. *Ex.* Maritsa hummed happily as she walked through the park. (p. 8)

humane   *adj.* Kind; showing sympathy. *Ex.* The Society for the Prevention of Cruely to Animals provides humane treatment for lost or sick animals. (p. 65)

hush   *n.* Quiet; silence. *Ex.* There was a sudden hush in the crowd as the band began to play the national anthem.(p. 96)

idle   *v.* To run (a machine) at very slow speed. *Ex.* His car idled quietly while he waited at the red light. (p. 160)

image   *n.* The way something looks; a picture. *Ex.* Ivan is the image of his grandfather. (p. 175)

imitate   *v.* To copy; to do the same thing. *Ex.* Have you ever seen Fernando imitate Elvis Presley? He's great! (p. 190)

impervious   *adj.* Not affected or influenced by anything. *Ex.* The mountain climber was imperious to the cold, the altitude, and the danger of his route. (p. 80)

implore   *v.* To beg. *Ex.* I implore you to give me another chance! (p. 7)

imply   *v.* To suggest; to say indirectly. *Ex.* When you say "this soup is unusual," are you implying that my cooking doesn't taste good? (p. 79)

impose   *v.* To use your authority to make something happen. *Ex.* The parents imposed strict limits on how much TV their children could watch. (p. 65)

inadequate   *adj.* Not good enough; unsatisfactory. *Ex.* Inadequate housing is a major problem in many large cities around the world. (p. 38)

influence   *n.* Something that causes change or has an effect. *Ex.* African sculpture had a major influence on Picasso's art. (p. 107)

influx   *n.* Many things coming in at the same time. *Ex.* The new housing development brought in a great influx of shops and restaurants. (p. 34)

ingredient   *n.* One part of a whole thing. *Ex.* Strength and speed are the main ingredients for a fast runner. (p. 78)

inhibit   *v.* To prevent. *Ex.* A lack of food inhibits normal growth in children. (p. 151)

initiative   *adj.* Using your own judgment about something and then doing it without being told what to do. *Ex.* When Mr. Veloria arrived in Toronto, he used his own initiative to open a small grocery store. (p. 35)

innovation   *n.* (innovative, *adj.*) A new idea; a new way of doing something. *Ex.* Computers are responsible for many innovations in business as well as in scientific research. (p. 38)

input   *n.* Information that you receive from other people or sources. *Ex.* Let's get input from Ricardo and Ana before we make a decision. (p. 176)

insipid   *adj.* Dull; uninteresting. *Ex.* The book was so insipid that I couldn't finish it. (p. 220)

instinct   *n.* Something that happens naturally (without thinking about it). *Ex.* Plants have an instinct to turn towards the light. (p. 128)

insular   *adj.* Isolated; not knowing much about the world. *Ex.* They lived in an insular valley and resisted any change. (p. 35)

integrate   *v.* To combine several things into one; to unite. *Ex.* Opera integrates orchestral music, singing and drama. (p. 176)

intrigued   *adj.* Extremely interested. *Ex.* I am intrigued by butterflies. (p. 162)

intriguing   *adj.* Extremely interesting; fascinating. *Ex.* Do you find any insects intriguing? (p. 161)

intuition   *n.* Knowing that something is true even though you cannot prove it. *Ex.* Trust your intuition when you are trying to solve a problem. (p. 159)

investment   *n.* Devoting time, money or energy to something. *Ex.* Ms. Shakarian made a large investment of time and effort to get a college degree. (p. 110)

invigorating   *adj.* Filling you with energy and strength. *Ex.* The climate in the Swiss Alps is invigorating. (p. 36)

ironically   *adv.* Being opposite or different from what you want or expect. *Ex.* Ironically, now that I can afford to take long vacations, my business is so busy that I never have time to get away. (p. 128)

irritably   *adv.* Easily angered or annoyed. *Ex.* He spoke to everyone irritably because he was angry. (p. 78)

jarring   *adj.* Shocking; irritating. *Ex.* The teenagers listened to some very loud and jarring music. (p. 78)

joint venture   *phrase*. Starting a project together. *Ex*. The Canadian Wood Products Company began a joint venture with a Siberian lumber company. (p. 34)

just so   *phrase* In a certain, specific way. *Ex*. I like my eggs boiled just so—not too soft, not too hard. (p. 95)

kindly-disposed   *adj*. Feeling friendly to other people. *Ex*. I feel kindly-disposed to all my neighbors. (p. 4)

label   *v*. To put information on something; to identify. *Ex*. The clerk labeled all the soup cans with a sticker that said "10 cents off." (p. 65)

lapse   *v*. To let something end and not continue it. *Ex*. My membership in the health club lapsed, and I didn't renew it. (p. 95)

lately   *adv*. Recently. *Ex*. Have you been to a movie lately? (p. 77)

leave   *n*. Time away from your job; holiday (British usage). *Ex*. I took four days of sick leave when I had the flu. (p. 3)

legacy   *n*. Something handed down from generation to generation. *Ex*. The problems in the banking industry are a legacy of years of mismanagement. (p. 131)

legitimate   *adj*. Acceptable; permitted. *Ex*. Having a bad cold with a fever is a legitimate reason for staying home from work. (p. 108)

line   (bring someone in line   *phrase*). To persuade someone to conform to the rules of the group. *Ex*. If the coach can't bring all the players in line, he will be fired. (p. 110)

linger   *v*. To stay for a while; to be slow to leave. *Ex*. We lingered at the museum because there was so much to see. (p. 207)

link   *n*. A connection; something that joins one thing to another. *Ex*. A satellite link connects TV stations all over the world. (p. 32)

loaded   *adj*. Having more significance than it might seem at first; having several meanings. *Ex*. The newspaper reporter asked some loaded questions about air pollution, and the factory manager refused to answer. (p. 78)

long-term   *adj*. Lasting for a long time into the future. *Ex*. The scientists are seeking a long-term solution to the water pollution problem. (p. 65)

longing   *n*. Great desire (for something you probably can't get). *Ex*. All my life, I've had a longing to visit Nepal. (p. 210)

lure   *v*. To attract strongly; to draw you towards something. *Ex*. Advertisements for Hawaii lure you with gorgeous pictures of palm trees and beautiful beaches. (p. 151)

macho   *adj*. Very masculine (informal). *Ex*. The little boy imitated the macho walk of the cowboy. (p. 112)

make fun of *v.* To say rude or bad things. *Ex.* The children made fun of Mary's old-fashioned clothes and she began to cry. (p. 77)

marital intimacy *phrase.* Concerning sex in one's marriage. *Ex.* There are many books that give advice on marital intimacy. (p. 18)

mat *n.* A small carpet to protect the floor. *Ex.* We put a welcome mat at our front door to greet our visitors. (p. 31)

match *v.* To equal; to be the same. *Ex.* The color of that shirt matches the jacket exactly. (p. 31)

matrimony *n.* Marriage. *Ex.* Carlos and Elena entered into matrimony on April 6, 1992. (p. 221)

means see **by all means**

miniature *adj.* A very small copy of something. *Ex.* My uncle collects miniature cars. (p. 146)

minority *n.* Less than half of a whole group. *Ex.* Only a small minority of people voted for Mr. Jones, so he lost the election. (p. 111)

mode *n.* A particular way (of doing something). *Ex.* What mode of travel do you prefer, airplanes or trains? (p. 222)

modesty *n.* Not drawing attention to yourself; keeping quiet about your accomplishments. *Ex.* Although Grace has top grades and won a scholarship, she is known for her modesty about her success. (p. 18)

modify *v.* To change somewhat. *Ex.* I modified the recipe to use chicken instead of beef. (p. 146)

motivation *n.* Having a strong desire to do something. *Ex.* My parents gave me the motivation to study hard. (p. 110)

nag *v.* To annoy someone by constantly complaining. *Ex.* Stop nagging me! I'll wash the car when I have time. (p. 193)

norm *n.* The usual and typical way of behaving. *Ex.* Day care for young children is the norm in Israel because most mothers work. (p. 113)

notorious *adj.* Famous for something bad. *Ex.* Al Capone was a notorious gangster in the 1920's. (p. 177)

nourish *v.* To provide with enough food. *Ex.* The birds nourished their babies by bringing them worms and insects. (p. 164)

nurture *n.* The way a child is raised by its parents. *Ex.* The lion nurtured her young until they were old enough to hunt for themselves. (p. 165)

nutrition *n.* The study of food and health. *Ex.* Good nutrition depends on eating a balanced diet. (p. 53)

obligingly *adv.* Willing to help or to please other people. *Ex.* Mrs. Menton obligingly makes her famous chicken stew for the club picnic every summer. (p. 79)

obsession   *n.* Something you think about all the time. *Ex.* Dmitri's childhood obsession with animals led to his career as a veterinarian (animal doctor). (p. 126)

obstinately   *adv.* Stubbornly; determined. *Ex.* The child obstinately refused to go to bed. (p. 6)

offset   *v.* To balance or compensate. *Ex.* This month's profits will offset last month's losses. (p. 36)

offspring   *n.* The child of a particular parent. *Ex.* This year's winner of the Kentucky Derby is an offspring of the famous racehorse Secretariat. (p. 64)

ostracism   *n.* Being left out (or sent out) of a group deliberately. *Ex.* In ancient Greece, ostracism was a form of punishment. (p. 110)

output   *n.* The amount of work produced. *Ex.* The output of the factory is 500 pairs of shoes every day. (p. 110)

overhaul   *v.* To examine and then make changes or fix something. *Ex.* The mechanic had to completely overhaul my car's engine. (p. 32)

overlap   *n.* When one thing partly covers another thing. *Ex.* You work from 8 a.m. to 4 p.m. and I work from noon to 6 p.m., so we have a four hour overlap. (p. 165)

overreact   *v.* To respond too much or too strongly. *Ex.* If you overreact every time you get a little scrape, no one will believe you if you really get hurt. (p. 126)

paralyzed   *adj.* Unable to move or feel. *Ex.* Mr. Williams was paralyzed from the neck down after the auto accident. (p. 175)

paraphernalia   *n.* All the items needed for a special activity. *Ex.* The baseball players use bats, catcher's mitts, and other paraphernalia when they play ball. (p. 94)

pardon me   *phrase.* A phrase you say when you didn't hear or don't believe something. (p. 78)

parsimonious   *adj.* Stingy; willing to give only a very small amount. *Ex.* Mr. Hughes was very parsimonious with his money. (p. 21)

pause   *v.* To stop for some time. *Ex.* The diver stood at the edge of the pool, paused, and then dived into the water. (p. 97)

peculiar   *adj.* Special; unique. *Ex.* That type of harmony and singing is peculiar to Bulgaria. (p. 4)

penalty   *n.* Punishment; a loss. *Ex.* What is the penalty for cheating on a test? (p. 131)

perception   *n.* (perceive *v.*) An understanding. *Ex.* Do you think that animals can have a perception of right and wrong? (p. 176)

perfunctorily   *adv.* With very little interest; in an unconcerned way. *Ex.* The guard looked at my admission ticket perfunctorily and let me in the door. (p. 7)

persevere   *v.* To continue your efforts in spite of difficulties. *Ex.* Ambroise persevered through good times and bad, and he finally graduated from college. (p. 7)

perspective   *adj.* Viewpoint; a particular way of thinking about something. *Ex.* The biologists are studying the rainforest from a scientific perspective. (p. 35)

phantom   *n.* An unreal thing; a ghost. *Ex.* Frauke told the children a story about phantom ladies living in an old castle. (p. 175)

phenomenon   *n.* An unusual event or occurrence. *Ex.* The concern about water pollution is a fairly recent phenomonon.

pinpoint   *v.* To find the exact spot. *Ex.* The doctor tried to pinpoint the exact location of the pain in my knee. (p. 161)

placebo   *n.* Something that you think is a medication but it actually contains none. *Ex.* Half the people in the experiment received the real drug and half received a placebo. (p. 177)

pound   *v.* To hit or beat hard. *Ex.* The carpenter pounded the nails with a big hammer. (p. 206)

practical joke   *n.* A trick that embarrasses a person or makes someone look foolish. *Ex.* As a practical joke, my class took the pronunciation tape out of my tape recorder and put in a popular music tape; I got so confused!

preclude   *v.* To prevent; to make impossible. *Ex.* The lack of oxygen on the moon precludes humans from living there. (p. 222)

predator   *n.* An animal that catches and eats other animals. *Ex.* Lions and tigers are predators of the African plains. (p. 146)

prediction   *n.* Guessing what will happen in the future. *Ex.* The weather prediction for tomorrow is sunny and warm. (p. 151)

preoccupation   *n.* Involvement; taking one's attention. *Ex.* Please pardon my preoccupation with my work, but I must finish this report by 5 p.m. today. (p. 209)

prestige   *n.* High status or position in society; admired. *Ex.* Mr. O'Brien gained prestige by donating the money to build a new hospital. (p. 111)

primitive   *adj.* Very basic; belonging to an earlier period of time or life. *Ex.* A worm is a fairly primitive form of life. (p. 160)

probation   *n.* The time when a criminal is under close supervision but not in prison. *Ex.* After he was released from prison, Frank spent two years on probation.

progressive   *adj.* Forward looking; having modern ideas. *Ex.* That school is considered quite progressive in its science classes. (p. 18)

promptly   *adv.* Immediately, right away. *Ex.* When Jack told Jane the funny story, she promptly began to laugh. (p. 64)

prone   *adj.* Tending toward something; likely. *Ex.* Sadia is very accident-prone; she's always breaking things. (p. 161)

proportion   *n.* Percentage; one part compared to the whole thing. *Ex.* I spend a large proportion of my income on rent. (p. 55)

protracted   *adj.* Lasting a longer time than you expect. *Ex.* Tim's protracted illness kept him away from class for almost three months. (p. 177)

provocation   *n.* Trying to make (someone) angry or excited. *Ex.* I was just walking down the street, and without any provocation, the dog attacked me. (p. 151)

provocative   *adj.* Trying to make you curious or interested. *Ex.* The newspaper printed a provocative article on why teenagers like loud music. (p. 160)

quiver   *v.* To tremble; to shake slightly. *Ex.* The spider web quivered when the moth flew into it. (p. 20)

raid   *n.* A sudden attack. *Ex.* The wolves made raids in the sheep herds at night. (p. 93).

randomly   *adv.* Without any order or pattern. *Ex.* The winning numbers in the lottery are randomly selected. (p. 165)

rationality   *n.* The ability to reason and think logically. *Ex.* Judge Wapner is known for his rationality and fairness. (p. 164

raw   *adj.* Not cooked. *Ex.* Carrots taste good either cooked or raw. (p. 78)

recital   *n.* Saying a list of things. *Ex.* At the graduation ceremony, there was a recital of the names of all the graduates. (p. 95)

refrain   *v.* To hold back; to avoid doing something. *Ex.* Please refrain from talking during the ceremony. (p. 111)

regulate   *v.* To control according to some rules. *Ex.* Ms. Leung's mother takes pills to regulate her blood pressure. (p. 65)

regulation   *n.* A rule; a law. *Ex.* The accountant knew all the regulations in the tax code. (p. 65)

reiterate   *v.* To repeat. *Ex.* The candidate reiterated her promise to lower taxes. (p. 130)

rejection   *n.* (**reject** *v.*) Not being accepted. *Ex.* Peter was rejected from the army because he is so nearsighted. (p. 110)

relevance   *n.* Importance; connection. *Ex.* What is the relevance of your past experience to this job? (p. 112)

reliably   *adv.* Can be trusted; generally accurate. *Ex.* That ancient Greek vase has been reliably dated to the era 800-750 B.C. (p. 166)

reluctantly   *adv.* Unwillingly; with hesitation. *Ex.* He ate the strange food reluctantly. (p. 78)

remorse *n.* Feeling regret and sorrow for something you did. *Ex.* Ahmed felt remorse for speaking rudely to his mother. (p. 8)

repertoire *n.* All the things you know. *Ex.* The pianist's repertoire included sonatas by Mozart and Beethoven. (p. 145)

reptile *n.* (reptilian, *adj.*) An animal from the group that includes snakes, turtles, lizards, and crocodiles. (p. 145)

rescind *v.* To take back; to reverse. *Ex.* The legislature rescinded the unpopular sales tax. (p. 128)

resentment *n.* A feeling of anger when you think you are being treated unfairly. *Ex.* Sabrina felt resentment when Paolo got a raise and she didn't. (p. 20)

reside *v.* To live in a place. *Ex.* Thirty percent of Japan's population resides in and around Tokyo. (p. 151)

resist *v.* To fight against; to try to prevent something from happening. *Ex.* I take lots of Vitamic C to resist getting a cold. (p. 63)

resolution *n.* Strong determination. *Ex.* The new president spoke about his resolution to help the country. (p. 7)

retrieve *v.* To find and bring back. *Ex.* Wilhelm retrieved his homework pages from the garbage after he accidentally threw them away. (p. 130)

reveal *v.* To make known. *Ex.* You don't have to reveal your secret if you don't want to. (p. 190)

rift *n.* A wide space; a large break. *Ex.* The argument caused a rift in their friendship, and they never spoke to each other again. (p. 128)

right *n.* Something you have by law. *Ex.* In some countries, women don't have the right to drive a car. (p. 108)

ritual *n.* and *adj.* A custom; something that a group always does in the same way. *Ex.* The funeral ritual included prayers and songs. (p. 19)

roam *v.* To wander around. *Ex.* I have roamed the wide world over and decided there is no place like home. (p. 207)

rocketing *adj.* Going up very quickly and high. *Ex.* Rocketing prices have made it difficult for many people to buy a house. (p. 31)

rot *v.* To spoil; to get bad. *Ex.* The raw chicken will rot if you leave it out of the refrigerator. (p. 66)

sake (**for their sake,** *phrase*). For someone's benefit. *Ex.* Please do it for my sake even if you don't want to do it for yourself. (p. 79)

salute *n.* A movement of your hand showing respect. *Ex.* The soldier gave the general a sharp salute. (p. 95)

scarcely *adv.* Almost none; hardly. *Ex.* Vanessa felt sick and scarcely ate any dinner. (p. 5)

scrutiny *n.* Careful examination. *Ex.* Mr. Sampson gave every section of the contract close scrutiny before he signed it. (p. 67)

scurry *v.* To hurry; to move quickly. *Ex.* The mouse scurried through the grass. (p. 22)

security *n.* Something that gives you confidence; without worry. *Ex.* ob security is very important to me. (p. 54)

seize *v.* To grab quickly. *Ex.* Seize the rope and pull the boat to the shore. (p. 197)

sequence *n.* The order in which something happens. (p. 195) *Ex.* Be sure to follow the directions in sequence, or else you'll have trouble! (p. 192)

service economy *phrase.* An economy that depends more on jobs that provide services to people than on manufacturing or farming jobs. (p. 36)

setback *n.* Something that causes a delay or stops your progress. *Ex.* The vote of "no confidence" was a terrible setback for the prime minister. (p. 162)

sheer *adj.* Pure; absolute. *Ex.* Patricio learned how to fly a small plane for the sheer pleasure of being alone in the air. (p. 221)

short run (in the short run, *phrase*). As an immediate result; initially. *Ex.* Your restaurant may not make a profit in the short run, but eventually it will be successful. (p. 33)

shrink *v.* To become smaller. *Ex.* Oh no! My favorite shirt shrank in the wash and it doesn't fit anymore. (p. 165)

shunned (shun, *v.*) Deliberately avoided or not accepted by other people. *Ex.* He made many enemies and was shunned by everyone in town. (p. 37)

side effects *phrase.* Additional results (often unpleasant). *Ex.* For most people, aspirin has no serious side effects, but some people are allergic to it. (p. 131)

simultaneously *adv.* Happening at the same time. *Ex.* Can you pat your head and rub your stomach simultaneously? (p. 164)

sip *n.* A little taste of a liquid. *Ex.* She took two sips of the coffee and said it was delicious. (p. 78)

skinny *adj.* Thin. *Ex.* I was skinny when I was a child, but now I'm fat. (p. 77)

smother *v.* To surround and cover something completely (sometimes killing it). *Ex.* The weeds smothered the flowers. (p. 145)

sob *v.* To cry loudly. *Ex.* Katrina sobs whenever she watches that sad movie. (p. 7)

sparsely *adv.* Having a small amount spread out over a large area. *Ex.* The Sahara Desert is sparsely populated. (p. 19)

spectacle *n.* An unusual sight; something interesting to look at. *Ex.* The circus parade was quite a spectacle with all the elephants, clowns, and dancing horses. (p. 220)

speculative *adj.* Guessing; theoretical rather than based on fact. *Ex.* It is speculative whether life could exist on another planet. (p. 177)

spontaneous *adj.* Happening suddenly without any cause; unplanned. *Ex.* There was a spontaneous cheer from the crowd. (p. 223)

spy *v.* To notice suddenly; to see. *Ex.* Mrs. Starses spied the first tulips coming up in her garden in April. (p. 130)

stand out *v.* To be different or individual; to attract attention. *Ex.* You will certainly stand out in a crowd if you wear that hat! (p. 111)

standard *n.* An acceptable level; a level used to judge the quality of something. *Ex.* This office has high standards for all its employees. (p. 54)

stem *v.* To originate; to come from. *Ex.* Hanmei's research on wasps and bees stems from his childhood interest in insects. (p. 110)

stereotype *n.* A general image of a group (but this image may or may not be true). *Ex.* That adventure movie is full of stereotypes—a strong hero, a helpless woman, a wicked villain. (p. 159)

still *adj.* Quiet. *Ex.* It is so still and peaceful in the forest. (p. 192)

stimulate *v.* To encourage; to cause a sudden increase. *Ex.* The smell of the roast chicken stimulated my appetite, and I said "let's eat"! (p. 192)

stimulus *n.* Something that encourages or excites you. *Ex.* The good smell of the soup was a stimulus to my appetite. (p. 192)

stool *n.* A small bench or chair without a back. *Ex.* Barnett sat on a stool at the snack bar. (p. 94)

store *v.* To save and use later; to put away in order to keep safe. *Ex.* During the summer, squirrels store lots of nuts to eat in the winter. (p. 51)

strain *v.* To stretch something beyond its limits. *Ex.* The increased population is straining the water supply, so sometimes there are water shortages. (p. 7)

strategy *n.* A careful plan. *Ex.* Mr. Nielsen has developed a strategy for expanding his real estate business. (p. 112)

stray *v.* To wander away from the place where you are supposed to be. *Ex.* My dog strayed from my house and it took all day to find him. (p. 6)

strike *v.* (struck, past tense) To hit; to crash into. *Ex.* The car struck the fence and caused a lot of damage. (p. 221)

striking *adj.* Very noticeable. *Ex.* She bears a striking resemblance to her grandmother. (p. 111)

stumble *v.* To fall over something. *Ex.* Melissa stumbled over the chair in the dark room. (p. 159)

stun *v.* To surprise greatly; to shock. *Ex.* Nadia was stunned when she won first prize in the contest. (p. 127)

substantially *adv.* In many ways; generally. *Ex.* The movie about Napoleon was substantially true, but some scenes were fictional. (p. 67)

subtle *adj.* Delicate; not obvious. *Ex.* Japanese food is known for its subtle flavor and beautiful appearance. (p. 159)

suit yourself   *phrase.* To do just what you want to do. *Ex.* You can go there either today or tomorrow; suit yourself. (p. 4)

superfluous   *adj.* Extra; unneeded. *Ex.* Don't carry any superfluous clothes on your trip; your suitcase is already too heavy. (p. 163)

superstitious   *adj.* Believing in things that cannot be proven by fact. *Ex.* Some superstitious people believe it is bad luck to walk under a ladder. (p. 6)

surge up   *v.* To rise up quickly. *Ex.* The waves surged up over the little boat during the storm. (p. 207)

susceptible   *adj.* Easily affected by something. *Ex.* I am very susceptible to colds and the flu every winter. (p. 177)

sustenance   *n.* Food; nourishment. *Ex.* People in Asia derive much of their sustenance from rice. (p. 222)

swelling   *n.* (**swell** *v.*) Something that expands beyond its original size. *Ex.* The swelling on my knee went down after I put ice on it. (p. 147)

tact   *n.* Consideration; politeness. *Ex.* Try to use some tact when you tell him that he is wrong. (p. 195)

tantalizing   *adj.* Tempting; raising your interest. *Ex.* The smells from the bakery are so tantalizing that I always go in and buy a bread or some cookies. (p. 166)

tap   *v.* To draw from; to take from. *Ex.* The irrigation system in Egypt taps the Nile River for its water. (p. 33)

target   *n.* The thing that someone is aiming at and trying to hit. *Ex.* Shoot the arrow into the middle of the target. (p. 110)

tend   *v.* To move in a certain direction. *Ex.* Jane tends to take her vacations in Florida because she likes warm weather. (p. 6)

tentative   *adj.* Subject to change; not final. *Ex.* I made tentative plans to go skiing next weekend if it snows. (p. 209)

texture   *n.* The way something feels. *Ex.* Silk has a soft, smooth texture. (p. 55)

threatening   *adj.* Intending to harm or to cause a problem. *Ex.* Those storm clouds look very threatening; let's hurry home before it rains. (p. 5)

thrilling   *adj.* Very exciting and enjoyable. *Ex.* Barbara and Charlotte took a thrilling plane ride through the mountains of Alaska. (p. 131)

transfer   *v.* To move from one position to another. *Ex.* Albert transferred some money from his savings account to a checking account. (p. 65)

traverse   *v.* To move across. *Ex.* The camels slowly traversed the Sahara Desert. (p. 191)

tremendous   *adj.* Very large. *Ex.* There was a tremendous wedding cake for the 400 guests. (p. 7)

trickle *v.* To flow slowly (like water in a little stream). *Ex.* Tears began to trickle down her face after she heard the sad news. (p. 166)

trivial *adj.* Minor; unimportant. *Ex.* Please don't bore me with the trivial details. (p. 126)

tyrant *n.* A ruler who has complete power and is cruel. *Ex.* The tyrant ordered his subjects to pay very high taxes. (p. 20)

unanimity *n.* Complete agreement by everyone. *Ex.* There is unanimity in my family about where we should go on vacation; we all love the mountains. (p. 110)

unappealing *adj.* Unpleasant; undesirable. *Ex.* That food looks so unappealing I can't eat it. (p. 113)

unarmed *adj.* Not having any weapons. *Ex.* The unarmed villagers were caught between the two armies. (p. 107)

uncomprehending *adj.* Not understanding. *Ex.* He tried to describe the danger to the uncomprehending crowd, but they didn't believe him. (p. 190)

undiluted *adj.* Very strong concentration; needing water to become thinner and usable. *Ex.* The frozen orange juice is undiluted, so you have to add water before you can drink it. (p. 78)

undisputed *adj.* Without any question; definitely true. *Ex.* The documents prove that the farmers have undisputed ownership of that land forever. (p. 145)

uneasy *adj.* Uncomfortable; anxious. *Ex.* Carlotta felt uneasy as she walked down the dark, empty street. (p. 93)

unintelligible *adj.* Impossible to understand. *Ex.* They spoke so quickly that they were unintelligible to me. (p. 19)

unprecedented *adj.* Never happened before. *Ex.* The increased population has created an unprecedented demand for new housing. (p. 32)

unrepressed *adj.* Allowed to happen; not held back. *Ex.* She laughed with unrepressed happiness. (p. 178)

upscale *adj.* Expensive; high fashion. *Ex.* The Champs-Elysées is an upscale boulevard in Paris. (p. 18)

urge *v.* To recommend strongly. *Ex.* My sisters urged me to get a better job, and now I'm much happier. (p. 65)

vague *adj.* Unclear; slight. *Ex.* I have a vague memory of meeting you before. (p. 191)

vent *v.* To express strongly; to let out. *Ex.* Maureen vented her anger at the driver who hit her car. (p. 20)

vice versa   *phrase.* In the reverse order. *Ex.* You can study now and eat later or vice versa; it doesn't matter which you do first. (p. 165)

virtually   *adv.* Almost entirely. *Ex.* Virtually every home in my country has a television set. (p. 65)

vivid   *adj.* Strong; described clearly. *Ex.* My grandmother told vivid stories of her life on a farm in the early 1900s. (p. 208)

ward of the state   *legal term.* A person who is taken care of or protected by the courts. *Ex.* The orphan became a ward of the state. (p. 37)

withstand   *v.* To resist successfully. *Ex.* The engineers built the dam with thick walls so it can withstand floods and earthquakes. (p. 128)

wound   *v.* To hurt. *Ex.* The man was wounded in the car accident. (p. 208)

wrinkle   *v.* To have many small creases caused by crushing or shrinking. *Ex.* No matter how carefully I pack my suitcase, my clothes always wrinkle. (p. 147)

Credits for Excerpts